Crossing the Divide

Crossing the Divide

Precarious Work and the Future of Labour

Edited by

*Edward Webster, Akua O. Britwum
and Sharit Bhowmik*

UNIVERSITY OF KwaZulu-Natal Press

Published in 2017 by University of KwaZulu-Natal Press
Private Bag X01
Scottsville, 3209
Pietermaritzburg
South Africa
Email: books@ukzn.ac.za
Website: www.ukznpress.co.za

© 2017 University of KwaZulu-Natal

All rights reserved. No part of this publication may be reproduced or transmitted in any form or by any means, electronic or mechanical, including photocopying, recording, or any information storage and retrieval system, without prior permission in writing from University of KwaZulu-Natal Press.

ISBN: 978 1 86914 353 4
e-ISBN: 978 1 86914 354 1

Managing editor: Sally Hines
Editor: Lisa Compton
Proofreader: Alison Lockhart
Typesetter: Patricia Comrie
Indexer: Christopher Merrett
Cover design: Marise Bauer, MDesign
Cover photographs (*clockwise from top left*): Incense stick roller in Ahmedabad, India, Leslie Vryenhoek; low-income Ghanaians working in Agbogbloshie, a suburb of Accra, Ghana, Marlenenapoli / Wikimedia Commons / Public Domain; a farmworker loading grapes in the Western Cape, South Africa, Eric Miller / Independent Contributors / Africa Media Online; workers at Serendipalm Company's processing mill, Ghana; a tea plantation worker in Northeast India, Toby Sinclair; a casual worker on a farm in the Western Cape, South Africa, Eric Miller / Independent Contributors / Africa Media Online.

Print administration by DJE Flexible Print Solutions, Cape Town

We dedicate this volume to Sharit Bhowmik (1948–2016).

Contents

Preface ix
Abbreviations xiii

1 A Conceptual and Theoretical Introduction 1
    Edward Webster, Akua O. Britwum and Sharit Bhowmik

Part I   Agricultural Aspects

2 Organising Casual Workers on an Oil Palm Plantation
    in Ghana 33
    Akua O. Britwum and Angela D. Akorsu

3 Ethnicity and Class: Issues in Organising Tea Plantation
    Workers in India 54
    Sharit Bhowmik

4 From Flexible Work to Mass Uprising: The Western Cape
    Farm Workers' Struggle 74
    Jesse Wilderman

5 Organising Farm Workers in Gauteng: Economic Upgrading
    and Social Downgrading 97
    uMbuso we Nkosi

Part II   Urban Considerations

6 Implications of Private Participation in Solid Waste
    Management for Collective Organisation in Accra, Ghana ... 121
    Owusu Boampong and Benjamin Y. Tachie

7 Hybrid Organisations, Complex Politics: When Unions
  Form Cooperatives   143
    Malati Gadgil and Melanie Samson

8 Sword of Justice or Defender of Vested Interest? The Struggles
  of Johannesburg's Municipal Workers   165
    Edward Webster and Carmen Ludwig

9 Dickensian England in Twenty-first-century Delhi – Without
  Great Expectations: Informal Labour Organising in the
  Manufacturing Sector   187
    Mouleshri Vyas

10 Organising Vulnerable Home-based Workers in India   206
    Indira Gartenberg

11 Collective Agency and Organising among Domestic Workers
   in Ghana   228
    Angela D. Akorsu and Amanda Odoi

Contributors   250
Index   254

Preface

This book is the outcome of a collaborative research project funded by the International Center for Development and Decent Work (ICDD) of the University of Kassel, Germany. The project was undertaken by a consortium of leading researchers based in South Africa, Ghana and India. The first phase of this project resulted in a book titled *Socio-economic Insecurity in Emerging Economies: Building New Spaces*, edited by Khayaat Fakier and Ellen Ehmke, and published by Routledge in 2014.

The second phase of the project, of which this volume is the product, focuses on the growing informalisation of work under neoliberal globalisation and the implications this has for the future of the labour movement. Informalisation has eroded the regulatory framework and undermined the standard employment relationship that defined the role of trade unionism in the second half of the twentieth century. Informal employment now comprises between half and three-quarters of non-agricultural employment in developing countries.

This volume is the outcome of four workshops, the first three of which heard draft papers by various authors. The first workshop was held in December 2013 in Johannesburg, the second in August 2014 at the University of Cape Coast in Ghana, and the third in December 2014 at the Guwahati Campus of the Tata Institute of Social Sciences (TISS) in India. The volume editors then met in January 2016 at the University of the Witwatersrand in Johannesburg to finalise the manuscript.

Crossing the Divide moves beyond a traditional academic study to engage directly with marginalised workers. The contributing authors combine years of academic research with active involvement with grassroots organisations. They blend their scholarly exploration of the informal economy with a commitment to empower and give voice to these precarious workers.

In order to capture the experiences of precarious workers effectively, we partnered with major trade union movements in the three countries to prepare key chapters in this volume: in South Africa, the Congress of South African Trade Unions (COSATU) Task Team on Organising Vulnerable Workers; in Ghana, the Trades Union Congress (TUC); and in India, the Labour Education and Research Network (LEARN) and the New Trade Union Initiative (NTUI).

The questions we address in this book include: How do informal workers organise? What forms does this organisation take? What strategies do vulnerable workers use? What sources of power do they draw on? What are their relationships with traditional unions, and how are traditional unions responding? The methodology followed is predominantly ethnographic, drawing on the experiences of vulnerable workers through in-depth interviews, observation and, in some cases, large-scale surveys. We believe that this is the most authentic way of uncovering the invisible world of the informal economy and vulnerable workers.

We would like to acknowledge the support received from the ICDD, which included funding for the four workshops. In addition, four of the contributing authors were supported during their research by ICDD fellowships: Indira Gartenberg, Amanda Odoi, Benjamin Tachie and Jesse Wilderman. We also wish to thank Karin Pampallis, publications manager of the Hidden Voices Project at the Society, Work and Development Institute (SWOP), University of the Witwatersrand, for her highly professional role in the development and production of the manuscript.

Edward Webster, Akua O. Britwum and Sharit Bhowmik

Postscript: September 2016

As we were editing what is now Sharit Bhowmik's last written piece, we received the very sad news that he had unexpectedly passed away due to heart failure on 8 September 2016 in Bangkok. The book was in its final stages; even the preface had been jointly written. The chapter we were editing – Chapter 3 in this volume – is classic Sharit. In meticulous detail he records the wages and working conditions of precarious tea plantation workers trying to find a voice through a union. There is no pretentious postcolonial theory in Sharit's work, just solid empirical evidence combined with a passionate and lifelong commitment to giving marginalised workers a voice. Our heartfelt condolences go to his wife and children, and to all the colleagues and students that his distinguished career touched. It has been a great privilege working with Sharit Bhowmik on this volume, and with great respect and gratitude we dedicate this book to him.

Edward Webster, Akua O. Britwum and Karin Pampallis

Abbreviations

AITUC	All India Trade Union Congress
AMA	Accra Metropolitan Assembly [Ghana]
ANC	African National Congress [South Africa]
AVP	Adivasi Vikas Parishad [Tribal Development Council, India]
BMWU	Black Municipal Workers' Union [South Africa]
CBA	collective bargaining agreement
CBD	central business district
CCP	consignment control process
CCTPW	Coordination Committee of Tea Plantation Workers [India]
CLOGSA	Civil and Local Government Staff Association [Ghana]
COSATU	Congress of South African Trade Unions
CPI	Communist Party of India
CPI(M)	Communist Party of India (Marxist)
DGHC	Darjeeling Gorkha Hill Council [India]
DPA	Dooars Planters Association [India]
EPWP	Expanded Public Works Programme [South Africa]
ESI	Employees' State Insurance [India]
ESPA	Environmental Service Providers Association [Ghana]
FAWU	Food and Allied Workers Union [South Africa]
FFB	fresh fruit bunch
GAMA	Greater Accra Metropolitan Area [Ghana]
GAWU	General Agricultural Workers Union [Ghana]
GDP	gross domestic product
GEAR	Growth, Employment and Redistribution programme [South Africa]

GJM	Gorkha Janmukti Morcha [Gorkha Liberation Front, India]
GJMC	Greater Johannesburg Metropolitan Council [South Africa]
GNLF	Gorkha National Liberation Front [India]
GOPDC	Ghana Oil Palm Development Corporation
GRMES	Garam Rolla Mazdoor Ekta Samiti [workers' collective, India]
HACCP	hazard analysis and critical control points
HMS	Hind Mazdur Sabha [Indian Workers Council]
HR	human resource
HRM	human resource management
ICU	Industrial and Commercial Workers Union [Ghana]
ILC	Indian Labour Conference
ILO	International Labour Organization
ITA	Indian Tea Association
ITPA	Indian Tea Planters Association
ITUC	International Trade Union Confederation
JCC	Johannesburg City Council [South Africa]
KAD	Women Workers Union [Denmark]
KKPKNSPS	Kagad Kach Patra Kashtakari Nagri Sahakari Pat Sanstha [savings-linked cooperative, India]
KKPKP	Kagad Kach Patra Kashtakari Panchayat [waste workers union, India]
LAWA	Leadership and Advocacy for Women in Africa [Ghana]
LEARN	Labour Education and Research Network [India]
LGWU	Local Government Workers Union [Ghana]
LMKS	LEARN Mahila Kamgar Sanghatana [LEARN Women Workers Union, India]
MMDA	metropolitan, municipal and district assemblies [Ghana]
MoU	memorandum of understanding
NCEUS	National Commission for Enterprises in the Unorganised Sector [India]
NCR	National Capital Region [India]
NEDLAC	National Economic Development and Labour Council [South Africa]
NFPM	National Fresh Produce Market [South Africa]

NGO	non-governmental organisation
NTUI	New Trade Union Initiative [India]
PLA	Plantation Labour Act [India]
PMC	Pune Municipal Corporation [India]
PPP	public-private partnership
RDP	Reconstruction and Development Programme [South Africa]
RSP	Revolutionary Socialist Party [India]
SAMWU	South African Municipal Workers Union
SER	standard employment relationship
SEWA	Self-Employed Women's Association [India]
SSNIT	Social Security and National Insurance Trust [Ghana]
SWaCH	Solid Waste Collection and Handling [cooperative, India]
TOPP	Twifo Oil Palm Plantations [Ghana]
TUC	Trades Union Congress [Ghana]
WIA	Wazirpur Industrial Area [India]
WIEGO	Women in Informal Employment: Globalizing and Organizing

1

A Conceptual and Theoretical Introduction

Edward Webster, Akua O. Britwum and Sharit Bhowmik

Under pressure to become more globally competitive, employers in the 1980s began to accept the neoliberal argument that the labour market was too rigid and needed to become more flexible (Standing 1999). Managers began changing 'the rules of the game' by departing from the standard employment relationship (SER) (Webster and Von Holdt 2005: 291). In the process we witnessed changing production forms and the blurring of relations between the formal and informal. Enterprise cost-cutting measures through outsourcing and subcontracting lengthened production chains. This resulted in several nodes along the elongated production chain, transforming the occupying workforce from secure to new levels of vulnerability (Bhowmik 2007; Britwum 2011). The erosion of the SER over the next three decades shifted employment towards a wide variety of income-generating activities that were 'unregulated by the institutions of society, in a legal and social environment in which similar activities are regulated' (Castells and Portes 1989: 12).

In the face of this structural transformation of the economy, we have seen the emergence of a kind of populism fuelled by nationalist entrepreneurs favouring isolationism and xenophobia. In the United States, Republican presidential candidate Donald Trump won widespread support in the 2016 electoral campaign for his attacks on globalisation and his 'fear-mongering demagoguery'. Jan Breman and Marcel van der Linden write about Europe:

> *Blut* and *Boden* [blood and soil] jargon has indeed a stark fascist slant; it feeds on sentiments which resist integration in a united

Europe and reject forces of globalisation even more strongly in an ideology that brazenly postulates fundamental inequality between creeds and races . . . There seems to be a close relationship between the unfettered free market mechanism and religious or ethnic fundamentalism (Breman and Van der Linden 2014: 936).

In India, we have seen an increase in communal clashes between the dominant Hindus and the Muslim minorities in different urban areas. There are also clashes between upper-caste Hindus and the traditionally marginalised lower-caste communities (who were viewed as untouchables in the past). The recent issue is over the banning of beef and slaughter of cows, which are considered holy by upper-caste Hindus. Most of the states have imposed a ban on cow slaughter. Alongside this, there are volunteer groups of 'cow protectors' who attack people they suspect of trading in cows or their flesh. The targets are Muslims and the lower-caste Hindus who either eat beef or skin dead animals. This issue serves mainly to polarise the communities and divert them from the failed promises of development and employment. In states bordering Bangladesh, Hindu fundamentalists have created the bogeymen of immigrants from Bangladesh who are taking away work from the local population. In fact, in one state, Assam, the issue of ethnic/religious cleansing has helped the ruling party at the centre to sweep the state elections. We have to wait and see whether promises of jobs are fulfilled or if further divisionary tactics will be used to divert the public from the main issues.

In Ghana, violent clashes between rural communities and pastoral Fulani herders and traders have arisen over land claims between sedentary communities where extreme land pressure makes coexistence with nomadic life untenable. In South Africa, violent attacks on cross-border immigrants have been ongoing, fuelled by thinly veiled racial and ethnic fear-mongering in the public discourse. Many of these migrants risk their lives in dangerous livelihood strategies, such as the so-called zama-zamas searching for gold in abandoned deep-level mines. When fatal accidents happen, as they do frequently when a mine collapses or toxic gases spread, xenophobic attitudes come to the fore.

With the growing informalisation of work, traditional forms of trade union organisation are proving inadequate, leading to a growing representational gap. Many believe that this process of work informalisation is leading to a convergence in the conditions of work across the globe (Siegmann and Schiphorst 2016: 111). Increasingly large numbers of workers in the Global South and North are experiencing similar insecure employment and livelihoods. Indeed, work insecurity and precarity have become very popular concepts in social science research.[1]

Over the past decade a wide range of book-length manuscripts have appeared on a number of related issues: the challenge informalisation presents to the labour movement (Standing 2009); the challenge facing precarious health workers in Pittsburgh (Lopez 2004); outsourced cleaners in the global economy (Aguiar and Herod 2006); undocumented immigrant workers in Los Angeles (Milkman 2006); insecure workers manufacturing white goods such as fridges in Korea, South Africa and Australia (Webster, Lambert and Bezuidenhout 2008); and temporary caddies and health workers in Korea and the United States (Chun 2009). In Ghana, tensions have arisen from the incorporation of informalised workers into trade unions without alterations to the traditional structures (Britwum 2011). In India, trade unions, with the exception of the Self-Employed Women's Association (SEWA), have traditionally focused on permanent workers in the formal sector. By the mid-1990s the adverse effects of liberalisation policies were felt by the working class, resulting in the widespread growth of low-paid insecure labour and leading the national trade unions to turn their attention to labour in informal employment (Bhowmik 2013). Even so, their combined efforts are little more than a drop in the ocean of vulnerable labour.

It was Guy Standing (2011), however, who popularised the concept of the 'precariat' with his book *The Precariat: The New Dangerous Class*.[2] The term now refers to a growing global workforce of casual labourers whose lives are precarious. Their experience of the world of work is marked by 'precarity' in terms of low wages, temporariness, uncertainty and dangerous working conditions. 'It is a term,' Karin Siegmann and Freek Schiphorst (2016: 111) suggest, 'designating a historical moment marked by the emergence of a new global norm of contingent employment, social risk and fragmented life situations – without security, protection or predictability.'

While work-related insecurities are undeniably affecting an increasing number of workers in the Global North and South, this collection of research-based essays suggests that the history and legacy of colonialism, as well as the policies of liberalisation, has impacted on the Global South in ways that are quite different from workers' experiences in the North. It is not only that there has never been a 'golden age' of decent work in the colonial workplace (Scully 2016). When one goes beyond the workplace into the hidden abode of reproduction – the household and the community – these differences become clear (Lee and Kofman 2012: 393). In the Global South the crisis is not simply over jobs; it is a crisis over the very reproduction of society itself (Webster and Von Holdt 2005).

Our concern in this volume is how informal workers organise, what forms this organisation takes, what strategies these workers use, what sources of power they draw on, what their relationships are with traditional unions, and how traditional unions respond to the challenge of informalisation.

Nobel laureate Elinor Ostrom (1990) has critically examined how theoretical models – advocating privatisation, for instance – are used for prescribing one-size-fits-all solutions, and has found this approach wanting. She makes a point of basing her analysis not on theoretical models but on a number of well-studied practical cases. We have adopted a similar approach in analysing the informalisation of work and preparing the contributions to this volume.

In this chapter we provide a conceptual and theoretical introduction to the case studies that follow. We have divided the introduction into four parts. We begin by tracing the growing interest in organising precarious and informal workers in the age of neoliberal globalisation. The use of the concept of precarity can be traced to Pierre Bourdieu's (1963) portrayal of a nascent colonial working class in Algeria in the 1950s; he distinguished between the precarious racialised, casual or contingent workers (*travailleurs intermittents*) and the permanently employed workers. But its derivative 'precariat', Carl-Ulrik Schierup and Martin Bak Jørgensen (2016) suggest, is attributed to French activists campaigning for irregular migrants' rights at the turn of the millennium. This has led to two quite separate academic and policy debates on the informalisation of work: in developing countries debates on the informal sector took place, and in industrialised countries debates were on precarious work.

In the second part of this introduction, we discuss the intellectual history of the concept of informality. In the third part, we introduce the power resources approach to the revitalisation of labour and identify four sources of union power. In the fourth part, we give an overview of the ten case studies in this volume, showing how they illustrate the inability of traditional trade unions to respond to the needs of informal rural and urban workers and how new forms of organisation and sources of power are emerging in tentative and often experimental ways.

We conclude by suggesting that predictions of the 'end of labour' have been common but that new forms of collective solidarity have emerged in the past. The challenge facing labour is to identify and build these new forms of organisation and sources of power that are developing alongside the decline of traditional trade unions.

Labour's challenge: Organising informal workers

In large part, the studies in this volume suggest that workers are rejecting traditional trade unions and forming new types of organisations that bring workers together to promote their rights and interests. In South Africa, vulnerable workers are turning to legal advice offices for support (Wilderman et al. 2016). In India, informal workers in some cases use the democratic electoral competition among different political parties to promote their demands (Agarwala 2014). Ghana's long-standing trade union presence in the informal economy, beginning in 1979 with the General Agricultural Workers Union (GAWU) organising rural agriculture workers, takes advantage of existing formations of informal workers' organisations (Britwum 2011).

New forms of resistance are emerging to deal with increasing informalisation. The struggles of mineworkers on the platinum belt of South Africa that culminated in the Marikana massacre of August 2012 is one example; the November 2012 uprising by rural workers in the farmlands of South Africa's Western Cape province, discussed in Chapter 4 of this volume, is another. In both instances, protest took place outside of traditional trade unions, and the Western Cape farm workers won their demands by, among other strategies, blockading a national highway.

There are increasing numbers of national and international union organisations that support organising initiatives by informal workers. Christine Bonner and Dave Spooner (2012) discuss an increased interest by the International Trade Union Confederation (ITUC) and the Global

Union Federations in organising informal workers, and the growing number of informal workers' associations of varying origins. Some of these have been created by informal workers themselves, and others by unions traditionally organising in the formal economy but now reaching out to organise informal workers; still others have been conceived and sponsored by external actors such as women's organisations, migrant workers' organisations and non-governmental organisations (NGOs) (Bonner and Spooner 2011).

The Women in Informal Employment: Globalizing and Organizing (WIEGO) is one of the best known of such initiatives. WIEGO was started in 1997 by a group of academics, researchers and activists. The organisation was set up because of the need to link academics and researchers in labour studies with grassroots activists and trade union organisations, largely in response to the statistical invisibility of informal workers, especially women. WIEGO works with organisations of street vendors, home-based workers, waste recyclers and domestic workers. It is closely associated with ITUC and its affiliated unions, including SEWA. WIEGO's uniqueness lies in its having created a single space in which a diverse range of actors with different capacities and interests – statisticians, economists, activists and organisers, policy analysts and academics from different disciplines – can work together to improve the situation of informal workers (Batliwala 2004: 73).

Documentation on the burgeoning role of both new actors and traditional representative forms of informal work in emerging and developing economies remains scanty (Lindell 2010). Writers like F.L. Cooke and G. Wood (2011) encourage a widening of efforts to clarify the conceptual and analytical scope of industrial relations actors and their related powers. Such observations underscore the need to expand research on the existence, viability and effectiveness of various actors engaged in promoting the labour rights of informal economy workers.

Despite the foregoing examples of successful organising initiatives of informal workers, their organisations are often dismissed as irrelevant or, in some cases, as being incapable of collective mobilisation (Lindell 2010). As late as the 1990s, trade unions affiliated to the Indian national trade union federations did 'not appear to be interested in unionizing workers in the informal sector' (Bhowmik 2002: 142). Sharit Bhowmik cites studies showing that workers in the informal sector constituted less than 1 per cent of the total membership of the national federations. This was despite the fact that employment in the informal sector had been growing, while it was declining in the formal sector due to strategies (such as outsourcing) adopted by large firms (Bhowmik 2002: 142).

Gunilla Andrae and Bjorn Beckman are sceptical of the role of traditional unions in organising informal workers, and make a persuasive case for informal workers to develop their own organisations:

> [It is] an illusion to believe that unions can either integrate or effectively organise the workers in the informal economy. Each segment of the population must find its own means of organising that takes its point of departure from the contradictions that specifically apply to them (1998: 87).

They identify a range of common interests in their case study of a garment workers' union and a tailors' association in Nigeria, such as access to stable and reasonably priced supplies of electricity and water as well as regulating and restricting foreign imports, notably through smuggling (Andrae and Beckman 1998: 93-4). However, they warn against the tendency to gloss over the differences at the two ends of the divide, leading to what they describe as 'a voluntaristic approach' to organising in the informal economy (86).

Despite these different experiences, countries such as Ghana show some levels of success in 'crossing the divide' between the informal economy and trade unions. Some trade unions have initiated attempts to overcome structural challenges and offer meaningful representation to their informal economy members (Britwum 2011). In India, as mentioned earlier, although the mainstream unions initially had little interest in the informal economy, they have more recently turned their attention to organising this sector. Recent membership surveys of the eleven national trade union federations show that each has increased its membership by three to five times. For example, the oldest federation, the All India Trade Union Congress (AITUC), had a membership in 1990 of around 830 000, but by 2012 it had increased its membership to 3.5 million. The expansion of membership has been mainly in informal employment occupations such as agricultural workers, small factory workers, child-care centre workers, domestic workers, construction workers and street vendors. Moreover, the largest trade union federation of women in informal employment, SEWA, has been accepted as a mainstream union. It is one of the eleven centres that are recognised as a national trade union federation based on its membership of over one million workers spread over four trades in at least eight states.

Class boundaries are blurred in the small enterprises in the informal economy. Many of the managers and owners are sitting at machines working alongside their workers. Kinship social networks play a role in recruitment. Organising in this sector implies that other social identities such as ethnicity, caste, community and gender should be foregrounded along with class.

Informal economy workers have used several organisational modes drawing on traditional norms. In Ghana, for example, market traders use a mix of traditional and secular notions of power and authority to mobilise and regulate their trades and to engage state and other players (Britwum 2013). Thus organisational forms are dependent on the immediate environment and spaces within which they operate. Not surprisingly, the only community groups that clothing workers in Johannesburg's Fashion District belong to are faith-based organisations, opening up the possibility of the self-organisation of informal organisations involving union–community coalitions (Webster and Joynt 2014).[3] Indeed, in 2012 a union of migrant workers was launched in the inner city of Johannesburg with Bishop Paul Verryn of the Methodist Church as the patron. In India, the different associations working with street vendors, including NGOs and trade unions, have come together to form the National Association of Street Vendors of India. They pressurised the state to frame a national policy on street vending and later, in early 2014, to pass a law protecting and regulating street vending (Bhowmik 2014a).

As Edward Webster and Bhowmik argue:

> In the South there has been a transition to capitalism, but it has been uneven. This is not merely because of the coexistence of different socio-economic formations but also because this transformation happens within a capitalist structure. The existence of urban informal employment may be an innovative response to insecurity, but it also emphasizes the widespread use

of manual, unskilled labour in the production process. Instead of contributing to a Northern Polanyian-type transformation, it [the countermovement] leads to the reproduction of traditional occupations within the urban informal sector (Webster and Bhowmik 2014: 5).

The artisanal and small-scale mining taking place in abandoned gold mines at the edge of Soweto near Johannesburg and around Obuasi and Tarkwa in Ghana are examples of what could be described as 'combined and uneven development' (V.I. Lenin, cited in Lowy 1981: 65).

Rather than engaging in traditional scholarship on industrial relations, many labour scholars are exploring the transformations occurring at the periphery of mainstream labour movements (Bonner and Spooner 2011; Britwum 2011; Webster 2011; Bhowmik 2014b). Jennifer Chun (2009) has called these new sources of power 'symbolic leverage' – where union organisers have successfully drawn on the public arena with the aim of restoring the dignity of and justice for socially devalued and economically marginalised workers.

In this volume we engage with these 'new political subjects' in three different countries – Ghana, India and South Africa. We chose these three countries for their similarities but also because of their differences. Although all three countries have experienced the dislocating effects of British colonialism, they achieved democracy at different moments following the Second World War – India in 1947, Ghana in 1957 and South Africa in 1994. More importantly, they began to liberalise their economies in the 1980s and early 1990s, leading to growing informalisation. But for our purposes the central difference lies in the degree of informalisation of their labour markets and the response of labour to this.

Asef Bayat (2010: 43–62) speaks of informal economic activities as 'the quiet encroachment of the ordinary'. He documents the everyday practices of families in Cairo as they struggle under the effects of neoliberal restructuring during the Mubarak regime in Egypt. Unable to challenge restructuring politically, or to adjust financially to rising living costs, families undertake 'individual and quiet direct action instead of collective decision-making to make ends meet'. Such action involves non-legal urban arrangements where goods circulate in an informal way through pirate networks, tapping into services such as electricity and water.

While we found examples of 'quiet encroachment' in our own research, our central interest is in the growing evidence that innovative organisational strategies to bridge the informal-formal 'divide' are emerging in the Global South. Ilda Lindell (2010) has documented successful attempts at collective organising and the emergence of alliances across this divide in Africa. An example of a new organising strategy in Ghana is an alliance of informal port workers with national trade unions. 'Through the alliance with the national union, the local union of casual workers gained the necessary political status to influence their working conditions' (Boampong 2010: 148). In India, the fairly powerful Mumbai Port Trust, Dock and General Employees' Union has successfully initiated a trade union for shipbreakers at Alang, the country's largest centre for the shipbreaking industry. Unlike the permanent workers who form the core of the union's membership, these workers are migrants who work in precarious conditions with low pay (Noiseux 2016). Rina Agarwala (2014: 2) has challenged the conventional view that informalisation is the 'final nail in the labour movement's coffin'. Informal workers in India, she demonstrates, are creating new institutions and forging a new social contract between the state and labour. She shows how informal worker movements are most successful when operating within electoral contexts where parties must compete for mass votes from the poor. Agarwala calls this 'competitive populism'. These informal worker organisations are not attached to a particular party, nor do they espouse a specific political or economic ideology. Ebbe Prag (2010) makes a similar observation in the Dantokpa market of Cotonou in Benin, where women traders use their influence in the market to secure political capital from politicians. These are examples of attempts by informal workers to organise for interest representation. We turn now to the evolution of the concept of informality.

An intellectual history of the concept of informality

In development discourse it was assumed in the 1950s and 1960s that, following modernisation theory, the 'dual economies' of developing societies would be transformed into dynamic industrial economies that would absorb the rapid flow of people to the cities. This did not happen. Instead, the urban populations of the developing world grew dramatically, surviving on small-scale informal economic activities rather than on formal employment. It was a paper by Keith Hart (1973) and the International Labour Organization (ILO) mission to Kenya (ILO 1972) which established the importance of a dichotomy between formality and informality. These two studies marked the rise of the concept of the 'informal sector' to describe the unregulated and invisible activities of the urban poor of the Third World to support themselves. The urban poor were not unemployed, these studies argued; they were working, although often for low and irregular returns. The implication of these research findings, policy advisers suggested, was that unemployment statistics gave a misleading impression of the level of inequality, and that the informal sector was potentially a major contributor to the national economy.

Over the next three decades an outpouring of research, debate and policy focus followed. Theoretically, perhaps the longest-standing discussion in the literature on informality considers whether informal work is dualist (a holdover of archaic forms of work organisation originating outside the modern economy), legalist (entrepreneurship seeking alternative channels due to overly restrictive regulations) or survivalist (the last resort of those with no viable economic alternative) (Smith and Stenning 2006).

Many argue that the extensive growth of informal employment comprising marginalised workers can be seen as a different version of what Karl Marx (1976: 781–870) called the reserve army of the unemployed. Marx's contention was that capitalism creates large groups of unemployed workers which can be used as weapons to control the wages of the employed. There are parallels with informal employment. The large sections of poorly employed workers, especially those engaged in outsourcing, are used not merely to lower costs through low wages but also to reduce the bargaining power of those in formal employment. A situation of this type leads to divisions within the working class, with the more secure formal workers on one side and the lower-paid insecure informal workers on the other. Beyond the creation of a reserve army to reduce the bargaining power of formal workers, there is the capture into mainstream capitalist sectors in developing countries of the so-called traditional production forms such as peasant and unpaid household labour. This incorporation facilitates, for example, the expropriation of value from rural non-waged agricultural workers (Wolpe 1972; Roberts 1982). This is in fact an important reason why those in informal employment are being organised. It will enable them to collectively articulate their own problems and put forth their demands rather than be used by the capitalist class to further its interests by dividing the working class.

Originally the informal sector concept was applied to the self-employed urban poor in developing countries. In 2003 the International Conference of Statisticians expanded the definition of the informal economy from enterprises that are not legally regulated to employment relationships that are not legally regulated or protected. 'Informal employment' is now defined as being without formal contracts, worker benefits or social protection. This includes self-employment in informal enterprises – workers in small unregistered or unincorporated enterprises, including employers, own-account operators and unpaid family members. It also includes wage employment in informal jobs – workers without formal contracts, worker benefits or social protection for formal or informal firms, for households or with no fixed employer, including employees of informal enterprises and other informal wage workers such as casual or day labourers, domestic workers, unregistered or undeclared workers, and temporary or part-time workers as well as industrial outworkers (also called home-workers) (Chen 2005: 7–8).

This broadening of the scope of the informal sector to include informal employment has led some to question the usefulness of the concept. Hart argues:

> The extension of the scope of the concept of the 'informal economy' – to embrace rich and poor countries, government and business, casual labour and the self-employed, corruption and crime – when taken with the wholesale devolution of central bureaucracies compared with forty years ago, leaves a question mark over its continuing usefulness today (Hart 2007: 5).

But, as Hart (2007: 5) goes on to argue, the value of the concept is that it allows one to understand how people devise their own means of survival in ways that are not 'organised immediately as ruling elites would like'. Similarly Henry Bernstein and Philip Woodhouse (2001) write of the 'classes of labour' in Africa and Leo Panitch and Colin Leys (2001: ix) describe the 'growing numbers . . . who now depend – directly and indirectly – on the sale of their labour power for their own daily reproduction'. They pursue their reproduction 'typically through insecure and oppressive – and in many places increasingly scarce – wage employment, often combined with a range of likewise precarious small-scale farming and insecure informal sector [survival activities]'.

This heterogeneity of work in Africa and the ambivalence in class positions that this leads to are not new to African labour scholars. As Robin Cohen and Peter Lawrence wrote more than three decades ago:

> There is a large group of the population which is simultaneously and ambiguously semi-proletariat and semi-peasant . . . Equally within the favelas and shantytowns, large numbers of individuals who are sometimes described as unemployed or as sub or lumpen proletariat are in fact intermittently employed performing services or in small workshops employing a handful of workers and apprentices. In the case of this group, the ambiguity arises from the fact that it comprises people who can at the same time be considered self-employed or employees (Cohen and Lawrence 1982: 1, 4).

James Heinz (2006) has provided a useful way of overcoming the ambiguity in differentiating a worker from a self-employed entrepreneur. He suggests that the common denominator between the two is that both individuals earn income by selling their labour in some kind of a market – either directly on a wage-labour market or indirectly through some form of product market. The dividing line between 'worker' and 'entrepreneur' may not be clear-cut, he concludes, but individuals who derive the vast majority of their income from their labour and are dependent on others for the realisation of these earnings can be considered workers.

This shift in views of the informal economy over the past three decades is captured in Table 1.1.

Table 1.1 Old and new views of the informal economy

The old view	The new view
The informal sector is the traditional economy that will wither away and die with modern, industrial growth.	The informal economy is here to stay, and is expanding with modern, industrial growth.
It is only marginally productive.	It is a major provider of employment, goods and services for lower-income groups. It It contributes a significant share of gross domestic product (GDP).
It exists separately from the formal economy.	It is linked to the formal economy – it produces for, trades with, distributes for and provides services to the formal economy.
It represents a reserve pool of surplus labour.	Much of the recent rise in informal employment is due to the decline in formal employment or to the informalisation of previously formal employment relationships.
It comprises mostly street traders and very small-scale producers.	It is made up of a wide range of informal occupations – both resilient old forms such as casual day labour in construction and agriculture, self-employed rural agriculture workers, as well as emerging new ones such as temporary and part-time jobs plus home-work for high-tech industries.
Most of those in the sector are entrepreneurs who run illegal and unregistered enterprises in order to avoid regulation and taxation.	It is made up of non-standard wage workers as well as entrepreneurs and self-employed persons producing legal goods and services, albeit through irregular or unregulated means. Most entrepreneurs and the self-employed are amenable to, and would welcome, efforts to reduce barriers to registration and related transaction costs and to increase benefits from regulations. Most non-standard wage workers would welcome more stable jobs and workers' rights.
Work in the informal economy comprises mostly survival activities and thus is not a subject for economic policy.	Informal enterprises include not only survival activities but also stable enterprises and dynamic growing businesses. Informal employment includes not only self-employment but also wage employment. All forms of informal employment are affected by economic policies.

Source: Chen (2005: 12).

We turn now to the third part of the introduction: a new approach to organising these new types of workers in the developing world, which has become known as the power resources approach.

Identifying sources of power among vulnerable workers

The power resources approach takes as its point of departure the assumption that the labour movement was built around the capacity of workers to disrupt the economy (its structural power within the workplace) and their ability to organise collectively into trade unions and political parties (associational power) (Piven 2000; Wright 2000; Silver 2003). Structural power can take two forms. Marketplace bargaining power is a form of structural power that evolves from tight labour markets, scarce skills in demand by employers, low levels of unemployment, or the ability of employees to exit the labour market. In contrast, workplace bargaining power results from a specific strategic position of a group of workers within production (Silver 2003: 13). In particular, the dynamics of production and, in the broader sense, of capitalism shape this particular form of workers' power. For instance, the location of workers in key industrial sectors and in highly integrated production lines or value chains enhances their ability to effectively interrupt production through collective action.

While structural power has been weakened by liberalisation and globalisation, and associational power is under attack by the ideologues of the 'free market', two other sources of power exist: societal power and institutional power. Societal power depends on building coalitions with social movements and influencing public discourse around issues of social justice (Chun 2009). Institutional power embeds past social compromises by the incorporation of associational and structural power into institutions and legislation (Dörre, Holst and Nachtwey 2009).

As Donna McGuire (2014) argues, institutional power continues to be applied during ongoing economic cycles, even where power relations within society may have changed. It may take the form of labour law, wage-setting and bargaining arrangements, as well as institutionalised forms of social dialogue such as the National Economic Development and Labour Council (NEDLAC), South Africa's premier peak-level social dialogue institution (Webster, Joynt and Metcalfe 2013.). The important point about institutional power is that it grants rights but also limits the space for action (Dörre, Holst and Nachtwey 2009). Institutions shape the relationship between structural and associational-organisational power, but power resources are not sufficient; they also need strategic capabilities – that is, the capability to detect power resources in order to make use of them as well as the organisational flexibility to optimise associational power (Lévesque and Murray 2013).

The fourfold sources of power – structural, associational, societal and institutional – provide the potential basis for a strategy for rebuilding collective solidarity; see Figure 1.1.

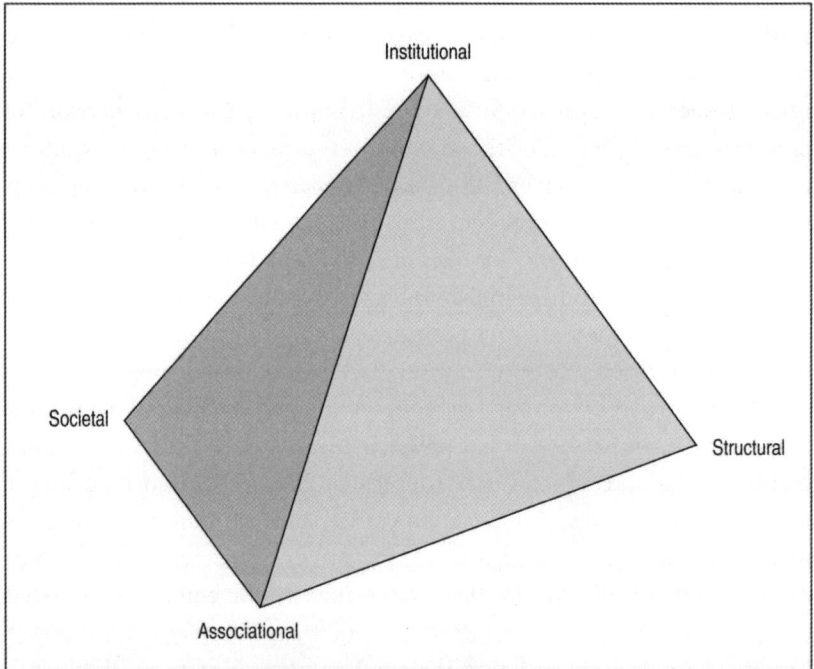

Figure 1.1 The pyramid of workers' power resources
Source: Schmalz and Dörre (2013).

Societal power and logistical power (which is a subtype of structural power) both seek to address 'the public' by extending disputes from the workplace into the public domain – for example, Western Cape farm workers blockading the roads. But tensions exist between logistical and societal/symbolic power: While the latter essentially depends on gaining public support, the former may turn citizens against the protests and delegitimise workers' demands in the eyes of the wider public. This points to the fact that the relationship between a union's power resources should be understood as not simply additive or complementary but also potentially conflictual.

New forms of organisation and sources of power

We have suggested that the increasing informalisation of work is leading to a growing representational gap as traditional forms of trade union organisation are proving inadequate. The case studies in this volume reveal the distinctive nature of precarious work in Ghana, India and South Africa, and show how this is leading to new forms of organisation and sources of power. Part I, 'Agricultural Aspects', consists of four case studies of agricultural labour: an oil palm plantation in Ghana, tea plantations in India, an uprising of farm workers in the Western Cape province of South Africa, and horticultural farming in South Africa's Gauteng province.

Chapter 2, by Akua Britwum and Angela Akorsu, deals with the plantation sector (oil palm) in Ghana and the painful (for workers) transition of ownership from public sector to privatisation. This change in ownership has weakened workers' structural and associational power by reducing the number of permanent workers and spurring the growth of insecure (non-standard) employment. These workers are excluded from protective legislation. The oil palm workers are mainly contract workers, with only a few having permanent employment. In Chapter 3, Sharit Bhowmik reveals that permanent workers outnumber temporary workers in tea plantations in West Bengal, India, but given their low wages and poor living and working conditions, the plight of these workers is no better than their counterparts in Ghana. The major difference is that the oil palm contract workers have started organising themselves, beginning in 2010, in order to articulate their interests in a collective manner. They have made major gains in improving their living and working conditions. In order to consolidate their efforts and ensure continuity, they have formed a trade union.

Tea plantation workers in West Bengal have been unionised since 1947, but the bane of the trade union movement is multi-unionism.

Workers of rival unions fight each other, and the main beneficiary is the management. The legal system also encourages multi-unionism. Although the Trade Unions Act allows for the registration of trade unions, there is no law that lays down conditions for recognition of any trade union as the principal bargaining unit. This is left to the discretion of the management. Unions therefore compete with each other to be recognised as a bargaining agent. Twenty-six unions signed the wage agreement of 20 February 2015. On the other hand, having a single union as labour's representative may not solve workers' problems, as the case of Assam has shown. The tea plantation workers in Assam, the largest tea-growing region in the country, are represented by one union. However, workers' power to bargain for better facilities is blunted by the union being soft on the plantation companies. Wages in Assam are lower than those in West Bengal.

The main difference between the oil palm workers and the tea plantation workers is that the former have come together to form a union after considerable struggle. They are thus in control of their union and they determine the bargaining agenda. However, the tea workers have less control over their unions as most of the leaders are not merely non-workers but are also of different ethnic origin. A look at the 26 signatories shows that almost all are Bengalis and not tribal workers.[4]

The struggle of the tribals for possession of their land becomes more effective when civil society organisations join in to support them. This is true not just of dispossession among the tribals but of other sections of the working population as well. The rights of plantation workers have long been ignored, not merely because they are isolated but also because most organisations, besides their trade unions, rarely come out in support. It is only when tea plantation workers start to die of starvation when their plantations close that people wake up to the fact that there is something wrong. In general, it seems difficult to sustain movements if they do not get support from civil society organisations or from the international labour movement. The struggle continues, however.

Chapter 4, by Jesse Wilderman, and Chapter 5, by uMbuso we Nkosi, deal with organising farm workers in South Africa. These chapters share a common thread – namely, the growing informalisation of work leading to insecure jobs and decreased social protection. These cases are similar to the ones in Ghana and India. The uprising of farm workers in the

Western Cape, discussed in Chapter 4, shows how collective action can be sustained through the collective leadership of precarious workers. The movement lasted several months and was different from earlier protests led by the trade unions. The latter were mild protest actions, whereas the Western Cape farm workers were more militant and at times took on violent tactics such as burning vineyards and blocking roads.

The study of the resistance of farm workers in the Western Cape shows how these workers used new tactics to organise. A large part of the organisation and mobilising was done through mobile phones. This is a comparatively new tool for organising, and Chapter 4 shows how the workers used these instruments effectively to strategise their struggle. Another aspect that helped the workers to build solidarity was the new housing system. The farm owners had earlier allowed the workers to reside on the farms. The workers stayed in their small houses at a distance from the farm owners and had little contact with workers from other farms. When the landowners evicted them from their homes, the workers moved to ghettos – informal settlements – outside the farms. This new spatial form in fact brought the workers closer to each other, and enabled them to plan their strategies in close coordination.

The militancy of the workers can be seen as a direct form of challenge to the authority structure on the farms, which is exercised through a mixture of racial paternalism and social distance. A similar situation exists in the tea plantations of India, where the managements have ruled through fear and the maintenance of social distance from the workers. This type of colonial relationship may be successful for managements as long as the workers are isolated and helpless. But once workers realise that their strength lies in their numbers, the situation can take a dramatic turn. The workers may revolt against management, perhaps violently. For example, in September 2015, around 10 000 women plantation workers in the southern state of Kerala went on strike to demand higher wages and better living conditions. This strike was unique because male workers and the registered trade unions were excluded. The women were fed up with the mild stance of the trade unions that were mainly male-dominated. The women sat in front of the government offices and blocked the highway. The strike lasted for three weeks and more women joined in as almost all plantations had to shut down. Women constitute a little more than half the labour force on plantations in India. The women were able to make some gains, but ironically the agreement was signed by the trade unions and management. Nonetheless, the women's strike gave a jolt to the trade unions, especially the two supported by communist parties.

Such protest actions are spontaneous and they arise when the workers realise that something is wrong but do not know how to oppose it in a sustained manner. Hence there is a sudden spurt in organisation that rises from within the group. In the cases of both Ghana and India, the existing trade unions could not meet the aspirations of the workers, who then organised their own independent movements. These spontaneous movements can be seen as healthy outbursts against oppression. However, they must develop institutional power to be sustainable or they will soon fizzle out. Trade unions are the main institutions for ensuring continuity. In the cases discussed, the movements were a result of the apathy of the existing trade unions to the problems of informal workers and women workers. In both cases the local trade unions were pressurised to take up the genuine issues of workers. In Ghana, informal workers in the oil palm plantations formed their own union. These instances show that pressure from rank-and-file workers can influence decisions of managements and trade unions.

Chapter 5 highlights the plight of the fresh fruit and vegetable growers in Gauteng. The problems of these farmers began when the government-sponsored National Fresh Produce Markets (NFPMs) declined. The NFPM was the largest purchaser of fresh fruit and vegetables, and farmers found it convenient to market their produce through this organisation. However, large grocery chains began bypassing the NFPMs and started purchasing directly from the farmers. Normally in such a case, when market forces prevail the farmers would get better prices as large buyers would compete with each other. Unfortunately, this did not happen, as the four major buyers formed a cartel that became a monopsony (a monopoly buyer) for the farmers' products, and they lowered the purchase prices. Thus the income for farmers was lowered, resulting in reduced wages for farm workers. The chapter examines the value chain in horticulture starting from the farm workers and ending in markets in the cities. There are a number of local and national retailers in between that push up retail prices but depress the value of the farmers' produce. India is likely to proceed in the same way. The right-wing government elected in May 2015 has stated that producers need not market their products through the Agricultural Products Marketing Co-operative. This organisation exists in all major cities and is the main source of distribution for retailers in the urban areas.

The chapters in Part I show that there are similarities in the agrarian situation in the three countries. The need to oppose anti-worker and anti-peasant positions of the state is important, but there is a greater need to involve civil society institutions in this fight so that the public at large can become aware of the exploitative processes. Another important similarity is that in almost all cases the workers have either started movements without the support of the conventional trade unions or they have pressurised the unions to take up their cause. This certainly underscores how the precariat is trying to put forward its demands through its own understanding of the situation instead of depending on other agencies to do so for them.

Part II, 'Urban Considerations', consists of six urban case studies of precarious work ranging from municipalities in Accra in Ghana, Pune in India and Johannesburg in South Africa, to grassroots organising of informal work in metal factories in Delhi, garment workers in Daravi slum in Mumbai and domestic workers in Ghana. These chapters highlight worker vulnerabilities necessitating organising for redress and the specificities that constrain organising efforts. The diversity in the nature and composition of the workforce within the sectors in the respective countries, the authors point out, is dictated by neoliberal economic policy of minimal state intervention and a large private sector.

The chapters on waste management workers in Ghana (Chapter 6, by Owusu Boampong and Benjamin Tachie), India (Chapter 7, by Malati Gadgil and Melanie Samson), and South Africa (Chapter 8, by Edward Webster and Carmen Ludwig) draw out the conditions that dictate the organisational modes of the workers. The state, represented by the municipal authorities in the three countries, has a different presence in the working life of waste workers as a result of the levels of private intrusions into public service delivery and attendant employment informalisation. They are characterised by different forms of privatisation and state control. At one end is the extreme informalisation of the waste management system in India, with the weakest workforce and municipal authority connections. The Pune Municipal Corporation (PMC) of India is almost invisible as an employer. Ghana operates at the midpoint: even though the Accra Metropolitan Assembly (AMA) continues to be directly engaged in waste collection and disposal, it is in control of just 20 per cent of the service delivery. The Greater Johannesburg Metropolitan Council (GJMC) in South Africa is visible in the employment lives of workers, more directly for its employees and indirectly through labour brokers and the quasi-private entity Pikitup.

The commonalities presented in these chapters include the increasing privatisation and attendant informalising of work and employment forms and the high levels of precarity generated. Thus privatisation of waste workers, represented at one end of the spectrum of informalisation, is driven by the state's desire to cut costs. Privatisation takes a number of forms with various actors. There is the quasi-private Pikitup created and owned by the GJMC in South Africa, and the fully private companies such as Zoomlion Ghana Limited and Asadu Royal Waste contract partners of the AMA in Ghana. In India a union-formed entity, the Solid Waste Collection and Handling (SWaCH) cooperative, signed a memorandum of understanding with PMC to collect waste. At the other end of the spectrum are efforts located in what has always been informal, such as domestic work. These make the case for a continuum of formal public service casualisation of the workforce, including labour contractors and the self-employed in contract employment relations.

Collective action by urban informal economy workers is analysed by Mouleshri Vyas in Chapter 9. Steel utensil manufacturing workers in Delhi, India, have been mobilised into an association on the basis of their economic status and are able to pursue strike actions, although with minimal results. The chapter highlights the struggles of these workers at an early stage of mobilisation; it points to the fact that the Wazipur Industrial Area (WIA), with its tough Dickensian-type physical and social conditions, as well as the extremely difficult nature of work and working conditions in the industry, pose an immense challenge to any initiative aimed at collectivising labour. It is clear that for many workers involvement in organising efforts is unlikely, and the only form of agency possible for such workers is individualised resistance, coping strategies or stoic endurance.

Chapter 10, by Indira Gartenberg, and Chapter 11, by Angela Akorsu and Amanda Odoi, demonstrate that organising invisible or 'hidden' workers is possible, and that innovative strategies of organising such as the use of cellphones and social media, as well as door-to-door solicitation, are effective in bringing together diverse groups of informal workers to create spaces for dialogue among them. Despite these similarities, the two chapters present contrasting examples regarding NGO efforts at organising such workers and offer little to settle divergent positions on the matter. Gartenberg's contribution on India provides a positive account of NGO efforts at organising informal workers and seems to confirm Bonner's (2010) suggestion that NGOs are useful in organising domestic workers. However, Akorsu and Odoi's divergent finding seems to confirm the view that NGO efforts at organising domestic workers only secure nominal rights protection, which is merely a means to an end – political voice and representation of the workers (Hayashi 2010). This is also true of the Indian case, as the NGO, aware of its limitations, initiated a trade union of women workers in informal employment.

Organising depends on the ability to mobilise members and connect them with a common purpose. Sustaining the mobilisation requires power to engage the parties with which workers are in contention. In Johannesburg, as described in Chapter 8, the connection with city authorities is clear and a stronger union presence allows workers to use traditional union power resources, such as strikes and public protests, to give visibility to their work and concerns. Connecting the right of citizens to accountability and quality service from the GJMC gave legitimacy to the workers' cause. In India, feminists at the SNDT Women's University in Pune drew on different power sources, what we have called societal power, by connecting their organising to the conditions of women within the economic and social sphere of the communities in which they live. The concerns were expressed in terms of efficiency: reducing drudgery and time employed and increasing income. In this instance, the cooperative system, which operated on the notion of self-help, is ideal.

The connections with traditional trade unions varied. The strongest example of traditional union sources of power is the case of the South African Municipal Workers Union; the weakest is Ghana, where waste workers were organised by the Local Government Workers Union of the Ghana Trades Union Congress and the Civil and Local Government Staff Association. There was very little commerce between the unions and workers. Traditional union methods in the case studies presented illustrate weak options for pursuing workplace rights even in the formal workplace. The use of traditional trade union methods is very weak in Ghana. In Pune, an innovative attempt to use the cooperative and activist approach to address developmental and political needs of workers was initiated. Chapter 7 persuasively illustrates that different organisational modes are required to address the variety of workers' needs in this situation. In the case of the GJMC waste workers discussed in Chapter 8, union power to protect workers was contingent on internal solidarity and union ability to utilise its power.

The case studies of waste management workers illustrate the variety of modes of organisation required to deal with the various actors and work-related needs of informal workers in urban areas. In the South African case, there is a need to connect community rights to waste management services and the accountability of the GJMC to city dwellers. In India, it is a question of efficiency and reducing working hours while increasing income sources. In Ghana, however, even the workers' claim to make a living and access to waste is in contention. These are the concerns that framed organising and gave players such as private contractors an interest in organising informal waste workers.

Informal workers are using a multiplicity of organisational forms to negotiate with city authorities their right to collect the waste generated in the city. The inability of the traditional trade unions to fill the emerging organising needs and the efforts to organise support from civil society as well as workers' individual and collective agency are evident in the case studies in this section. The heterogeneity of circumstances and needs of urban informal workers points to the variations in their organising strategies. It is clear that for some workers, collective organising efforts are unlikely to succeed and the only forms of agency possible are individualised resistance, coping strategies or endurance. For the majority, however, participation in organising initiatives is conceivable, although with minimal success.

Undeniably, internal and external limitations constrain urban informal workers' associations from maturing into a strong political voice through consolidating their gains in what we are calling institutional power. But what our case studies demonstrate is that urban informal workers, though vulnerable, are not passive victims of globalisation. Rather, they have representation capacities that can be harnessed into strong political agency in claiming their rights. Significant progress in organising will be made only if there is a concerted effort to develop innovative associational strategies that recognise the potential for societal power as an alternative to the erosion of structural power. Building symbolic power requires an emphasis on contesting the public arena, both physically in streets and neighbourhoods and cities, as well as in the media. It also necessitates the construction of a new discourse drawing on symbolic meanings that have a resonance in communities as well as with the broader public – for example, the injustice of poverty, the right to make a living, discrimination suffered by women and street traders, and so on.

Conclusion: Searching for new forms of solidarity

The concept of solidarity is central to any discussion of crossing the formal–informal divide. Solidarity is, as Ingemar Lindberg (2014) observes, often used more rhetorically than analytically. He distinguishes between two distinct interpretations of this concept. The first is value-based, defining solidarity as a 'moral imperative that . . . is a fundamental value in all the major religions of the world: Do to the other what you would like her to do to you. Love your neighbour as yourself' (Lindberg 2014: 136). Lindberg suggests that a union approach to solidarity is different because

> [it] has a constitutive element of mutual self-interest. Solidarity in a union context means moving from an individual self-interest, or the self-interest of a smaller group, to a broader self-interest – for example, of all metalworkers in Sweden, or all dockworkers in Europe – and perhaps eventually to the mutual self-interest of a global working class. But even so, union solidarity will always have an element of shared self-interest. Unions are interest-based organisations (Lindberg 2014: 136).

But Lindberg goes on to add a third element to his definition of solidarity – identity. Solidarity has, he says,

> an element of identification that is typically based on a shared position in the organisation of production. Identity as a worker, being part of the working class, is a vital element in union

solidarity – [solidarity] is expressed in a willingness to stand up for each other and fight together (Lindberg 2014: 136).

The history of labour has been marked by constant predictions of the 'end of labour'. This is best illustrated by a comment by David Brody, a leading labour historian in the United States:

Perhaps one of the more famous stories illustrating the labor movement's unpredictable course is the one historians often tell of the multitude and solemn pronouncements made by august labor experts in 1932 heralding the certain death of the American labor movement. These dire predictions, of course, were issued literally on the eve of the dramatic and widespread upsurge of labor organizing that began in 1932 (Brody 1980, cited in Cobble 1992: 82).

The rise of Fordism in the 1930s in North America had led to a shift from craft unionism, where the power of workers lay in their skill (market-based power), to industrial unionism, where their power lay in a new political subject, the semi-skilled worker, and their new source of power at workplace level (workplace bargaining). Whether we are at the beginning of a new type of labour movement is unclear. However, what is clear from our case studies is that a new political subject of labour has emerged, creating new forms of organisation and sources of power among the labouring poor of Ghana, India and South Africa.

Notes
1. Three special editions on precarious work appeared in the first half of 2016: *Progress in Development Studies* 16(2); *International Labor and Working Class History* 89; *Global Labour Journal* 7(2).
2. There are three main books by Standing that popularised the concept of the precariat: *Work after Globalization: Building Occupational Citizenship* (2009); *The Precariat: The New Dangerous Class* (2011); and *A Precariat Charter: From Denizens to Citizens* (2014).
3. See Bonner (2010: 11) for examples of domestic unions with links to faith-based organisations, and Ally (2010: 166–7) for the role of religion in the lives of domestic workers in Johannesburg.

4. The term 'tribe' may now be politically incorrect in sociological literature, but in India the word has a specific connotation. These indigenous people are identified in the schedule of the Constitution of India as a 'Backward Class' and they are entitled to protection of their culture and their land. The state has to make special provisions for their education, and a quota of 7.5 per cent is reserved for admissions in all educational institutions and for jobs in the public or government sector. The fact that despite all this protection tribals in India remain the most backward section of the population is another matter.

References

Agarwala, R. 2014. *Informal Work, Formal Politics and Dignified Discontent in India*. New York: Cambridge University Press.

Aguiar, L. and A. Herod (eds). 2006. *The Dirty Work of Neoliberalism: Cleaners in the Global Economy*. London: Blackwell.

Ally, S. 2010. *From Servants to Workers: South African Domestic Workers and the Democratic State*. Pietermaritzburg: University of KwaZulu-Natal Press.

Andrae, G. and B. Beckman. 1998. *Union Power in the Nigerian Textile Industry: Labour Regime and Adjustment*. Uppsala: Nordic Africa Institute.

Batliwala, S. 2004. 'Movements as Transnational Actors: Implications for Global Civil Society'. In *Creating a Better World: Interpreting Global Civil Society*, edited by R. Taylor. Bloomfield, CT: Kumarian.

Bayat, A. 2010. *Life as Politics: How Ordinary People Change the Middle East*. Amsterdam: University Press Amsterdam.

Bernstein, H. and P. Woodhouse. 2001. 'Telling Environment Change Like It Is? Reflections on a Study in Sub-Saharan Africa'. *Journal of Agrarian Change* 1(2): 283-324.

Bhowmik, S. 2002. 'India'. In *Worlds of Work: Building an International Sociology of Work*, edited by D. Cornfield and R. Hodson. New York: Kluwer Academic/Plenum.

———. 2007. 'Delhi'. In *UN-HABITAT: Improving the Regulatory Framework for Income Enhancement for the Urban Poor*. Nairobi: United Nations.

———. 2013. 'The Labour Movement in India: Fractured Trade Unions and Vulnerable Workers'. *Rethinking Development and Inequality* 2: 45-61.

———. 2014a. 'Street Vendors in India Get Legal Protection'. *Global Labour Column* No. 174.

Bhowmik, S. (ed.). 2014b. *The State of Labour: The Global Financial Crisis and Its Impact*. New Delhi: Routledge.

Boampong, O. 2010. 'The Possibilities for Collective Organization of Informal Port Workers in Tema, Ghana'. In *Africa's Informal Workers: Collective Agency, Alliances and Transnational Organizing in Urban Africa*, edited by I. Lindell. London: Zed.

Bonner, C. 2010. 'Domestic Workers around the World: Organising for Empowerment'. Paper presented at the Social Law Project Conference, 7–8 May, Cape Town.

Bonner, C. and D. Spooner. 2011. 'Organising Labour in the Informal Economy: Institutional Forms and Relationships'. *Labour, Capital and Society* 44(1): 5–18.

Bonner, C. and D. Spooner (eds). 2012. *The Only School We Have: Learning from Organising Experiences across the Informal Economy*. Cambridge, MA: WIEGO and Harvard University.

Bourdieu, P. 1963. 'The Attitude of the Algerian Peasant toward Time'. In J. Pitt, 'The Sociological Vision of Pierre Bourdieu'. *Theory and Society* 14: 723–44.

Breman, J. and M. van der Linden. 2014. 'Informalizing the Economy: The Return of the Social Question at a Global Level'. *Development and Change* 45(5): 920–40.

Britwum, A.O. 2011. 'Trade Unions and the Informal Economy in Ghana'. In *Trade Unions in West Africa: Historical and Contemporary Perspectives*, edited by C. Phelan. Oxford: Peter Lang.

———. 2013. 'Market Queens and the Blame Game in Ghanaian Tomato Marketing'. In *The Food Crisis: Implications for Labor*, edited by C. Scherrer and D. Saha. Labor and Globalization series, Vol. 2. München: Rainer Hampp. Available at https://kobra.bibliothek.uni-kassel.de/bitstream/urn:nbn:de:hebis:34-2013082143542/1/ScherrerFoodCrisis.pdf.

Castells, M. and A. Portes. 1989. 'World Underneath: The Origins, Dynamics and Effects of the Informal Economy'. In *The Informal Economy: Studies in Advanced and Less Developed Countries*, edited by A. Portes, M. Castells and L.A. Benton. Baltimore, MD: Johns Hopkins University Press.

Chen, M.A. 2005. 'Rethinking the Informal Economy: Linkages with the Formal Economy and the Regulatory Environment'. Research Paper No. 2005/10. New York: United Nations University.

Chun, J.J. 2009. *Organizing at the Margins: The Symbolic Politics of Labor in South Korea and the United States*. Ithaca, NY, and London: Cornell University Press.

Cobble, D. 1992. *Dishing It Out: Waitresses and Their Unions in the Twentieth Century*. Urbana: University of Illinois Press.

Cohen, R. and P. Lawrence. 1982. 'A Tribute to Ruth First'. *Review of African Political Economy* 9(25): 1–4.

Cooke, F.L. and G. Wood. 2011. 'Introduction'. *Relations industrielles / Industrial Relations* 66(1): 3–10.

Dörre, K., H. Holst and O. Nachtwey. 2009. 'Organizing – a Strategic Option for Trade Union Renewal?' *International Journal of Action Research* 5(1): 33–67.

Hart, K. 1973. 'Informal Income Opportunities and Urban Employment in Ghana'. *Journal of Modern African Studies* 11(1): 30–49.

———. 2007. 'The Urban Informal Economy in Retrospect'. Special issue, *Habitat Debate* 13(June): 17–18.

Hayashi, R.R. 2010. 'Empowering Domestic Workers through Law and Organising Initiatives'. *Seattle Journal for Social Justice* 9(1): 486–535.

Heinz, J. 2006. 'Three Ways of Enhancing the Analysis of Informal Labour Markets'. Unpublished paper.
ILO (International Labour Organization). 1972. *Employment, Incomes and Equality: A Strategy for Increasing Productive Employment in Kenya*. Geneva: ILO.
Lee, C.K. and Y. Kofman. 2012. 'The Politics of Precarity: Views beyond the United States'. *Work and Occupations* 39(4): 388-408.
Lévesque, C. and G. Murray. 2013. 'Renewing Union Narrative Resources: How Union Capabilities Make a Difference'. *British Journal of Industrial Relations* 51(4): 777-96.
Lindberg, I. 2014. 'Unions and Trade: What Kind of Solidarity?' *Globalizations* 11(1): 131-41.
Lindell, I. (ed.). 2010. *Africa's Informal Workers: Collective Agency, Alliances and Transnational Organizing in Urban Africa*. London: Zed.
Lopez, S. 2004. *Reorganizing the Rust Belt: An Inside Study of the American Labor Movement*. Berkeley: University of California Press.
Lowy, M. 1981. *The Politics of Combined and Uneven Development: The Theory of Permanent Revolution*. London: Verso.
Marx, K. 1976. *Capital: A Critique of Political Economy, Volume One*. Introduction by E. Mandel. Harmondsworth: Penguin.
McGuire, D. 2014. 'Analysing Union Power, Opportunity and Strategic Capability: Global and Local Union Struggles against the General Agreement on Trade in Services (GATS)'. *Global Labour Journal* 5(1): 45-67.
Milkman, R. 2006. *L.A. Story: Immigrant Workers and the Future of the U.S. Labor Movement*. New York: Russell Sage Foundation.
Noiseux, Y. 2016. 'Organising the Informal Sector: A Case Study in Mumbai's Shipbreaking Yards'. *International Critical Thought* 6(2): 12-20.
Ostrom, E. 1990. *Governing the Commons: The Evolution of Institutions for Collective Action*. Cambridge: Cambridge University Press.
Panitch, L. and C. Leys. 2001. 'Preface'. In *Socialist Register 2001: Working Classes, Global Realities*, edited by L. Panitch and C. Leys. London: The Merlin Press.
Piven, F.F. 2000. 'Power Repertoires and Globalization'. *Politics and Society* 28(3): 413-30.
Prag, E. 2010. 'Women Leaders and the Sense of Power: Clientelism and Citizenship at the Dantokpa Market in Cotonou, Benin'. In *Africa's Informal Workers: Collective Agency, Alliances and Transnational Organizing in Urban Africa*, edited by I. Lindell. London: Zed.
Roberts, R. 1982. 'Peculiarities of African Labour and Working Class History'. *Labour / Le Travail* 8/9: 317-33.
Schierup, C-U. and M.B. Jørgensen. 2016. *Politics of Precarity: Migrant Conditions, Struggles and Experiences*. London: Brill Academic.
Schmalz, S. and K. Dörre. 2013. 'Arbeitskreis Strategic Unionism: Jenaer Machtressourcenansatz 2.0'. In *Comeback der Gewerkschaften? Machtressourcen, innovative Praktiken, internationale Perspektiven*. Frankfurt and New York: Campus.

Scully, B. 2016. 'Precarity North and South: A Southern Critique of Guy Standing'. *Global Labour Journal* 7(2): 160–73.

Siegmann, K. and F. Schiphorst. 2016. 'Understanding the Globalizing Precariat: From Informal Sector to Precarious Work'. *Progress in Development Studies* 16(2): 111–23.

Silver, B. 2003. *Forces of Labor: Workers' Movements and Globalization since 1870.* Cambridge: Cambridge University Press.

Smith, A. and A. Stenning. 2006. 'Beyond Household Economies: Articulations and Spaces of Economic Practice in Postsocialism'. *Progress in Human Geography* 30(2): 190–213.

Standing, G. 1999. 'Global Feminization through Flexible Labor: A Theme Revisited'. *World Development* 27(3): 583–602.

———. 2009. *Work after Globalization: Building Occupational Citizenship.* Cheltenham: Edward Elgar.

———. 2011. *The Precariat: The New Dangerous Class.* London: Bloomsbury Academic.

———. 2014. *A Precariat Charter: From Denizens to Citizens.* London: Bloomsbury Academic.

Webster, E. 2011. '"The Wages Are Low But They Are Better than Nothing": The Dilemma of Decent Work and Job Creation in South Africa'. In *New South African Review 2: New Paths, Old Compromises,* edited by J. Daniel, P. Naidoo, D. Pillay and R. Southall. Johannesburg: Wits University Press.

Webster, E. and S. Bhowmik. 2014. 'Work, Livelihoods and Insecurity in the South: A Conceptual Introduction'. In *Socio-economic Insecurity in Emerging Economies: Building New Spaces,* edited by K. Fakier and E. Ehmke. London: Routledge.

Webster, E. and K. Joynt. 2014. 'Precarious Workers, Different Voices: Johannesburg's Inner-City Clothing Workers'. In *Socio-economic Insecurity in Emerging Economies: Building New Spaces,* edited by K. Fakier and E. Ehmke. London: Routledge.

Webster, E., K. Joynt and A. Metcalfe. 2013. 'Repositioning Peak-Level Social Dialogue in South Africa: NEDLAC into the Future'. Johannesburg: NEDLAC.

Webster, E., R. Lambert and A. Bezuidenhout. 2008. *Grounding Globalisation: Labour in the Age of Insecurity.* Malden, MA, Oxford, and Carlton, Australia: Blackwell.

Webster, E. and K. von Holdt (eds) 2005. *Beyond the Apartheid Workplace: Studies in Transition.* Pietermaritzburg: University of KwaZulu-Natal Press.

Wilderman, J., R. Grawitzky, L. Lenka, C. Morris, J. Munakamwe and A. Riabchuk. 2016. 'Worker Advice Offices in South Africa: Exploring Approaches to Organising and Empowering Vulnerable Workers'. Johannesburg: CHI and NALEDI.

Wolpe, H. 1972. 'Capitalism and Cheap Labour-Power in South Africa: From Segregation to Apartheid'. *Economy and Society* 1(4): 425–56.

Wright, E.O. 2000. 'Working-Class Power, Capitalist Class Interests and Class Compromise'. *American Journal of Sociology* 105(4): 957–1002.

PART I

Agricultural Aspects

2

Organising Casual Workers on an Oil Palm Plantation in Ghana

Akua O. Britwum and Angela D. Akorsu

Economic globalisation and the attendant desire on the part of capital to maximise profit at the expense of labour has led to several cost-cutting measures. These measures include various modes of employment informalisation, such as production fragmentation along value chains, casualisation and outsourcing. Over time, standard employment relations, characterised by lifelong employment in a permanent job with a known employer, are gradually disappearing. Increasing labour fragmentation and liberalisation pushes workers outside the traditional confines of trade unions, creating what Edward Webster (2005) calls a representational gap. The emerging situation occurs in an environment of a diminishing of the state role in policy formulation and of union political clout (Jessop 2011). In response to the restive workplace environment, and to retain absolute control over workers and their representative trade unions, employers have resorted to union-busting tactics, thus generating even greater insecurity for workers. Workers and their movements have not been passive victims, but have used various means in an effort to protect their right to decent work and living conditions.

A challenge facing labour movements is the rigidity of their traditional structures based on standard employment relations. As unions struggle to maintain their space, alternative forms of engaging workplace rights have emerged, particularly among informal workers, with varying degrees of power, legitimacy and relevance. Labour movements have also attempted to enhance their relevance and expand their institutional power through formations such as the Global Union Federations and by linking up with other civil society groups such as social movements, consumer pressure groups and faith-based organisations (Abbott 2006; Akorsu 2010; Cooke 2011; Cooke and Wood 2011). Not all these actors are new, but as F.L. Cooke and G. Wood (2011) report, they are acting more strongly and adopting new roles in (re)shaping employment relations. In addition, Cooke (2011) observes that, under certain circumstances, such formations are used to complement resource or capacity inadequacies of labour movements.

However, the ability of new formations to fill the representational gap has limitations. Such formations and the actors that drive them are informed by neoliberal ideology, whose prime agenda is to promote the interest of capital (Akorsu 2010). The use of trade agreements and multinational firm-specific codes of conduct as tools for maintaining labour standards, for example, has been criticised as largely motivated by political efforts to shrink the remaining policy space available to developing country states (Frenkel 2001; Chan and Ross 2003; Chang 2005; Cooke and He 2010). Neoliberal institutions and actors therefore cannot provide a viable solution to the problem of defending workers' right to decent work and living conditions. The task of organising workers to engage in collective action to defend their working rights remains relevant, and is primarily the responsibility of workers themselves.

The value of organising to defend their interests has not been lost on workers irrespective of their location, whether in standard employment relations or the expanding informal workplace. A number of studies have captured an array of organisational forms beyond trade unions, pointing to numerous players that provide avenues for informal workers to engage policy and other actors in production relations. In Ghana, studies have recognised the motivating factors and the tools such workers employ for engaging their interests and the centres of power they challenge. Accounts of success stories in Ghana and elsewhere in the West African subregion note how some informal economy groups command considerable economic and political influence (Boampong 2010; Brown and Lyons 2010; Lindell 2010; Britwum 2013). Studies on vibrant organisational forms remain limited to a small but influential group of urban-based informal economy workers (Boampong 2010; Britwum 2013). Rural informal economy workers remain largely outside the ambit of organisational forms, and their main concerns have been welfare and enterprise survival. But writers such as Ilda Lindell (2010) want the debate on the conceptual and analytical scope of actors regulating employment forms and working conditions widened, while Cooke and Wood (2011) regret the dearth of documentation on the nascent role of new actors in emerging and developing economies. A related concern is the intention of such actors and their relative effectiveness (Cooke 2011). Such observations underscore the need to expand research on the existence, viability and effectiveness of these new actors in a developing country like Ghana. This and the extent to which trade unions are positioned to recover their traditional labour-protection clout and fill the representation gap remain crucial for labour's claim to decent work and commensurate reward for its inputs into production.

Plantation agriculture in Ghana has been going through forms of restructuring usually presented as motivated by efficiency concerns, with implications for workers' organising. The interest in the oil palm industry, particularly the Ghana Oil Palm Development Corporation (GOPDC), stems from a number of factors. First, palm oil is a global commodity with a strong global production chain; it has several uses in the food, cosmetic, detergent and pharmaceutical industries. Furthermore, it has generated renewed interest worldwide as a result of the search for bio-fuels (Väth and Kirk n.d.). Unlike Ghana's major export cash crop, cocoa, oil palm has always been cultivated on plantations. Beginning as highly formalised state-owned employment concerns, oil palm plantations employed their entire workforce directly in standard employment relations, and provided the majority with accommodation within the nucleus estate. In the 1980s and 1990s, structural adjustment policies in the form of deregulation and privatisation of state-owned enterprises saw most workers retrenched. Those retained were shifted into various informalised employment arrangements, straddling contract work, outsourced concerns and household peasant enterprises in smallholder and out-grower schemes (Britwum, Ghartey and Agbesinyale 2006). The recourse to informalisation generated several forms of informal and insecure employment, with complicated relations with the nucleus plantation. The plantation owner shed the ultimate responsibility for overhead costs of the workforce responsible for the production of the raw materials on which the enterprise depended. This loss of social wages heightened the vulnerability of workers occupying the various nodes on the oil palm production chain.

This chapter reports on a study of the collective action of casual workers at GOPDC in their attempt to secure labour rights that guarantee them decent living and dignified employment conditions. It seeks to capture the strategic avenues deployed by workers in their drive for representation in a hostile working environment. The main research interest was the emerging organisational forms and strategies adopted by these workers to pursue their interests and the organisational players that they engaged. Additional interests were their relations with traditional unions and the response of these unions in assisting the workers in their effort to improve their wages and living conditions. The chapter unpacks employment relations between workers and the nucleus plantation by tracing GOPDC's value chain and identifying labour forms and relations situated on the various nodes. In addition, the chapter captures the working conditions and labour-force needs identified by these workers in order to illuminate how they craft their demands, their level of awareness and their willingness to organise.

Specific data-gathering methods included focus group discussions and key informant meetings through semi-structured and unstructured interviews with management, local union representatives, and officials of the General Agricultural Workers Union (GAWU) and the Industrial and Commercial Workers Union (ICU). Individual employees (permanent and casual) as well as out-growers and smallholders were also interviewed. The first set of research participants were interviewed in October 2013, with a follow-up conducted in June 2014. These primary sources were complemented by secondary sources such as GOPDC company documents including collective bargaining agreements (CBAs), annual reports, human resource management (HRM) documents, as well as newspaper reports, court judgments and timesheet records. The researchers had the opportunity to tour the mill and observe workers processing fresh fruit bunches (FFBs) into palm oil and other derivatives. They also sat in on a union meeting of permanent workers.

The first section of this chapter describes GOPDC and its place in the Ghanaian oil palm industry. The second section traces the nature and types of workers employed along the GOPDC oil palm value chain, identifying their working conditions as well as their needs and interests. The third section traces the strategies adopted by unions to organise oil palm workers, as well as sources of organisational power within the group of casual workers. The fourth section addresses the nature of relations between the organising of casual workers at GOPDC and traditional trade unions. The fifth section concludes the chapter by positing that in order to amplify the voices of workers' groups, the internal disabilities and self-centred interests of individual union leaders have to be addressed. Such contradictions threaten the principle of solidarity on which unions operate and can further weaken workers' ability to build a viable labour movement to confront capital in its strengthened form.

GOPDC and the Ghanaian oil palm industry

GOPDC is an integrated agro-industrial company specialising in the cultivation of oil palm, the extraction of crude palm and palm kernel oil, and the refining of specialty oils and fats for use by the food and chemical industries in Ghana and the export market. Established in 1975, GOPDC is a major player in sub-Saharan Africa and the largest of the seven main oil palm plantations located within the forest belt of Ghana. It covers 22 352 of the 41 086 hectares owned by all Ghanaian oil palm companies, and has a milling capacity of 60 tons per hour (the country's total combined milling capacity is 172 tons per hour). GOPDC is an industry leader, providing the majority of products from the oil palm. About 21 000 hectares of oil palm plantations are located at Kwae and Okumaning estates in Ghana's Eastern Region. In total, there are over 2.9 million oil palm trees spread over a radius of 30 kilometres, creating direct or indirect income for more than 50 000 people. According to a report on GOPDC's website, Ghana currently has an unmet annual demand of 35 000 tons of palm oil, and the unmet demand for the Economic Community of West African States subregion is 850 000 tons (MOFA n.d.).

GOPDC was set up by the state to produce and process FFBs into palm oil and other derivatives for the food and chemical industries. The company was privatised in 1995 and Siat Group, a Belgian company, took over the majority share. Other shareholders at the time included the state pension fund scheme, the Social Security and National Insurance Trust (SSNIT). The sale of the government's 20 per cent share for a paltry US$2.3 million instead of the expected US$18.1 million attracted condemnation, and the minister of finance and economic planning, under whose watch the sale was conducted, was subjected to a police inquiry (*The Insight* 2010; *Joy Online* 2010). The main producers of FFBs are plantation workers, smallholders, out-growers and independent farmers. Under the public ownership in the 1980s and 1990s, production was by workers in permanent employment of the nucleus estate. A small quantity was produced by smallholders – that is, peasant farmers resident on the land acquired by the plantation concern who were allowed to remain on their land and sell their FFBs to the nucleus plantation, the GOPDC. After privatisation, out-growers' schemes were introduced (Väth and Kirk n.d.). At the time of data gathering in October 2013, the nucleus estate was estimated to be producing 30–40 per cent of FFBs, while out-growers produced 50–60 per cent of GOPDC's FFB requirements. Smallholders produced less than 1 per cent. The use of peasant farmers in smallholder and out-grower schemes provides the nucleus estate an opportunity to share entrepreneurial risk while holding on to the relative security of profit (Väth and Kirk n.d.).

Workers and working conditions at GOPDC

The company relies on a vast array of workers for its operations. At the time of data gathering, out of a total of 2 880 direct workers, 401 were permanent (14 per cent) and 2 191 were on contract (76 per cent). In addition, GOPDC had contractual relations with 7 000 out-grower and 500 smallholder farmers who supplied FFBs to the mill. These out-growers and smallholders engage their own set of workers ranging from unpaid household labour to part-time and contract-waged workers. Thus the majority of workers whose labour ensures GOPDC's survival are in informal employment.

There is a gender dimension to GOPDC's direct workforce as well. Of the permanent staff of 401 workers, 90 per cent were men and 10 per cent were women. Females were more likely to be in casual employment, where they constituted about 43 per cent of the workforce.

The majority of contract workers (94 per cent) were engaged in the agricultural services department of the company, while 5 per cent were engaged at the mill and the remaining 1 per cent in the corporate, finance and workshop departments. Contract workers were employed on a three- to six-month contract. Occasionally they were engaged to undertake road and building construction on the nucleus estate. In the mill, they tended to be cleaners and helpers during the peak season of production, which falls between January and July. The human resource (HR) officer explained that the few designated contract workers in the corporate, finance and workshop departments were more temporary workers than contract workers in the sense that the positions they held were yet to be filled by qualified permanent workers.

The contract workers were engaged in diverse activities on the nucleus plantation such as planting, slashing, pruning, circling, spraying, applying fertilisers, loose picking, harvesting and carrying fruits. These activities were classified as non-skilled, semi-skilled or high-skilled tasks, and this classification determined who was engaged for what activity. Focus group interviews with the plantation workers revealed that harvesting and fertiliser application were classified as skilled jobs, while picking loose fruits and carrying FFBs were non-skilled jobs. According to field workers, task allocation was informed by some elements of sex stereotyping. Women were considered better at circling, loose picking and carrying FFBs, and men better at harvesting. Such considerations possibly explain the larger number of female contract workers relative to female permanent workers. The skill classification also determined the minimum wage level attached to a particular activity. The minimum daily wages were GH₵7.20, GH₵9.00 and GH₵12.00 for non-skilled, semi-skilled and highly skilled (special) contract workers respectively.[1] Meanwhile, the majority of contract workers were field workers on the plantation, and nearly all field workers were classified as unskilled and paid a daily minimum wage of GH₵7.20. This translated into a monthly wage of GH₵144.00, which was below the officially accepted monthly minimum wage of GH₵162.00.

Before 2010, when casual workers began organising, the terms and conditions of contract work denied contract workers a number of the workplace benefits enjoyed by permanent workers. A typical contract contained the statement 'Do not consider yourself a worker of GOPDC', a strong indication of the precariousness of the workers. Yet, as revealed by interviews during data gathering, most if not all contract workers had worked with GOPDC for years. The least number of years worked was 5, and the longest period captured was 30 years. In fact, permanent workers objected to this situation. In the words of one worker: 'How can you recycle one worker for 10 to 17 years, even 32 years? Some of them came here as young as 16 years and have worked for 20 or 30 years. That is the fate of some Ghanaian workers: they will go home with nothing.'

The continuous rehiring of these workers is illegal in Ghana. The Labour Act 651 clearly prohibits the hiring of the same contract workers beyond three consecutive times or six months. The company justified its heavy use of contract workers by claiming the seasonality of some of the activities on the plantation. The HR officer insisted that the isolated location of the company meant that the same people kept applying for the contract positions. This assertion was challenged in interviews with the casual workers and their group leaders, overseers and supervisors, as well as a management representative. They maintained that, given the annual production cycle of GOPDC, there was no point in the company's insisting that it had a reduced seasonal need for workers. Contract workers are engaged throughout the year to perform diverse activities and are utilised in areas such as the mill and workshop. The real reason for the continuous use of contract workers by the company, though downplayed by management, is the heavy financial implications of having permanent workers. Until workers began organising, GOPDC had no obligation towards the overhead costs of contract workers. On the part of contract workers, there were very few employment opportunities in their community.

GOPDC relies heavily on its 7 500 smallholders and out-growers to meet nearly 60 per cent of its FFB needs. Approximately 7 000 farmers cultivate palm fruits for GOPDC on about 13 000 hectares of land. Smallholders are allocated plots of land on the GOPDC-owned concession; the out-growers farm on their own lands. Both groups of farmers are given inputs such as palm seedlings, fertilisers, chemicals and agricultural extension services as loans; they have to pay back these loans with compound interest to the company. The loan payment is deducted from the payments that GOPDC makes to the farmers when they deliver their FFBs to the mill. The company also outsources cleaning of the factory, transportation, security and catering services. The HR officer hinted that there are thoughts of outsourcing field work on the plantation. This would mean pushing casual workers further into precariousness.

The constant fear of being left without work or income is the most fundamental concern of casual workers at GOPDC. This is in spite of the fact that the company continuously re-engages the same workers on contracts over the years. Women are the most vulnerable in terms of job security: they are not entitled to maternity leave, so pregnancy means loss of income. According to the HR officer, GOPDC avoids hiring pregnant women because of the belief that their condition compromises their work output.

Casual workers contacted during the study expressed extreme dissatisfaction with their working conditions. Specific issues of contention included low wages, occupational hazards, inconvenient hours of work and constant change of working rules. Field workers were paid a daily piece rate of nine pesewas (Gp9) per palm tree they cover, with each worker expected to cover a minimum of 82 trees a day. This yields a typical day's wage of GH₵7.20, or GH₵144.00 per month. One research participant asked: 'How on earth can one live on this income? But we hold on to this because there are no other job opportunities in this community. They [GOPDC] have taken our entire land.'

Common occupational health and safety problems encountered by casual workers include snake bites, cutlass wounds, sand and stone particles in the eye, and, rarely, electrocution from the high-tension lines that are run overhead in the plantations. One casual worker lost his limbs through electrocution while harvesting palm fruits. Protective apparel is rarely provided. One female research participant mentioned that in her seventeen years of work as a casual at GOPDC, she had received only two pairs of wellington boots from the company. The women field workers also indicated that cutlasses used for the work are sold to them on hire purchase, with the cost deducted from their wages. This was confirmed by the HR officer, who explained that the practice was to discourage indiscriminate collection of cutlasses by workers. Casuals keep their cutlasses once issued, so the company had no control over their use outside working hours.

Closing hours are flexible and workers can leave the company premises once they have completed their daily quota. However, casual workers were unhappy about the hours they had to start work. Though there was no set reporting time, the schedule run by the company bus forced workers to leave home at 4 a.m. GOPDC transport services have been outsourced to a school located in one of the communities. The company reached an agreement with the school to use its bus to transport casuals to work. For the school, transporting workers to the plantation in the early hours of the morning allows it time to transport students to school. This schedule is particularly inconvenient for female casual workers with childcare responsibilities. One female worker described her emotional turmoil each morning watching her toddler cry as she disrupted his sleep at dawn to get him ready for the day. Missing the bus means walking a lonely 10-kilometre path to work and getting there too tired to work. All short-cut routes into the plantation have been made inaccessible by a deep trench dug by GOPDC, ostensibly to keep livestock out of the plantation.

Group leaders indicated that during working hours a worker could spend ten minutes to two hours each day walking within the plantation. They think that a shuttle bus or, less desirably, motor bikes sold on hire purchase to workers would facilitate their movement within the plantation.

GOPDC had no HRM policy. According to the HR officer, HR decisions are guided by the provisions in the Labour Act 651 and the CBA. In the case of casual workers, GOPDC practices show that the Labour Act and CBA do not apply. First, the continuous use of the same casual workers contravenes the dictates of Ghana's Labour Act. Second, the CBA is the only collective agreement operating at GOPDC and is signed between the company and the unionised permanent workers; it does not apply to casual workers. The working conditions of the casual workers appeared to be at the discretion of the managing director. Our interviews with union executives, casual workers and outgrowers revealed a high turnover of managing directors, who tended to be expatriate staff. The implication was that the rules governing casual workers kept changing. Before the casual workers attempted to organise, they had no access to social security provisions such as pensions, medical and ambulance services, company school for their children, funeral support or welfare provisions, among many others.

Casual workers and unionisation
Union awareness and willingness to organise
The study informants confirmed a high level of union awareness and willingness to organise among casual workers at GOPDC. Their feedback revealed the following:

- Some casual workers were permanent workers when GOPDC was state-owned and thus were very aware of the benefits of unionism.
- The permanent workers' union co-opted the casual workforce to back their demands for higher wages. According to one union executive, 'After we had emboldened them, they took the initiative to organise themselves.'
- Some casual workers had been members of trade unions in other workplaces.

The desire to organise was exceedingly high among GOPDC casual workers, and they had made varying attempts to organise and affiliate with trade unions, with different levels of success. Box 2.1 provides an account of their organising efforts as narrated by their leaders during the time of the study.

> **Box 2.1 Organising efforts of GOPDC casual workers: A narrative**
>
> Our organising story as casual workers at GOPDC started in 2010, when we were cajoled by the local union affiliated to GAWU to support the permanent workers in their demand for higher salaries. The assumption was that increases enjoyed by the permanent workers would trickle down to us. Indeed, the permanent workers received increases: 10 per cent for junior staff and 12 per cent for senior staff. No mention was made of casual workers. With dashed hopes, we decided to fight for ourselves. Some of us were outspoken and emerged as leaders. Over time, management requested us to select leaders and so we selected eleven representatives from each department.
>
> With the help of the local union, we drafted a conditions-of-service document for casual workers. It was called a 'memorandum of understanding', but we did not like that title so we ignored it and drafted our own conditions of service and proceeded to negotiate with management. We did as a result obtain a 100 per cent increase in the daily mark, which changed from GH₵3 to GH₵6. We also got management to agree in July 2012 to grant us access to medical and ambulance services and our children access to the company's school.

Our demands for SSNIT pension contributions and representation on the welfare committee were upheld. But by September 2012, these agreements were yet to be implemented, so we embarked on a two-day protest (not a strike, mind you).

In the meantime, we had petitioned the presiding officer of the Kwaebibrim District Assembly with another concern. This was the frequent accidents resulting in the death of casual workers who were transported to work in KIA trucks. A meeting was arranged at the District Assembly with us (casual workers) and management. It was after this meeting that buses were hired to transport workers. Otherwise, it was trucks, often overloaded with workers like animals. The owner of the company then came and instructed that casuals in certain key positions should all be made permanent workers and the rest of the casual workers categorised into unskilled, semi-skilled and skilled casuals. This we saw as discrimination and a way to weaken our front; in fact, we saw it as a GAWU plot.

It was at this point that we decided to form a union, and as an initial step we invited officers of GAWU and the ICU to address the workers. After the interactions we opted to join ICU because the industrial relations officer from ICU was more convincing; and besides, we have been witness to how unresponsive GAWU has been to its members, our colleague permanent workers.

But subsequent developments indicated that management was in our way. First, they kept postponing the date for inaugurating our local union. Second, for some strange reason all efforts by the labour office to conduct a verification of our intention to form a union failed. Third, management issued a promise to change the status of casuals into permanent workers and proceeded to do so for some 150 of us in certain key positions such as in the workshop, mill, clinic, school and corporate departments. Management sent their dues deducted at source to GAWU and so they automatically were covered by GAWU's CBA.

Meanwhile, so many things were happening that we did not quite understand. For instance, pension deductions failed to reach SSNIT. Some deductions on our payslips were not clear because no details were given. This really infuriated us and we decided we

> would rather be casual workers than permanent under GAWU membership. So we embarked on another protest (again, this was not a strike action). We went ahead and registered 2 700 casual workers and they willingly contributed GH₵1per month to support our agenda. The protest lasted about a week, and on 15 May 2011 we the leaders were dismissed for having vacated our posts – 24 of us. We were given 24 hours to leave our homes on the company premises. About 40 police officers were brought in to forcefully eject us, but we would not budge. Later the company took the case to court and lost.
>
> It's all been a struggle. Apart from the internal tug-of-war with management, we have used the press, the local chiefs and politicians to garner support; we have resorted to religion; and we are currently resorting to the law courts to fight the unfair termination of our appointments. We hope to win the case and to be reinstated, but even if that does not happen, we will have left a legacy for all casual workers at GOPDC. Despite the struggle, it has been worthwhile, in view of what we have been able to obtain for casual workers at GOPDC up to this point.

The story was confirmed by management and by union leaders of permanent workers. Management representatives accused the causal workers' leaders of being too militant and not following due process. Their militancy, management contended, accounted for their failure to secure unionisation. During interview sessions, management representatives were at pains to point out that GOPDC was not averse to the decision of the casuals to unionise. The objection was to their choice of union, the ICU. First, management took serious exception to the presence of two unions in the same organisation. Second, management also insisted that GAWU is the legitimate union for the agricultural sector and GOPDC is an agro-based industry; the ICU therefore has no business unionising GOPDC workers.

But casual workers believe that GAWU has a hand in the refusal of management to grant approval for workers to join the ICU. They also accuse GAWU national leadership, the deputy general secretary in particular, of being compromised by management. In short, they have little confidence in GAWU's ability to defend their rights. Casual workers were not alone in their suspicion of GAWU's lack of readiness to pursue their interests. Some permanent workers, members of the GAWU local, indicated their displeasure with the national union, accusing the national officers of inertia. Such members hoped that the attempt of the casual workers to join the ICU would succeed, though few were willing to declare open support for the casuals.

Converting the employment status of a number of casuals to permanent workers was received with suspicion. For the casuals, it was a management tactic to break their front. According to the leaders, 'The casuals, seeing that all the executives have been made permanent and automatic members of GAWU, became unhappy, angry and disappointed.' This feeling of dejection was also noticed during the interviews with the group of women casual workers. They looked and sounded perplexed when the matter was raised, and actually mentioned, 'Now we don't know our fate, we don't know what next.' While granting casual workers permanent employment may indeed be a union-busting tactic on the part of management, it seems that there is also a managerial realisation that wholesale casualisation is not always beneficial.

Sources of organisational power among casual workers at GOPDC
The casual workers revealed a remarkable sense of agency and resourcefulness in their attempts to secure their interests. The conditions-of-service document they drafted was rich in content, and close examination revealed many similarities with the CBA of the permanent workers. Unfortunately, however, this document had not been finalised at the time of data gathering. The workers were in the process of developing a third draft when the appointments of the leaders were terminated. Having seen their latent power and the effect their numbers could yield in terms of negotiations, the workers took the initiative to contact unions and make their own informed choice. Their numerical power is a resource that permanent workers are aware of and seek to benefit from. The senior staff union leader stated: 'Our backbone is the number of casuals we have and we had thought we could use them to negotiate. Casuals are important to changing the conditions of work here; yes, because they are our numbers.' The casual workers' leaders

were convinced of workers' entitlement to improved working conditions and their choice of action to defend their rights. They had also been at pains to secure support from a variety of institutions and well-placed individuals in their district and region. They appealed to the press, chiefs, an aspiring Member of Parliament (MP), the district assembly, the labour office and the ministry of employment and social welfare. Some of these were able to offer critical backing, but their support was sporadic. For example, the aspiring MP was able to stop the ejection of leaders from company housing. The dismissed leaders remained disappointed with the failure of state officials especially to offer consistent defence. The ICU, however, has been strategic in its support and is currently paying the legal bills for the dismissed leaders. This heavy involvement on the part of the ICU raises questions about how GAWU can sustain its presence as the main union at GOPDC.

In terms of the future for casual workers' organisational efforts at GOPDC, all categories of interviewees, including the casual workers themselves, no longer believed that it could happen without some violent disruption. This could be seen in the general feeling of insecurity among all categories of workers, including the permanent workers. The police presence on the premises attested to the feeling of insecurity, even on the part of management. According to one management representative, 'Organising casual workers at GOPDC is a difficult endeavour, which can only be achieved through a revolution, and from the look of things that revolution is imminent.'

Trade unions' attitude to organising casual workers

Of the two national unions in contention over the organising of casual workers at GOPDC – namely, the ICU and GAWU – the latter has been in a strategic position for well over three and a half decades. It has been in the forefront in organising rural self-employed agricultural workers since the late 1970s at the instigation of the International Labour Organization (ILO); through this, GAWU had gained experience in extending union coverage to informal workers (Britwum 2011). However, this experience is at variance with GAWU's failure to organise casual workers in an enterprise where it has been representing permanent workers for well over 30 years. GAWU failed to utilise its strategic location to organise the casual workers despite facing severe membership loss as a result of the privatisation of plantation agriculture in the late 1980s and 1990s. Its membership has dwindled further as a result of casualisation and outsourcing. GAWU's success with organising informal economy workers, particularly in rural agriculture, can be attributed largely to the influence of the ILO and other foreign partners. In the absence of foreign funding, leadership discretion appears to be the guiding factor. This, unfortunately, has been slow to come.

The ICU's quest to expand membership, on the other hand, has resulted in a rather aggressive and somewhat unorthodox organising strategy, including outright poaching of already organised workers. The ICU relies on its diverse jurisdiction to intrude into the organising space of other unions. Interviews with union officers of Ghana's Trades Union Congress (TUC), GAWU and the ICU confirmed that the ICU had already taken over GAWU locals in other major oil palm plantations, such as the Benso Oil Palm Plantation (BOPP) and the Twifo Oil Palm Plantations (TOPP), and were about to take over members in a banana plantation (GAWU 2012). The ICU appears to be exploiting a weakness in GAWU. This takeover is not without its own challenges for the ICU.

Workers at GOPDC are receptive to union organising, and recognise that backing from a vibrant national union will stand them in good stead at the negotiating table. This is working in the ICU's favour. Seeing the potential in such a captive membership, the ICU is making heavy investments by supporting the workers in their legal battle with the company. Such investments include lawyer's fees and transportation costs for all workers to and from court. These are large investments, especially when one realises that between 6 December 2012 and 25 February 2014, workers had made 26 court appearances (interview, ICU regional officer, 2014).

While the ICU makes inroads with the casual workers dismissed by GOPDC, GAWU has been paralysed by an intractable leadership struggle between the general secretary and his deputy. Follow-up interviews revealed that the general secretary had been asked to take leave as an interim measure. It is not certain how the deputy can turn the union around. For the casuals at GOPDC, it is this deputy who was involved in the negotiations that shortchanged them. The present predicament of casual workers and the restive workforce at GOPDC is partly the result of GAWU's failure to utilise its strategic advantage. Local union members at GOPDC believe that GAWU's national leadership has been compromised. The sentiments are best captured in the words of one of the local union leaders:

> He [the deputy general secretary] comes here alone and goes straight to meet with management over three hours and workers were not part of the meeting. It is obvious that they [GAWU's national leaders] have compromised their position with management. We have had the occasion to confront them because the juniors were very angry and we had to cool tempers, just this year [2013]. The workers did not agree that the national union leaders should meet with management over four hours without the local union leaders. The deputy general secretary got infuriated because workers openly told him the truth and he thought he was too big for the workers to confront him. We have sent letters of protest to express our sentiments about how [the national union leaders] approach the work they have to do for the local union. We added a caution that if they do not improve we will abandon them for another union.

For both permanent and casual workers at GOPDC, management's preference for GAWU only confirms the compromised relations with national union leaders, which further discredits GAWU as a viable representative. Workers believe that the powers of the regional officer have been muted as a result of the direct contact between GAWU national leadership and the local union at GOPDC. In the words of one worker: 'GAWU does not empower the regional to deal with the locals. We hold meetings, and always there are questions that regional officers cannot answer.'

GAWU leadership insists, however, that it is a case of differences in union negotiation approaches. GAWU is using methods that insist on dialogue and mutual understanding, while the ICU prefers more militant adversarial methods that workers find appealing. GAWU leaders are convinced that their less adversarial approach to negotiation yields better results and that the ICU is building expectations that cannot be met. They cite the case of TOPP to support this claim. The ICU succeeded in taking over from GAWU as the local at TOPP in 2011 (GAWU 2012).

But for the casuals, such methods as GAWU claims to adopt do not serve their interests and did not deliver on their demands.

The two national unions have different attitudes to unionising the casuals at GOPDC. While the ICU sees its potential coverage as an asset worth investing in and is quick to deploy resources, GAWU has been slow to realise this, a failing that looks set to cost it members. When asked about union policy on casual workers on plantations where GAWU organises, the deputy general secretary was evasive. There was no attempt to convince the research team that GAWU was considering extending coverage to casuals. It is clear that GAWU's national leadership is misreading the dynamics of the changing labour market, particularly in plantation agriculture. What this means for the future of worker organising and the main union located within this sector remains to be seen.

Conclusion

This chapter has highlighted several pertinent issues regarding organisational needs, forms, strategies and sources of power among casual workers in an oil palm plantation in Ghana. The poor working conditions and the associated vulnerability among GOPDC workers in general and casual workers in particular can in some measure be attributed to the representation gap in today's labour market. This situation cannot be treated as business as usual because of its threat to existing labour movements and workers' rights to decent work.

The organisational efforts of casual workers at GOPDC also reinforce the fact that informal workers in Ghana are not passive, uninformed victims of labour abuses but have the potential to organise to secure better working conditions for themselves. That these workers have a high awareness of their vulnerability and are prepared to confront it through organising gives some room for optimism. The organising efforts of GOPDC casual workers yielded remarkable gains in their working conditions and proved the benefits of collective action. The workers were innovative in marshalling various power sources to back their efforts. A consistent approach has been appealing to the social relations between company and community. This allowed them to call on traditional rulers of the landowning communities and political leaders as representatives of state power. They also sought to engage public opinion by calling on the electronic media, both radio and television. In addition, they drew not only on secular power sources, but also called on both Christian and traditional religious faiths to back their cause. This recourse to multiple power sources, although innovative, may reflect a lack of confidence in various sources. This relates not so much to the ability of office holders to utilise their institutional power but to the capacity of officials to resist co-optation by the powerful multinational GOPDC. Their example also illustrates the challenges of collective organising among informal workers. The forms of organising are highly dependent on workers' efforts to mobilise all forms of existing power sources within their reach.

Their relative powerlessness due to lack of resources and access to legal services, for instance, drove them to seek trade union coverage with the ICU. Although the association of informal workers' groups with trade unions has been applauded by some as strategic and beneficial, the experience of the casual workers at GOPDC indicates that such alliances can be disruptive. Where unions do not see the benefit that these workers bring, as in the case of GAWU, union coverage will not necessarily augment workers' power. The fact that casuals remained without union coverage for decades in an enterprise where GAWU had organised permanent workers shows that visibility is not the only factor underlying the representation gap. Union organisational policy is a matter to contend with here as it determines who gets covered and how. Granted, informal workers have the will and power to organise collectively to secure better working conditions no matter their levels of vulnerability. Pushing for alliances with trade unions can augment the power of informal workers only if the internal contradictions of traditional unions have themselves been overcome.

Note

1. GH₵2.30 was equivalent to US$1.00 at the time of data gathering (October 2013).

References

Abbott, B. 2006. 'Determining the Significance of the Citizens' Advice Bureau as an Industrial Relations Actor'. *Employee Relations* 28(5): 435–48.

Akorsu, A.D. 2010. 'Labour Standards Application in Ghana: Influences, Patterns and Solutions'. PhD thesis, University of Manchester.

Boampong, O. 2010. 'The Possibilities for Collective Organization of Informal Port Workers in Tema, Ghana'. In *Africa's Informal Workers: Collective Agency, Alliances and Transnational Organizing in Urban Africa*, edited by I. Lindell. London: Zed.

Britwum, A.O. 2011. 'Trade Unions and the Informal Economy in Ghana'. In *Trade Unions in West Africa: Historical and Contemporary Perspectives*, edited by C. Phelan. Oxford: Peter Lang.

———. 2013. 'Market Queens and the Blame Game in Ghanaian Tomato Marketing'. In *The Food Crisis: Implications for Labor*, edited by C. Scherrer and D. Saha. Geneva: ILO.

Britwum, A.O., N.K. Ghartey and P. Agbesinyale. 2006. *Organising Labour in the Informal Sector: The Case of Rural Agriculture in Ghana*. Accra: Ghana Universities Press.

Brown, A. and M. Lyons. 2010. 'Seen but Not Heard: Urban Voice and Citizenship for Street Traders'. In *Africa's Informal Workers: Collective Agency, Alliances and Transnational Organizing in Urban Africa*, edited by I. Lindell. London: Zed.

Chan, A. and R. Ross. 2003. 'Racing to the Bottom: International Trade without a Social Clause'. *Third World Quarterly* 24(6): 1011-28.

Chang, H.J. 2005. 'Policy Space in Historical Perspective: With Special Reference to Trade and Industrial Policies'. Paper presented to the Queen Elizabeth House 50th Anniversary Conference on Development Threats and Promises, University of Oxford, England.

Cooke, F.L. 2011. 'The Enactment of Three New Labour Laws in China: Unintended Consequences and the Emergence of "New" Actors in Employment Relations'. In *Regulating for Decent Work: New Directions in Labour Market Regulation*, edited by S. Lee and D. McCann. Geneva: Palgrave Macmillan and ILO.

Cooke, F.L. and Q. He. 2010. 'CSR and HRM in China: A Study of Textile and Apparel Enterprises'. *Asia Pacific Business Review* 16(3): 355-76.

Cooke, F.L. and G. Wood. 2011. 'New Actors and Employment Relations in Emerging Economies'. *Relations industrielles / Industrial Relations* 66(1): 7-10.

Frenkel, S. 2001. 'Global Athletic Footwear Commodity Chains and Employment Relations in China'. *Organization Studies* 22: 531-62.

GAWU (General Agricultural Workers Union). 2012. 'Report of the National Executive Council to the 9th Quadrennial Delegates' Conference, 20-24 February'. Accra: GAWU.

The Insight. 2010. 'Rot at GOPDC: The Full Facts Revealed!' *The Insight* 16(1137): 1.

Jessop, B. 2011. 'Rethinking the Diversity and Variability of Capitalism: On Variegated Capitalism in the World Market'. In *Institutions, Internal Diversity and Change*, edited by G. Wood and C. Lane. London: Routledge.

Joy Online. 2010. 'CID Questions Ex-minister over "Dubious Deal"'. 30 August. http://politics.myjoyonline.com/pages/news/201009/53039.php (accessed 22 July 2013).

Lindell, I. 2010. 'Introduction: The Changing Politics of Informality – Collective Organizing, Alliances and Scales of Engagement'. In *Africa's Informal Workers: Collective Agency, Alliances and Transnational Organizing in Urban Africa*, edited by I. Lindell. London: Zed.

MOFA (Ministry of Food and Agriculture, Ghana). n.d. 'Brief on the Oil Palm Sector in Ghana'. http://mofa.gov.gh/site/?page_id=8819 (accessed 22 July 2013).

Väth, S.J. and M. Kirk. n.d. 'Linkages between Investors and the Local Population: Evidence from the Oil Palm Sector in Ghana'. Marburg: Institute for Co-operation in Developing Countries.

Webster, E. 2005. 'New Forms of Work and the Representational Gap: A Durban Case Study'. In *Beyond the Apartheid Workplace: Studies in Transition*, edited by E. Webster and K. von Holdt. Pietermaritzburg: University of KwaZulu-Natal Press.

3

Ethnicity and Class

Issues in Organising Tea Plantation Workers in India

Sharit Bhowmik

India is the world's largest producer as well as the largest consumer of tea. In 2013 the country produced 1.2 billion kilogrammes of tea, of which 911 million kilogrammes were consumed in the domestic market (Tea Board 2015). The tea industry is also India's largest employer in the formal private sector, employing approximately one million permanent workers and 600 000 casual workers (Tea Board 2009: 153). Tea is cultivated mainly in four states: two in North India and two in South India. These four states account for 97 per cent of the country's total tea production (Tea Board 2009). In the north, Assam and West Bengal produce 75 per cent of the country's tea, while in the south, Tamil Nadu and Kerala produce 22 per cent. Tea is mainly grown on large plantations that average around 200 hectares each. These plantations are owned mainly by public limited companies, although a few are owned by individuals.

This chapter discusses the complex issues involved in organising workers in the state of West Bengal. These include the problems of poverty, marginalisation, class formation, ethnicity and gender. Three administrative districts in the state's northern region are the main tea producers: Jalpaiguri, Alipurduar and Darjeeling. Alipurduar is a new administrative district that was carved out of Jalpaiguri district in 2014. Darjeeling produces high-quality tea that is known for its flavour. The state produces 20 per cent of India's tea and employs around 250 000 workers, half of whom are women (Tea Board 2009: 10–11, 154).

The Tea Board of India has divided the tea-growing areas into three tea districts: Dooars, consisting of the tea-growing area of Jalpaiguri and Alipurduar districts; Darjeeling Hills, or the hill areas of Darjeeling district; and Terai, encompassing the plains region of Darjeeling district. These names are used in this chapter.

The data presented is based on my field research in the tea plantation regions of West Bengal over the past four decades. I started my research while pursuing my doctoral studies. Since then I have studied different aspects of the working class, including my studies on the urban informal economy, but my interest in tea plantation labour has continued and I am at present revisiting work on this subject and attempting to analyse the changes taking place. Hence, although a part of this chapter is drawn from secondary data, the major portion dealing with the situation in the past few decades is based on my fieldwork over the last 30 years.

Features of plantations

Historically, plantations were a product of colonialism and their produce was mainly for export. In some cases, such as rubber plantations, they were established to provide raw materials for Western industry. In other cases, such as tea, coffee and sugar plantations, their markets lay in the colonising countries.

There were two basic necessities for the development of tea plantations: firstly, large areas of cultivable land, and secondly, a large labour force. However, the areas most suited for plantations were initially sparsely populated and hence local labour was not sufficient. Furthermore, the planters were not inclined to take local labour, even if available, because they wished to retain their bargaining power over wages and conditions of work. Because tea cultivation is a labour-intensive industry, reducing labour costs would considerably increase the profits of the planters. Moreover, the planters needed to get the maximum amount of work from their labour force. What this actually meant was that the planters wanted cheap and hard-working labour under conditions of labour shortage. Such a situation appeared to be wishful thinking, but the planters managed to make it a reality.

The only way the planters could achieve this was by not allowing the labour market to develop. Normally, when the labour market is comparatively free, the demand for and supply of labour determines wages. If there is high demand for labour and low supply, wages rise. Plantations faced similar conditions, but the planters did not want to increase wages to attract workers. Instead they imported low-cost labour from outside the area. These immigrants were initially imported as slaves and later as indentured labour. The cotton plantations in the southern part of the United States, as well as the sugar plantations in the Caribbean islands and other places such as Guyana, Mauritius and Fiji, were all run on slave labour from Africa in their early stages of growth. After slavery was abolished, indentured labour from Asia was used. Besides procuring cheap labour, these systems of recruitment ensured that the labour force stayed on the plantation under the total control of the planters. Hence plantations came to be known as having not a resident labour force but more often than not 'one of alien origin' (Greaves 1959: 115).

Tea plantations in India

The tea industry in India began with the founding of the Assam Company in 1839. The potential for growing tea was discovered earlier, in 1824, by Major Robert Bruce when he came across indigenous tea bushes in Assam (ITA 1933: v–vi). At that time the British East India Company had a monopoly over trade with China and was importing tea from there. It had no interest then of opening other centres. But when the British Parliament cancelled the company's monopoly over trade with China in 1833, its directors decided to explore the possibilities of growing tea on a commercial basis in Assam, which had been annexed by the company in 1825 (Bose 1954: 1–2). The first consignment of tea was sent to London in 1838 as a trial (Tinker 1974: 29). Within a short time Indian tea was favoured over its Chinese rival because of its stronger brew, which increased its popularity among the working class. As a result, by 1839 there was a 'mad rush to clear the hillsides of Assam for new gardens' (Tinker 1974: 29). Three decades later, tea plantations were also started in West Bengal, Tamil Nadu and Kerala.

The areas suited for growing tea in India were covered with thick, unhealthy forests where malaria and *kalazar* (blackwater fever) were rife. These forests had to be cleared, but the local population was unwilling to work under these hazardous conditions and at the low wages offered. Wages of tea plantation workers in Assam and Bengal during the late nineteenth and early twentieth centuries were about half those of agricultural labourers in these areas (Bose 1954: 87).

Labourers recruited to the plantations were mainly migrants, and the planters ensured that they worked only on the plantation at the low wages offered. Labourers in Assam and in Dooars and Terai were recruited from the Chotanagpur region of Central India, whose tribal people had been reduced to penury due to frequent droughts, famines and ruthless land revenue policies set by the colonial rulers (Bhowmik 1981). Workers in Darjeeling Hills were recruited mainly from Nepal, where the situation was more or less similar. The peasantry were reduced to penury due to the high taxes imposed on them by the rulers (Regmi 1981).

The planters encouraged families rather than individuals to migrate to the plantations. This served a dual purpose. Firstly, since planters wanted cheap labour, they had to have workers who were permanently settled on the plantations and who had no opportunity for alternative employment. Therefore, by encouraging families to migrate, planters ensured that workers were cut off from their place of origin and were settled on the plantations. The entire family – males, females and children – worked at wages determined by the planters.[1] Secondly, family-based migration ensured that labour could be reproduced, thus solving to some extent the problem of future recruitment.

Until India became independent in 1947, the planters, with the backing of the colonial government, exercised total control over labour. The planters' interests were represented by their trade bodies, whereas the workers were prevented from forming trade unions. The report of the Commission of Enquiry on the Conditions of Tea Plantation Labour in India and Ceylon (also known as the Rege Commission, after its chairperson), set up in 1944, noted that 'the employers are highly organized and powerful whereas the workers are all unorganized and helpless' (Rege 1946: 96). The Commission recognised the necessity of trade unions but admitted that they were unlikely to appear in the near future (193). The report of the study group for the tea industry of the first National Commission on Labour noted that the main reason for the absence of trade unions in the pre-independence period was that 'access to the plantations was difficult, if not impossible' (NCL 1969: 64).

Origins of trade unions in tea plantations

Plantation workers in the tea districts showed signs of collective action after the trade union organisers of the Bengal-Assam Rail Road Workers' Union made attempts to organise them in early 1946. In that year the rail workers had voted for a leadership that was strongly linked with the Communist Party of India (CPI). Most of the union's organisers were communists. They tried to establish contacts with workers in tea plantations that were close to railway stations. The organisers performed their activities under the cover of night because contacting labourers in the daytime was almost impossible. Plantation managers imposed strict control over the movements of outsiders, who could be arrested or even shot for trespassing. In Darjeeling Hills trade union activists from the railway workshop at Tindharia contacted plantation workers in a bid to unionise them. The unionists in Dooars were mainly Bengalis and not local workers; in Darjeeling Hills, they belonged to Nepali middle-class families. In both cases the unionists were of the supervisory categories in the railways. Most of them later left their jobs to work full-time as organisers in the tea plantation trade unions. The communist unionists belonged to two political parties: the CPI and the Revolutionary Socialist Party (RSP). The RSP is ideologically close to the views of Trotsky, whereas the CPI is closer to the views of Lenin.

Despite the unfavourable odds, the trade unionists did organise workers in some tea plantations. By early 1946 they had formed a trade union called Zilla Cha Bagan Mazdur Union (District Tea Plantation Workers Union). A similar union was formed in Darjeeling. The union raised issues such as the lack of food supplies and drinking water for workers in some plantations. Around the last quarter of 1946, the union sent a memorandum to the labour commissioner of the government of Bengal, raising issues concerning wages, housing and the general welfare of plantation workers. The labour commissioner forwarded this document to the associations of tea planters – namely, the Dooars Planters Association (DPA) and the Indian Tea Planters Association (ITPA).[2] The executive committee of the ITPA (1946) decided 'that the Trade Union Act, Rules, Manual and Model Rules should be secured at once to see whether the Association could advise the gardens for formation of Employer-sponsored Unions'. This more or less reflects the attitudes of the planters towards trade unions.

The communist union leaders were able to stir up labour unrest on quite a few plantations. According to reports presented to the ITPA annual conference in 1946, both the ITPA and the DPA were very critical of the role of 'communist outsiders' who were fomenting unrest among the labour force (ITPA 1946: 14-44). The only solution, they believed, was to encourage employer-sponsored unions. Around this time the secretary of the Jalpaiguri District Congress Committee sent letters to the two planters' associations seeking their permission to form trade unions among plantation workers. This proposal came as a boon for the planters, who decided that the association should 'advise member bodies to give every possible help and assistance to the Congress' (ITPA 1947: 112).

The DPA was equally cordial to the Congress unionists. It had earlier supported the All India Gorkha League, which was at that time an anti-communist political organisation of Nepalis, to counter the communist influence on the workers (DPA 1947: 104). The trade union wing of the All India Gorkha League had tried to organise in areas employing Nepali workers, mainly in the Alipurduar district. The Darjeeling branch of the Indian Tea Association (ITA) had encouraged the same union in Darjeeling Hills in order to combat the growing influence of the communist-supported trade unions.

At a committee meeting on 11 August 1947, it was decided that the DPA should encourage the Congress to form unions. Therefore, 'Congress members with cards of identification will be given permission to hold meetings in gardens with a view to form trade unions' (DPA 1947: 119). Through these manipulations, the planters were able to split the tea industry's working-class movement.

The postcolonial situation

After India attained independence in 1947, the character of the state changed. The new government's attitude towards the working class was more favourable than that of the colonial regime. It tried to impose some regulations on employers while granting some protection to the workers, attempting to find a *via media* between the two.

At the Indian Labour Conference (ILC) meeting in 1951,[3] the representatives of workers put forward a strong plea for rational fixation of wages. A decision was taken to set up committees to formulate statutory minimum wages in various industries. In 1952, for the first time, statutory minimum wages were fixed for tea plantation labour (GoI

1966: 13-14). This provided some protection for plantation workers. The planters could no longer fix wages according to whims or by exploiting the weak bargaining power of the workers. They had to accept the concept of a living wage and that any violation would result in prosecution under the Minimum Wages Act of 1948.

Subsequently, other Acts were passed granting some facilities to the workers. Some of these Acts, such as the Payment of Bonus Act (legislation providing for a provident fund and gratuity), affected the working class in formal employment in general. There were other Acts passed after independence – such as the Industrial Disputes Act of 1947 and the Factories Act of 1948 – which granted security of employment and set safety conditions at the workplace. The planters initially ignored these Acts as there was no check on them and the state apparatus to enforce them did not exist. In the early 1950s, however, the state governments set up labour bureaus headed by a labour commissioner, and labour officers were appointed in different regions to ensure implementation of the provisions and to deal with conciliation between labour and management. Labour tribunals were also set up to decide on disputes.

All these changes resulted in the formalisation of relationships between planters and workers. The planters started losing the tight grip they once had over their workers, and the existing master–servant relationship changed to that of employer–employee. Workers were no longer wholly dependent on the mercies of employers, as they now had some legal protection.

Of all the legislation affecting plantation workers, the Plantation Labour Act (PLA) of 1951 is the most significant. This is the only Act that specifically seeks to raise the living standards of plantation workers. It contains several provisions related to housing conditions, health and hygiene, education and social welfare. The PLA, along with the Factories Act, regulates employment, working conditions and working hours. The Act provides for compulsory housing and stipulates that every year 8 per cent of workers' houses have to be converted into permanent structures (walls of brick and mortar with tiled roofs). There are provisions for sanitary facilities and water supply in the labour residences (known as labour lines), crèches for infants and primary schools for children. The PLA therefore has a great deal of potential for improving the working and living conditions of plantation labourers.

Fragmentation of trade unions

A strong trade union movement is essential if the interests of labour are to be protected and the provisions of labour law implemented. However, the trade union movement in India was fragmented into different unions shortly after independence. Before independence, there was only one trade union federation, the All India Trade Union Congress (AITUC). By 1944 the federation came under the control of the communists. This was resented by many in the AITUC, which had been in the forefront of India's freedom struggle. In 1947 some trade union leaders decided to form another federation, which they called the Indian National Trade Union Congress.

The split in the AITUC in 1947 paved the way for further splits based on narrow party lines. As a the result it almost became mandatory for every political party to have its own trade union front. When a political party splits, its trade union front also splits, thereby further fragmenting the working-class movement. Similarly, a new political party invariably floats its own trade union.

In 1948 the socialists within the AITUC decided to form a separate political party, and they took with them several trade unions to form another federation, known as Hind Mazdur Sabha (HMS, Indian Workers Council). The RSP-supported trade unions had initially joined HMS, but in 1949 they formed another federation, the United Trade Union Congress. In 1955, Bharatiya Mazdur Sangh (Indian Workers' Union) was formed by the Rashtriya Swayamsevak Sangh, a Hindu fundamentalist body. In this way new trade unions have sprung up along political lines. At present there are thirteen recognised central trade unions and scores of federations that are not recognised by the Ministry of Labour. With the exception of the Self-Employed Women's Association (SEWA), the remaining twelve have strong links with political parties (Bhowmik 2013).

Impact of trade unions

The trade union movement in tea plantations also has the problem of multiple unions. This has considerably weakened the bargaining power of the workers. There were 23 trade unions in the three tea districts in 2015. Nevertheless, the trade unions are well entrenched and almost all workers are members of a union. There are very few plantations that do not have a trade union; in most such cases, these plantations are isolated and no union has ventured there.

A major feature of trade unions in the three tea districts is that leadership at the district level has remained part of the non-worker middle-class unionists. The leaders belong to the political party that controls the union. Most of them have made no conscious effort to understand the social life of the predominantly tribal workers.[4] In fact, with the exception of a small minority, they cannot even speak the Sadri dialect, the lingua franca of the tribal workers. The general tendency of the union leaders is to confine themselves to the economic sphere and avoid involvement in the social life and activities of the workers except when they impinge on union activities. For example, if the unity of the union is threatened because of an intertribal marriage or if a section of workers starts a witch-hunt that threatens to split workers, the union leaders intervene to defuse the situation.

Trade unions operate at the district level, and almost all the central trade unions have branches in the tea districts. The union leadership at the plantation consists mainly of workers. However, at the district level workers are rarely leaders. All important positions such as general secretary, treasurer, president and vice president are held by middle-class Bengalis, most of whom are full-time organisers and paid by the parent political party. Workers are included in the executive committees and other similar committees with a large number of members. At the plantation, problems are tackled by the local union leaders. However, when important issues need to be discussed with management at the district level, the district-level union leader is called to negotiate. Major industry-wide issues such as wage increases, bonuses and workload are discussed in tripartite discussions (government, trade unions and employers' associations). The unions do not always consult workers when framing demands. The tribal workers are thus isolated from major issues concerning their living and working conditions. A similar situation exists in Darjeeling Hills, where the Nepali-speaking people dominate. The union leaders may belong to the same ethnic group (Gorkha), but they are from the middle class.

When trade unions entered the plantations, the isolated and unorganised workers looked upon them as saviours. They had total loyalty to their unions and trusted their leaders. Over the years, as a result of changes in their conditions of existence, the workers have become more aware of their problems and have grown more vocal. The union leaders could have used this growing awareness to build up leadership from below. Unfortunately, the leaders have chosen to maintain their distance from workers and to entrench themselves in positions of power.

Persisting poor conditions

Although conditions have improved since independence, plantation workers continue to form the less-developed section of the population in the state. A survey conducted in 1995 of 182 households in the three tea districts revealed workers' living conditions (Bhowmik 1996). This data is now twenty years old, but at the time of writing this chapter (early 2015), the situation was similar, if not more dire. In fact, a turn for the worse could be observed after 2001, when a large number of plantations in Dooars had shut operations, leaving their workers destitute.

The survey examined whether provisions of the PLA had been implemented. As discussed above, this Act stipulates a number of guidelines relating to living and working conditions of plantation workers, whose lives would improve substantially if these provisions were implemented. In reality, however, there is not a single tea plantation in the state that has fulfilled all provisions of the Act.

According to reports of the West Bengal government (GoWB 2005), in 2004 around 74 per cent of the workers' houses were permanent structures; the others were houses with mud walls and thatched roofs. Had the PLA been implemented, all houses should have become permanent structures by 1969. The government report indicated that house repairs were not carried out by the employers and in most cases workers had to bear these costs. Yet provision and repair of worker housing is mandatory for management, and forms a part of the workers' wages. Toilets did not exist; workers and their families went to the open fields to defecate (Bhowmik 1996). Doctors in the plantations indicated that infection from hookworms was quite high among the labour force as these worms breed in faeces.

The most depressing findings in the survey relate to education. The data on 182 heads of households showed that nearly half (49 per cent) were illiterate, 12 per cent were functionally literate, 22 per cent had primary education, and 14 per cent had reached middle school. But these heads of households were in their forties, and hence were born after the PLA came into force. Their educational levels indicate that they did not get the benefit of primary education.

The PLA states that every plantation having 25 or more children must provide primary schooling for them. The government, with the cooperation of the employers, runs the plantation schools. The plantation provides the schoolhouse, while the teachers are employees of the state's education department. Although the plantation schools are supposed to teach the first four years of schooling, visits to the plantations showed that most schools did not have more than two classrooms and two teachers, even if there were many children of school-going age. The smaller plantations had one teacher. One wonders how knowledge could be imparted or the children imbibe it.

The plantations in Dooars are in isolated areas; the workers and their children have little access to employment other than on the plantation or in low-productive agriculture in the neighbourhood. The vulnerable plight of tea workers became particularly apparent when a crisis arose in the industry from 2000 onwards. At that time tea prices started to fall, and by 2001 they had fallen below the costs of production. Around 55 tea plantations in West Bengal closed and their workers were left with no wages or alternative sources of income. This heavy dependence on the plantation took a heavy toll on plantation workers, especially those in Dooars. It is estimated that between 2001 and 2006 nearly 1 500 people died of malnutrition in tea plantations, most of them in Dooars.

Consequences of isolation

The present-day problems of tea plantation labour in West Bengal have their roots in the history of the plantation system. As indicated above, in the early years the planters, concerned with keeping wages low, did not allow the labour market to develop. They preferred to employ forced labour that was bound to work on the plantations at low wages, and they also ensured that the regions surrounding the plantations remained underdeveloped. This meant that the captive labour force had no alternative but to work on the plantations.

These methods may have served the objectives in the earlier phase, but when this system continued even after the labour shortage was overcome in the postcolonial period, it created new problems. Since there were hardly any employment opportunities outside the plantations, the unemployed family members of plantation workers looked towards the plantation for gainful employment. This gave rise to casual labourers, who get work for six months in a year. A study on casualisation conducted in 1992 showed that there were 50.6 casual workers for every 100 permanent workers in the three tea districts (Bhowmik 1992). Most of them were related to the permanent workers and even resided in the same households.

The availability of a large pool of unemployed within the plantations has put the planters in a strong position in wage negotiations. They use the existence of casual labour to depress wages by indicating to the trade unions that a higher wage would result in curtailed casual labour. Workers would lose because higher wages might increase the income of permanent workers, but a reduction in casual labour would reduce total household income. Hence, even though there is a labour market at present, it is heavily tilted towards the planters.

Persistent marginalisation

The factors discussed above have collectively led to the marginalisation of plantation workers, especially in Dooars and Terai. The ethnic factor (tribal workers and workers of Nepali origin) has also played a role in this process. The main problems of these people are rooted in the fact that they are immigrants and are ascribed low social status. The Bengali population in these districts are also immigrants from the eastern part of Bengal (this now constitutes Bangladesh), but they are politically and linguistically dominant in the area. Even though the predecessors of immigrant tea workers may have settled in the area before most Bengalis did, they are regarded as outsiders. This is despite the fact that the tribal plantation workers are responsible for creating the wealth in this region through their labour.

The situation in Darjeeling Hills is different. Despite a similar economic environment, the tea plantation workers and former workers constitute the majority, and they have been politically effective. Moreover, the household data from the 1995 survey showed that quite a few men had gained employment in the armed forces or in paramilitary services (Bhowmik 1996). Some young people found employment as tourist taxi drivers or shop assistants in the towns of Kurseong and Darjeeling.

These workers have been vocal in articulating their ethnic interests and have in fact been the driving force the of the Gorkhaland movement, which has been demanding a separate state for Gorkha-speaking people in Darjeeling.[5] Though both groups of plantation workers – the Gorkhas and the tribals – are marginalised within the state of West Bengal, their responses to the situation have been different. The Gorkhas, who form the majority in the area, have been assertive about the recognition of their language and the right to develop on the basis of their own culture. On the other hand, the tribal workers in Terai and Dooars have been unable to raise either issue. Although their total population is large, they form less than half the population of the tea-growing districts.

The trade unions leaders in Darjeeling may be from the middle class, but they are ethnically and linguistically similar to the workers. Their leaders speak the same language as the workers and belong to the Gorkha community. The tribals have depended on outsider (Bengali middle-class) leadership to articulate their problems as they have been unable to develop leadership from among their ranks. It is likely that the outside leadership has in fact prevented development of organic leadership, a point taken up again later.

Growing ethnic assertions

Over the past several decades the people of Darjeeling Hills have formed several movements for asserting their separate identity. The Nepali-speaking people of the hills are linguistically and ethnically different from the people of the rest of West Bengal. Their movement for autonomy has been an undercurrent in their politics since India won its freedom. Apart from the All India Gorkha League, which had been in the forefront of the movement for autonomy even before independence, the CPI too was in favour of a separate status for the Nepali speakers. Its district council had passed a resolution in 1950 stating that the Nepali-speaking people formed a nationality and should be treated as such. The CPI has stood by its resolution, but the Communist Party of India (Marxist), or CPI(M), which was formed after the CPI split in 1964, disowned it. The CPI(M) was the largest political party in the state; from 1977, it dominated the coalition government of the Left Front that ruled West Bengal for 35 years since it had an absolute majority in the state legislature.

By the early 1980s the government of India, then ruled by the Congress Party, included the Nepali language as a part of the Eighth

Schedule of the Constitution, giving it the status of a national language. This was a boost to the hill people. One of the most effective leaders of the movement for a separate state was Subhash Ghising. He formed an organisation called the Gorkha National Liberation Front (GNLF) in the 1980s and in a few years became its most popular leader. The backbone of his movement was the tea plantation workers. He campaigned for a separate state with renewed vigour. This demand was strongly opposed by the CPI(M)-led state government, which tried to portray it as a secessionist move. By 1988 the government of India entered into a pact with the GNLF that called for the establishment of the Darjeeling Gorkha Hill Council (DGHC); this gave autonomy to the hill areas but was a considerably watered-down version of a separate state.

While this attempt at state formation was going on, another movement was spreading silently in other parts of the tea-growing areas. This was based on the dissatisfaction and fear of the tribal tea plantation workers, who are ethnically different from the Gorkhas. The GNLF had included Terai and parts of Dooars in its demand for a separate state, which upset the tribal people in these areas. The tribals in Dooars and Terai are more numerous than the Gorkhas in the hills. The GNLF gave up the demand for a separate state after the DGHC was formed. Ghising was the chairperson of the DGHC until it was dissolved in 2008.

The tribal tea workers were slowly trying to assert their autonomy. There were growing numbers of educated tribals, some of whom found employment in the plantations, although many others were unemployed. These educated tribals became aware of the need for unity to assert their separate identity and their aspirations. They also realised that it was necessary to develop their own leadership and not depend on outsiders. These trends have been observed since the 1980s through intermittent instances of tribal workers challenging the views of their non-tribal leaders. Although such instances were sporadic and uncoordinated, they revealed the discontent among the workers. Most trade union leaders chose to overlook the significance of these events or tried to explain them away as instigations of outsiders (an argument similar to that made by the planters when the communists started unionising workers).

The Gorkhaland movement in fact served as an impetus for tribal workers to unite and protect their identities. The lead was provided by an organisation called Adivasi Vikas Parishad (AVP, Tribal Development

Council). This is a Delhi-based non-governmental organisation formed to support the social and cultural upliftment of tribals. The tribal workers in the two tea districts began to acknowledge that they had long been deprived of their rights and were marginalised in their trade unions. The new generation of educated tribals were conscious of their identity as being different from the others (Bengalis and Gorkhas) and they wanted to maintain it. Their first major show of strength was in 2007, when thousands of tribals in Dooars demonstrated against the treatment of the tea plantation workers in the neighbouring state of Assam. Since then AVP membership has grown tremendously.

As described earlier, tea plantation workers in Dooars, Terai and Assam come from the same places of origin. These communities are given the status of Scheduled Tribe in their states of origin and in West Bengal. However, the communities of tea plantation workers in Assam are not recognised as Scheduled Tribes, which deprives them of the facilities provided for tribal communities. Instead, they are referred to in Assam as 'tea garden tribes', which is not a statutory category; they are also known as Adivasis. (In other parts of the country, the terms 'tribal' and 'Adivasi', which literally means 'indigenous', are interchangeable, but in Assam they constitute separate categories. 'Tribal' refers to indigenous tribes in the state but excludes tribal tea workers.)

In 2010 the students' union of the Adivasis in Assam organised a demonstration in the state capital of Dispur to demand their inclusion among Scheduled Tribes. The demonstration was attacked by the local people and the students were badly beaten. A woman was stripped by the locals and made to run naked through the streets. The police joined in and beat up the protesting students. All this was televised live and seen by the whole country. The tribal tea workers in Dooars and Terai organised demonstrations to register their protest in solidarity. The AVP formed a trade union known as the Progressive Tea Workers Union, which put forth demands for increased wages for the workers. This union was formed mainly to challenge the hegemony of the outside leadership in the existing trade unions.

New developments in the Gorkhaland movement also helped increase the popularity of the AVP. There were rumblings among the people of Darjeeling against the way the DGHC was functioning under the leadership of Ghising and the GNLF. The tea workers who had been his main supporters had become disillusioned as the industry was in a shambles and their living standards had fallen. The revolt against Ghising was led by his one-time right-hand man, Bimal Gurung. He formed a new organisation called Gorkha Janmukti Morcha (GJM, Gorkha Liberation Front), which drew away most of Ghising's supporters. Primarily directed at Ghising, the revolt articulated the anger of the public against the GNLF for failing to improve the lives of the poor living in the hills. By 2008 the GNLF was disbanded and Ghising had to seek refuge in Jalpaiguri district.

The GJM was more aggressive than the GNLF in demanding a separate state. It organised many strikes and closures in the hills to press for its demands; some of these actions paralysed all activities in the hills for days. It got support from one of the mainstream political parties, the Trinamul Congress, which in 2011 replaced the ruling left coalition with a huge majority. A new hill council was set up with more financial powers, but this did not satisfy the GJM. Gurung's agitation for a separate state continued. A new aspect of the GJM's demand was that Dooars and Terai must be included in the proposed state. Gurung made it clear that his party would not attend any meeting on a separate state if these two areas were not included.

The tribals in these areas were equally adamant that they would not allow Dooars and Terai to be part of a Gorkha-dominated state. The AVP has aggressively opposed the spread of the GJM in Dooars and Terai. Its cadres have disrupted the GJM's efforts to hold public meetings in these areas. Bimal Gurung and his supporters have been unable to enter Dooars to canvas support for their cause. AVP tribal activists, armed with bows and arrows, blocked his convoy and forced it to return to the hills.

The Gorkha workers in Dooars have also tried to assert their identity along with the people in the hills. A large section supported the GJM, which caused tensions among the workers as the AVP, representing tribals, was opposed to the GJM. However, in 2011 the Gorkhas in Dooars started questioning the strategies of the GJM over the issue of wages for plantation workers. These wages are fixed every three years through tripartite meetings between the employers' associations, the trade unions and the state government's labour department. There was a great deal of confusion in early 2011 as wage revisions were to take place in the three tea districts. The existing wage rate was INR67 per day, which by all standards was very low. (At INR130, the minimum daily wage of unskilled workers in the state was double the wage of a plantation worker.) The 23 trade unions in this region formed a joint committee known as the Coordination Committee of Tea Plantation Workers (CCTPW), which was the main negotiator on behalf of the workers. The union affiliated to the AVP is not a member of this committee.

Before the CCTPW could put forth its demands, the AVP announced that it would not accept anything less than INR250 as a daily wage. This was a very steep increase, which would not be accepted by the employers' associations. The other unions were in a fix: if they opposed this wage, they would be appear to be anti-worker, but supporting it would send a message that it was not the CCTPW but the AVP that was the leader of the tea workers. Before any serious debate could take place, the GJM, on the suggestion of the state government, agreed that the minimum daily wage should be INR100. The employers gave in readily but pegged it at INR90 for workers in Darjeeling. The agreement was signed on 31 March 2011. The GJM leaders thought that they had staged a coup because the agreed wage marked a significant jump from the prevailing wage.

The workers in Dooars were not happy with this outcome for two reasons. First, the GJM did not consult their unions before agreeing on the wage. Second, the wage agreed to by the GJM was much lower than the minimum wage prescribed by the state (INR165) for all workers and well below the wage suggested by the AVP.

GJM's hasty move upset the Gorkha workers on the plains as they felt that the GJM was using them for its own interests. These people have since revised their support for a separate state. I spoke to some of their leaders when I visited Dooars in August 2013. They all told me that they had changed their opinion about having a separate state as it would ultimately mean the rule of the Gorkhas in the hills over the others, which would create further tensions. This was exactly the stand of the AVP. The demand for higher wages for Dooars was considerably weakened, and a few months later, when the new wage was announced, it was fixed at INR95, slightly higher than for Darjeeling (Bhowmik 2011: 27–9).

The wage agreement of 2011 was in effect for the next three years, but until January 2015, a year after the agreement expired, no decision had been taken on this issue. This time all trade unions, including those of the AVP and the GJM, joined with the CCTPW to fight for a just wage. The united body of trade unions organised a two-day strike on 10-11 November 2014. The strike was a success in so far as the industry in all three tea districts came to a standstill. However, this had no effect on the position of the employers.

Subsequent talks in the tripartite meetings have failed because the employers have taken the aggressive stand of providing only a marginal increase of a few rupees. The ruling party (Trinamul Congress) has a total majority in the state legislature, but the party is becoming increasingly ineffective. Its image has been considerably damaged because of a major financial scandal involving some of its ministers and Parliament members. The government is more involved in salvaging its image than with the future of workers living on the periphery. Tea industry workers, who are poorly paid and isolated, need the support of the state government to ensure justice. This is almost absent at present. On 20 February 2015, the planters' associations, the unions and the state government signed a new wage agreement that will increase the daily wage to INR127.50. This is still well below the minimum wage in the state, which is INR235 per day, and also well below the wages of plantation workers in other tea districts in southern India (Bhowmik 2015).

Another major reason for the rigid stand of the employers is that the government at the centre (led by the right-wing Bharatiya Janata Party) believes that the only way employment can increase is by removing all protection for labour. The prime minister has said in public meetings that there should be fewer controls on employers to fulfil commitments to labour. Instead, employers should be trusted to provide just deals for their workers (Pais 2014). By this logic, employers should be allowed to fix wages according to what they think is best for labour.

The present political situation shows that labour is likely to be pushed further to the wall. One of the ways of countering this is to form a unified trade union movement. This means that although ethnicity is an important issue for the workers, they have to rely more on their class strength to protect themselves. This can be achieved only if the trade unions are united and not as strongly divided as at present.

Notes

1. In fact, this is the only industry in the country that officially allowed employment of child labour because the family was taken as the unit of employment during colonial times. This was accepted even after India gained independence in 1947. The Plantation Labour Act, passed in 1951, recognises four categories of workers: males and females (those above eighteen years), adolescent (those between fifteen and eighteen years) and children (those below fifteen years). The Act did not stipulate a minimum age of employment. After 1991, however, when international tea buyers questioned the use of child labour, employers pressurised the Tea Board to change the categories of children and adolescent to 'non-adult'. The Act was subsequently amended in 2010 and the minimum age of employment was accepted as fourteen years, which is one year lower than the minimum age in the Child Labour (Prevention and Regulation) Act, 1984.
2. The DPA was part of the Indian Tea Association, which represented the interests of the European tea companies. Headquartered in London, the ITA played an important role in influencing government policies on tea. The ITPA represented mainly the Indian tea companies, which at that time were fewer in number than the European companies.
3. The ILC is a tripartite body comprising representatives of labour, management and government. Its unanimous decisions are binding for all. It meets every year.
4. The term 'tribal' is used in the Constitution of India for some sections of the population. These communities are known as Scheduled Tribes. They are designated as Backward Communities (along with the Scheduled Castes), and they are entitled to special provisions for their education and social development.
5. Ghorkhaland leader Subhash Ghising insisted that the Nepali-speaking people of Darjeeling should be known as Gorkha and their language was also Gorkha. He did this to draw a line between the Nepalis of Nepal and those in India. Gorkha is a district in Nepal.

References

Bhowmik, S. 1981. *Class Formation in the Plantation System*. New Delhi: People's Publishing House.

———. 1992. 'Tea Plantation Industry'. In *Unionisation and Employment in Indian Industry*, edited by S. Davala. New Delhi: Friedrich Ebert Stiftung.

———. 1996. 'West Bengal'. In *Tea Plantation Labour in India*, edited by S. Bhowmik, V. Xaxa and M. Kalam. New Delhi: Friedrich Ebert Stiftung.

———. 2011. 'Wages and Ethnic Conflicts in Bengal's Tea Industry'. *Economic and Political Weekly* 46(32): 27–9.

———. 2013. 'Labour Movement in India: Fractured Trade Unions and Vulnerable Workers'. *Rethinking Development and Inequality* 2: 84–96.

———. 2015. 'Living Conditions of Tea Plantation Labour'. *Economic and Political Weekly* 50(46–7): 30–2.

Bose, S. 1954. *Capital and Labour in the Indian Tea Industry.* Bombay: All India Trade Union Congress.
DPA (Dooars Planters Association). 1947. 'Detailed Report of the General Committee'. Calcutta: Indian Tea Association.
GoI (Government of India). 1966. 'Report of the Central Wage Board for Tea Plantation Industry'. Delhi: Ministry of Labour.
GoWB (Government of West Bengal). 2005. 'State of Labour in West Bengal, 2004'. Kolkata: Department of Labour.
Greaves, I. 1959. 'Plantations in the World Economy'. In *Plantation Systems of the New World,* edited by the Pan-American Union. Washington, DC: World Bank.
ITA (Indian Tea Association). 1933. 'Detailed Report of the General Committee 932'. Calcutta: ITA.
ITPA (Indian Tea Planters Association). 1946. 'Annual General Report for 1945'. Jalpaiguri: Jalpaiguri Printing Press.
———. 1947. 'Annual General Report for 1946'. Jalpaiguri: Jalpaiguri Printing Press.
NCL (National Commission on Labour). 1969. 'Report of the Study Group for Plantations (Tea)'. Delhi: Ministry of Labour.
Pais, J. 2014. 'The Limits of Self-Certification'. *The Hindu,* 6 November.
Rege, D.V. 1946. *Report on an Enquiry into Conditions of Labour in Plantations in India.* India: Manager of Publications.
Regmi, M. 1981. *Thatched Roofs and Stucco Palaces: Nepal from 1750 to 1950.* New Delhi: Oxford University Press.
Tea Board. 2009. 'Tea Statistics 2006-07'. Kolkata: Tea Board of India.
———. 2015. 'Annual Statistics'. http://www.teaboard.gov.in/TEABOARDPAGE/MjA= (accessed 5 February 2015).
Tinker, H. 1974. *A New Form of Slavery: Indian Indentured Labour.* London: Wiedenfeld and Nicolson.

4

From Flexible Work to Mass Uprising
The Western Cape Farm Workers' Struggle

Jesse Wilderman

In early November 2012, massive and unprecedented protests and strikes erupted among farm workers and the rural poor in more than 25 towns in the Western Cape, South Africa. These explosive actions eventually involved tens of thousands of workers and took place, intermittently, for over three months. The protests ended only when the government announced a historic increase of more than 50 per cent in the farm workers' minimum wage. The extraordinary nature and size of this uprising raises several questions: Why did the protests happen when they did? What allowed them to reach such a large scale against what most people thought of as nearly impossible odds?

The puzzle: Collective uprising in a world of paternalism and flexible work
The perceived power of the farm owners coupled with a lack of extensive, formal organisation among farm workers seemed to have stacked the deck against overt, collective resistance. Before the massive protests, many observers thought the narrative of the Western Cape fruit and wine farms implied that transformation of working and living conditions would not be prompted by action from below.

Yet not only was this uprising historic in scale and intensity, it also displayed a form of resistance outside the 'paternalistic' discourse that had come to characterise relationships between farm workers and farm owners. As Joachim Ewert and Andries du Toit (2005: 329) describe traditional farm worker resistance, 'they [the workers] rely on the "weapons of the weak", operating within the framework of the paternalistic moral universe itself, relying on individual appeals, consensual negotiations, and the avoidance of the appearance of open conflict'. The Western Cape uprising, however, was defined by open conflict, including burning of vineyards, protest marches and pitched battles with the police. Farm workers and their allies adopted an overt, confrontational and adversarial approach that, in this instance, was an apparent break from the traditional discourse.

If this were not puzzling enough, employment regimes on Western Cape farms, mirroring larger trends across the globe, were shifting to become more 'flexible', with a drop in permanent contracts, a rise in seasonal employment and decreased income security. Recent discourse might suggest that this shift creates a more vulnerable and transitory workforce, making the organising of collective resistance even more difficult. Yet it was these 'vulnerable' seasonal workers who were at the heart of initiating and mobilising the protests.

This chapter explores these puzzles in order to shed light on what allowed this uprising to emerge and gain unprecedented size and form. Here the central question is, what made it possible for these workers to mobilise and take collective action when more traditional attempts at building organisation and resistance had lacked scale and impact? More specifically, this chapter argues that the changing nature of the agricultural workforce, while creating less security, also undermined the key impediments to overt and confrontational collective resistance – namely, paternalistic social construction and isolation – while increasing social instability. These changes created more space for overt resistance. But farm workers and the rural poor lacked effective, large-scale institutional or organisational vehicles for channelling grievances into an orderly resolution process. This meant that mobilisation relied, at least initially, on an alternative set of structures, strategies and stories less mediated by traditional vehicles of large trade unions and formal, membership-based organisation. This gave the uprising a unique set of organising structures and resources of power. As Stephen Campbell (2013: 135, citing Hardt and Negri 2001) explains, 'contemporary transformations in capitalist production shape and make possible *certain forms* of struggle' (emphasis added).

This chapter is divided into four parts. First, it briefly sets the context by explaining conditions for farm workers, traditional impediments to organising and the basic events of the uprising itself. The second section explores how the ongoing transformation of the workforce among Western Cape farms has implications for the social construction of relationships of power as well as the spatial composition of farming communities and the rural poor, thereby opening the door for more collective forms of resistance. Third, the chapter turns to the forms of organisation, solidarity, resources and power that participants relied on during the uprising. Finally, the chapter closes by briefly exploring some of the challenges and opportunities that arise from this type of resistance by farm workers and the rural poor.

Farm workers, organising challenges and the uprising

Understanding the farm worker protests of late 2012 and early 2013 requires some account of the working and living conditions facing farm workers as well as what have been considered the traditional impediments to organising, organisation and collective action. The challenges for farm workers, farm dwellers and the residents of nearby settlements and townships are closely linked and overlap. At work, many farm workers face extremely long hours, lack access to basic workplace amenities such as drinking water and toilets, and are exposed to health and safety risks including pesticides and bodily injury. For their gruelling work, many farm workers – until the most recent uprising – were earning a minimum wage of R69 per day (just under US$6 per day at the time of writing). This wage level meant that farm workers were some of the lowest-paid workers in the formal sector of employment in South Africa (Human Rights Watch 2011).

Conditions for farm workers outside the workplace are also very poor. Fewer farm workers are housed on the farms than in the past, and the on-farm housing that exists is often substandard. Of those workers living off the farms, most live in nearby informal settlements, which are home to a broader group of the rural poor. Residents of these settlements experience substandard housing and often inadequate delivery of electricity, water, sanitation and other basic needs. Lack of access to health services and transport also poses significant challenges (Human Rights Watch 2011; NALEDI 2011; BFAP 2012).

Yet even with these many and significant challenges facing farm workers and the communities in which they live, trade unions have been mostly unsuccessful at organising among farm workers, with union density at around 3 per cent. Organisers cite a range of challenges including employer opposition and the vulnerability of workers as well as an embedded culture of domination and subordination, particularly for workers who live on farms and are dependent on the farm owner for housing and other basic needs. Other impediments to building organisation include the transitory nature of much of the agricultural workforce and the distances between workers who live on farms, which limit interactions between groups of workers (Human Rights Watch 2011; NALEDI 2011).

Despite these impediments to organising and the lack of large-scale membership-based organisation, massive protests erupted in the farming town of De Doorns in early November 2012, and by early December had spread to over 25 towns across the Western Cape, involving tens of thousands of workers, unemployed, youth and other poor people living in rural areas (interview, Wesso 2013). The exact nature and size of the protests varied from town to town, but generally protest activities involved farm workers and residents of rural settlements marching, blockading roads with burning tyres and debris, holding placards demanding R150 per day and, importantly, refusing to go to work. In many cases, the protests also involved some destruction of property and vineyards as well as confrontations with the police that featured tear gas, rubber bullets and arrests. Three deaths were reported over the course of the protests.

Large-scale protests flowed over the course of several months before finally coming to an end in early February 2013, when the Department of Labour announced its intention to increase the minimum wage by a whopping 52 per cent – a response to the primary rallying cry of the protestors for a daily wage of R150. The questions examined in this chapter are what kinds of changes among a workforce traditionally considered both weak and difficult to organise opened the door for this to happen, and what were the critical organising structures, strategies and stories that enabled farm workers and their communities to drive collective action.

The changing workforce: Breaking down barriers to collective action

Over the last twenty years, South African agriculture has faced increased global competition, decreased protection and subsidies from government, and greater demands on pricing and quality. These pressures have been particularly acute in the Western Cape, where fruit and wine farms are strongly oriented towards export markets. Global competition for coveted export markets lowers prices while creating pressure for tight production schedules and greater productivity. Meanwhile, government structures to regulate farm production and guarantee prices have been abolished since 1997. This has had a significant impact on farm owners, who now deal with a small number of dominant marketers and see themselves as newly 'at the will of the free market' with very little government support or protection (interviews: De Wet 2014; Gouws 2014; Mouton 2014). Large-scale and more consolidated buyers – primarily supermarket chains – are also exercising increased power within the global value chain. This enables buyers to demand higher-quality products that meet stringent requirements in terms of food safety and health, ethical production and environmental impact, and to claim a greater share of the value produced. Some statistics suggest that farm owners are now capturing only about 18 per cent of the value of their products (interview, Visser 2014).

Meanwhile, post-apartheid regulatory and legislative transformation within South Africa is also driving change within the agricultural sector. Post-1994, the African National Congress (ANC) government sought to extend labour and social protections to farm workers, adopting regulations and legislation that grant farm workers unemployment insurance, basic conditions of employment, the right to organise and strike, minimum wages, and some health and safety protections. The government also sought to improve land and housing rights by passing the Labour Tenants Act and the Extension of Security of Tenure Act to provide a legal framework around evictions (Barrientos and Kritzinger 2004; Pons-Vignon and Anseeuw 2009). During this same period, albeit quite slowly, the government also began building and providing more low-cost or free housing in the settlement areas of farming communities.

In response to all these changes, farm owners began shifting away from live-on-farm, full-time labourers, instead making greater use of off-farm, seasonal, casual and contract labour. Contract labour allows farmers to adjust the workforce size based on seasonal needs, while insulating them from responsibility for rights granted in employment legislation. Using off-farm labour further insulates farmers from requirements under tenant rights legislation (Barrientos and Kritzinger 2004; interviews: De Wet 2104; Gouws 2014; Knill 2014). As a result, more than half of the workers on fruit and wine farms in the Western Cape are now casual or seasonal;

in De Doorns, seasonal workers make up approximately 80 per cent of the workforce (interview, Visser 2014). The majority of farm workers are now living off farms (Human Rights Watch 2011). In addition to the dramatic increase in the use of seasonal and off-farm labour, the greater flexibility of the 'migrant labour system' over the last twenty years has increased the number of migrants working on farms and amplified the growth of settlement communities (interview, Mouton 2014).

At the same time, many people interviewed suggested that this influx of migrants was helping to shift the 'profile' of the traditional Western Cape farm worker. Organisers and farm workers used words and phrases like 'younger', 'more educated' and 'exposure to other things beyond the farm' to describe the changing nature of farm workers brought on by greater numbers of migrants (interviews: Jansen 2013; Witbooi 2013; Yanda 2013). And with the increasing reliance on seasonal rather than permanent labour, many households in the settlement communities – both migrant and non-migrant – have a connection to farm work for only part of the year and are forced to find alternative means to survive at other times, weakening their 'farm worker' identity (interview, Prins 2013).

Taking all these trends together, we see an agricultural sector where the number of seasonal labourers at least equals the number of permanent workers, where greater numbers of farm workers are living off farms, where more permanent migrant workers make up an expanding part of the workforce, and where larger formal and informal settlement communities occupy the hillsides of most farming towns. The question is, then, how does this transformation of the workforce and spatial arrangements in farming communities break down some of the moral and physical boundaries of social control? How do these changes – some of which might be expected to make workers more vulnerable – create a new potential for collective forms of resistance?

First, we must understand the key mechanisms of social control that existed (and still exist in many ways) in the agricultural sector: paternalism, isolation, fear and, in conflicting ways, vulnerability. The dominant paternalistic power relationship developed in a context of land dispossession and unequal power, with white-owned commercial agriculture built on the backs of cheap black and coloured labour (Pons-Vignon and Anseeuw 2009). Landowners were both the providers for the farm 'family', including farm workers, and the final authority over all those who lived on their land. Dependence on the farm owner for housing, transport, water and so many other basic necessities created a level of vulnerability unique to on-farm labour. Losing a job could also mean losing the roof over one's head.

But this social formation created much more than vulnerability. It significantly shaped and limited the arenas of contestation between farm owner and farm worker. As Ewert and Du Toit (2005: 318) explain, 'Generations of colonial settlement, slavery, and racial domination have knitted these concepts deeply into the social construction of white *and* black identities' (emphasis in original). Paternalism is a set of institutions and arrangements that create a 'deeply *organic* and *hierarchical* conceptualisation of the relationship between farmer and worker', where 'obligations between worker and farmer extend far beyond the labour-wage nexus' and where 'the most important day-to-day question is one's relationship to and one's place within this "family" that is the farm' (Du Toit 1993: 320; emphasis in original). This social construction, along with its arrangements, strategies and ideologies, tends to deny the possibility that farm worker and farm owner could be systematically opposed in their goals or relationship. Concerns may be raised, but always in the frame of their impact on the farm, with the farm owner having the final say. This social construction is also facilitated, at least partially, by the disconnection of farm workers from the outside world off the farm, where competing understandings and definitions of self and society might be found. Using this analysis, 'paternalism smothers any possibility of resistance' (Du Toit 1993: 316).

This paternalistic construction contributes to and works alongside other powerful obstacles to collective action – namely, isolation and fear. Farms are often spread across huge geographical areas, and without transport of their own, workers who live on the farms have traditionally been limited in their access to information and their ability to coordinate and collaborate. This spatial isolation, coupled with a strict enforcement of private property rights by farm owners opposed to any sort of organising, creates huge obstacles to gathering any sort of strength or safety in numbers.

The changing nature of the workforce – the use of more seasonal and off-farm labour along with the expansion of migrant labour –

weakens these traditional barriers to collective action. Paternalistic social dominance by farm owners is weakened as seasonal, off-farm labour is less dependent on the farm owner for basic needs and holds no place in the farm 'family'. The influx of migrants and the transitory nature of less stable and permanent employment relationships also weaken the bonds and history that help formulate the identities, institutions and norms of paternalism. As the farm owner is removed from his role as landlord, service provider and, in some cases, even permanent employer, the paternalistic connection is much less likely to hold. Seasonal and off-farm workers are more likely to have demands that focus on disparity in outcomes and rights rather than harmony and appreciation of the farm owner's 'gifts' to them (interview, Du Toit 2014).

This new leadership by off-farm labour was also evident in the primary demand of the protestors that, while more multifaceted in some regions, was primarily about demanding a daily wage of R150. Unlike on-farm labour, where survival is dependent on a range of services provided by the farmer, the seasonal workers who live in the rural settlements are dependent on their wages and the provision of municipal services and social grants. The connection of the seasonal worker to the farm is much more transactional and less susceptible to the relationship and power dynamics that breed paternalistic social construction.

Moreover, off-farm, migrant and seasonal workers are less subject to the isolation and lack of access to information that help maintain the dominance of paternalism (interview, Yanda 2013). These same workers also tend to move around more within and between the farming towns, building networks and sharing information and experiences. And the more transient nature of their jobs also means that these workers have less of a relationship with any one farm owner and are thereby less beholden to any one farm owner's wishes. A complaint that all interviewed farm owners regularly raised was that seasonal workers might be working for them one day and then the next day be working on another farm nearby (interview, Knill 2014).

These transformations of the workforce and living arrangements also impact on workers' perceptions of their own identities as 'farm workers'. As farm owners move away from year-round employment to more temporary employment arrangements, workers must find other means of employment or survival, particularly during the off-season.

In addition, the changing spatial make-up and work arrangements are shifting farm workers' dependency for social support away from farm owners and towards the service delivery, social grants and housing available from government. These shifts obviously weaken the inhibiting social construction of paternalism but do not greatly reduce the level of grievances among farm workers, given the government's limited success in delivering adequate services to meet increasing needs and rising expectations. In this way, the breakdown of paternalism not only provides some liberation for new possibilities of resistance but also amplifies the levels of social instability that might prompt action.

It was service delivery protests that, at least partially, allowed for a set of protest tactics or repertoires to emerge among rural communities that were collective and confrontational in nature, while targeting the state as the key actor for change. In other words, the lack of impeding social constructions and institutions of stability not only allowed collective action to emerge and amplified grievances but also helped shape the type of collective action undertaken. As one farm worker in Citrusdal reported, 'It [the protest] was a mixture of all the groups – unemployed, farm workers, township workers, people who worked in the town, youth, coloured workers – and even the mayor was sympathetic' (interview, Brink 2013).

Moreover, coordination, collaboration and the sharing of grievances, all critical for mass collective action, become much easier when everyone lives in one area. The first major component of the uprising arose in Stofland, a rural settlement of thousands of farm workers and their families living in shacks and government-provided houses off the farms in De Doorns. As explained by workers, the initial organisation of the strike and mobilisation of the entire settlement community – from twice-daily meetings on the local rugby field, to nightly house-by-house communication, to the use of whistles to bring people out of their houses in the morning – were critically facilitated by the concentration of farm workers in one area (interviews: Jacobs 2013; Witbooi 2013; Yanda 2013; Marowmo 2014). This living arrangement also made organising possible without the need for significant resources, while organisers from trade unions consistently raised concerns about their ability to reach large numbers of workers with few resources (interviews: Witbooi 2013; Yanda 2013).

These settlements were not only places where workers could share grievances but, in some cases, they were sites where 'influencing' organisations could train and support farm worker leaders who would later become key in the protest.[1] An organiser with Women on Farms, a non-governmental organisation that works with women in farming communities, explained that while she had limited access to farms, she would simply visit the rural settlement, stop women on the street or knock on their doors and talk to them about getting involved, eventually calling a meeting in the community itself to bring women together to share experiences and challenges (interview, Jacobs 2013).

It is important to note, however, that these dynamics are not without their internal contradictions. For example, while moving off-farm makes farm workers less dependent and therefore less vulnerable to the will of the farm owner, the transformation to a more seasonal employment adds to the economic vulnerability of these same workers. And because farm owners are able to – and do – pick and choose who will work for them season to season, it is reasonable to argue that seasonal farm workers might be less inclined to engage in collective action. In fact, in De Doorns, for example, farm owners are refusing to rehire seasonal workers who engaged in protest activity (interview, Yanda 2013). Yet it can also be argued that the increased economic vulnerability of seasonal workers creates a stronger set of issues and anger around which to mobilise and organise. In different ways, seasonal workers have both the most and the least to lose by taking the risk of engaging in collective resistance.

In conclusion, the dynamics of the changing workforce – more seasonal, off-farm and migrant labour – have been driven by farm owners' reactions to a specific kind of liberalisation and globalisation, along with increased tenancy and labour rights. This transformation is creating new spatial arrangements in farming communities while severing some of the key bindings of the paternalistic social construction.

Setting to scale, having an impact: Stories, structures and strategies
In terms of the uprising itself, the first large-scale action involving thousands of people in De Doorns was inspired by the spark of hope and sense of strategic possibility created by a relatively small but successful strike on an individual farm near the town.

The question of how information and – as importantly – inspiration was spread is in many ways a question about what kind of 'story' was being told by whom and how it reached people. Movement narratives that are successful in motivating people to act generally include the grievance that the community faces, a construction of common identity, and a picture of collective action that can redress the problem (Polletta 1998). Doug McAdam (in Killian 1984) refers to the use of story as part of his concept of 'cognitive liberation', whereby people are able to develop a collective definition of their situation as unjust and subject to change through collective action. The story of the De Doorns protest, as recounted by farm workers in towns to which the protest spread, had all of these elements. Every participant in the uprising who was interviewed for this research reported being first inspired to action by seeing this story on television.

A critical element of the television images and story – described as videos of large numbers of black and coloured people blockading the highway, marching in protest, burning tyres, throwing stones, holding placards demanding R150 per day, and speaking out against white farm owners who treat them unfairly – was that they were, at least initially, unmediated by professionalised voices and unfiltered in defining the conflict, risk and demand. Many farm workers saw themselves in the protestors, which provided them with courage and a sense of hope that collective action was possible. As a farm worker who was born and lived her whole life on a farm explained, 'We were afraid in the first place and now we are not afraid; we saw De Doorns on the TV and they were farm workers like us and not afraid so we decided we would not be afraid' (interview, Erumas 2014). These scenes of conflict also awakened a rights-based discourse – in contradiction to the traditional paternalistic discourse – that inspired almost an obligation to participate. As one farm worker described it:

> One day we are working on the farms and we see the De Doorns strike on the television and it is coming from farm workers themselves. We are doing nothing but we are sitting there in our houses and every night we see [on the television] the police shooting at them because they are talking about R150 living wage; no one will take them seriously if it is only just them in

De Doorns . . . if they are going to win, it will benefit all of us. After that, we decide we are going to join De Doorns (interview, Jacobs 2013).

The lack of formal organisational engagement and professional spokespeople, particularly at the beginning of the uprising, increased the moral power of the protest and stamped it with a more genuine and legitimate character. With headlines like 'Leaderless Farm Strike is "Organic"' (*Mail & Guardian*, 16 November 2012), the protestors suggested an action by moral urgency rather than planning and coordination.

In addition, the clarity of the demand and, more specifically, the size of the increase that workers were demanding – over 100 per cent – served to raise expectations and spark indignation. And more than simply increasing expectations, the scale of the increase signalled the demand for a much broader transformation of conditions for the rural poor in the Western Cape. The workers were articulating 'a wage demand so large as to signify a much broader rejection of the overall system underlying their conditions' (Fisher 1978: 203).

Mobilising structures: Coordinating units, networks and technology

The key structures that allowed much of the inspiration from the De Doorns protests to be turned into strategy and collective action across many of the farming communities were locally based organisations or vanguard groups – cadres of pre-existing community-based activists – that might be described as 'coordinating units' (Killian 1984). These coordinating units were able to use their know-how and networks to extend large, at times confrontational, collective action, seizing the moment to mobilise well beyond the scale of their membership, resources or previous efforts.

These units had several characteristics in common:
1. They were able to recognise the opportunity that the uprising presented for much broader mobilisation beyond the incremental organisation-building they had done in the past.
2. They were nimble enough to refocus and take action quickly.
3. They made use of local volunteer capacity, as well as local informal networks, to do outreach and mobilisation.
4. They had some experience with protest and organising.

5. They had a 'social base' which went beyond the workplace and farm workers.
6. They were linked with other activist and social movement organisations around the Western Cape.

Engaging with this continuum gave these organisations deeper networks and local volunteer capacity that, along with their understanding and history, put them at the centre of the action. A leader of the Mawubuye Land Rights Movement recalled that, after word of the De Doorns strike had spread, groups of unorganised farm workers walked long distances during the night to seek out Mawubuye members for help on how to *toi-toi* (protest) (interview, Jansen 2013). These same groups also had relationships with other organisations across the Western Cape, allowing for broader levels of collaboration and coordination, specifically in the form of a 'Farm Worker Coalition'. This is just one example of the many different kinds of coordinating units that were critical to translating the energy of the moment into concrete strategy and action in towns across the region.

While these coordinating units played a key role in facilitating participation, these and other organisations also engaged in 'influencing' work well before the uprising. Although not immediately directed towards confrontational collective action, this work helped establish the 'supportive organisational context' (McAdam in Killian 1984), leadership and networks that would later make the spread of the uprising possible. Activities including 'speak outs', political education schools, and training in basic workplace and human rights were used to develop leadership skills that could often be found among the leaders of the uprising (interviews: Jacobs 2013; Andrews 2014).

While locally based organisations, with their deep community roots, were the key to spreading the protest on the ground, there were different levels of organisational engagement. The Congress of South African Trade Unions (COSATU), for example, contributed to the spread (and at times the contraction) of the protest by using its standing and public prominence to encourage participation and provide legitimacy. In theory, these different sets of resources and strengths could be complementary in spreading and sustaining the protest. In reality, the challenges of coordination, collaboration and leadership – particularly when there was not a clear understanding of common purpose, roles and goals – probably amplified the uprising in the short term but ultimately led to significant infighting that was detrimental to longer-term collaboration.

In addition to the role of pre-existing organisations, informal networks also played a part in spreading information and expanding participation. The increasingly transient nature of agricultural work meant that farm workers could build networks as they moved between seasonal jobs or even between individual farms within an area. The shifting spatial make-up of the farming communities, particularly the growth of informal settlements, gave workers more opportunities to build networks with a broader group of other farm workers and also with non-farm workers living in the same area. Finally, the increasing numbers of migrants, particularly those who move between communities following seasonal work, allowed more and more networks to be built among these groups and between the farming towns.

Technology, particularly mobile phones, also played a role in the rapid spread of the strike. Every worker and community respondent who was interviewed had the use of a mobile phone, and many of the respondents used both Facebook and WhatsApp as tools to communicate with their networks and engage in group sharing. This technology-based interconnectedness has been part of the ongoing transformation that has broken down some of the isolation faced by farm workers. The increased technology has dramatically increased the speed at which rural communities can communicate with each other, heightened the ability to convey a common message, and helped farm workers gain exposure to outside ideas and influences.

Service delivery protests also played a role in building networks, leadership and informal organisation. These same protests served to engage the whole community of the rural poor in these areas and to develop a set of protest tactics that would be widely used during the uprising. As one activist and researcher of these rural communities explained:

> Seasonal workers [living in the settlements] were not organised and had no access to trade unions. People developed civic committees in these townships, with the big innovation of these

committees being service-related issues. First they organised around these issues and then also started to take on issues around farm employment and migrants in the area . . . service delivery issues drove them together (interview, Kleinbooi 2013).

Repertoires of contention: Replicable tactics and strategy

Along with formal and informal networks, the basic protest strategies and tactics that were used made it more likely for the resistance to gain scale. Strategy can be defined as 'turning the resources we have into the power we need to get what we want' (Ganz 2010: 82). Tactics are the means for putting this strategy into action. Tactics and strategy – the repertoires of resistance – are shaped by the experience and traditions of the collective actors; in other words, 'the repertoire is therefore not only what people *do* when they make a claim; it is what they *know how to do* . . .' (Tarrow 1993: 283; emphasis in original).

In this case, the experiences and leadership of the coordinating units were critical in spreading the protest and shaping the tactics being used. In addition, larger numbers of protestors, given that they resided in settlement areas, had some previous experiences with marches or collective action around service delivery issues. These tactics were also easily replicable, and this power of imitation – action that was easily recognisable and mimicked – helped spread the uprising. The main tactics of the De Doorns strikers included blockading roads, burning tyres, marching, refusing to work and stopping others from working. These were all tactics that could easily be emulated by others who wanted to join the protest. At the same time, these tactics could be adapted to local situations and facilitate broad participation beyond farm workers: anyone in the community could join a march, burn a tyre or help block a road (interviews: CSAAWU activist members 2014; Dube 2014). Moreover, the tactics did not require a lot of advance planning or external resources beyond what was easily accessible to most farm workers and the rural poor, most notably their bodies. Other materials – petrol, tyres, stones and handwritten placards – were relatively easy for farm workers to acquire and did not require coordination with outside support or organisations. In some sense, the protestors were recognising a range of sources of power and leverage, drawing on the resources of both the farm workers and the broader community to disrupt the normal functioning of society.

On the one hand, the results of the uprising suggest that structural power was not enough to win significant concessions from farm owners, particularly given their ability to bring in replacement workers. On the other hand, the government did feel compelled to intervene and raise the minimum wage by the significant amount of 52 per cent. In many ways, this demonstrates the power of combining broad community engagement with worker-based mobilisation and targeting the government as a key actor. Of course, the challenge of relying on the government as the chief actor is how to implement these gains when the enforcement and regulatory power of this same government is lacking.

The primary forms of power employed during the uprising – structural and disruptive power – can have an impact only with the participation of both workers and the broader community of the rural poor. If workers were to strike without the support of the settlement community, they would be quite easily replaced in their work, while disruption of the broader functioning of society, particularly when facing police repression, requires large numbers and broad support to have any chance of being sustained.

This analysis poses an important question about whether or not to describe this uprising as a farm workers' strike or as a community rebellion of the predominantly black, rural poor who are expressing their outrage at being politically marginalised and focusing their energy on challenging the state to fulfil its responsibilities. Given the broad community mobilisation beyond farm workers, the choice of public space rather than the farms for protest, the tactics borrowed from service delivery protests, some articulation of demands beyond the workplace, and the focus on government as a key target, there is a strong case to be made that this was a rebellion of the rural poor rather than simply a farm workers' uprising. At the same time, the case could be made that this was primarily an uprising led by black and coloured farm workers targeting white farm owners around a legacy of poverty-level wages and unbearable living conditions. This is supported by the central demand around farm workers' wages, the targeting of farms and farm equipment for destruction, the concentrated efforts at stopping farm workers from going to work, the timing of the protests around the beginning of the harvest, and a focus on trying to force the employers to reach an agreement to improve conditions. The answer might be that this uprising was both a community rebellion and a workplace strike rolled into one, where the protest was focused on challenging both the state and the employers as sources of authority, and where the changing nature of work and the arrangement of rural communities is narrowing the distinction between 'farm worker' and other identities of the rural poor.

In either case, the heavy reliance on disruptive power turned out to be effective at getting government to act. Yet there might have been a 'power mismatch' in the protests: many of the underlying power relationships are still defined on a day-to-day basis between owners and workers on farms, but the disruptive power of the protest and the aggregation of the protestors' resources were in the 'streets'. In the aftermath of the strike, many worker interviewees indicated that the relationship with the farm owner had not changed or become more equal (interviews: Erumas 2014; FAWU members at 1st Farm 2014; Shirleen 2014).

In other words, through this specific form of collective action, farm workers were able to challenge their conditions of poverty but were less able to confront the faces of power that dominate daily work life; the resistance and outrage were still 'outside the gate' and not 'on the farm'. This may explain why farm workers might have been willing to engage in major conflict and confrontation in these protest actions but still indicated high levels of fear around organising trade unions on the farms. As one farm worker put it, 'You can lose your job when you join the union, but it is easy to throw stones at the police' (interview, FAWU members at 1st Farm 2014).

The nature of the protest, then, may also point to an ongoing difficulty for farm workers in converting temporary mobilisation into more permanent organisation which could come through workplace-based recognition by the employer and the shared consent of a collective agreement (Kuzwayo and Webster 1978). The lack of 'recognition' and 'shared consent' by farm owners may mean that farm workers must rely either on ongoing mobilisation and higher levels of conflict or on outside parties such as government for enforcement and further engagement with farm owners.

The farm workers' protest thus gained its scale and impact through a motivation driven by widely disseminated television images of the De Doorns struggle told by participants with a clear and aspirational demand, a set of locally based coordinating units with a specific set of organisational characteristics, an array of relationships built on informal networks that have been expanded and strengthened by the changing nature of farm work and the spatial living arrangements of the rural communities, and communication technology that allowed for the rapid sharing of information. These core factors were aided by an easily repeatable set of tactics and strategies that existed within the experience of the rural poor, exercised both structural and disruptive power, and allowed for broad participation.

These elements give us clues as to how organisers and organisations might engage with the emerging leaders and increasing confidence of some of the protestors to determine whether the gains of the protest can be institutionalised and built upon or prove to be fleeting and temporary.

Key lessons and continuing challenges

The question for social movement organisations, particularly trade unions, is how to support and amplify the energy of the farm workers' uprising without seeking to control it. How can organisations contribute to a supportive organisational context where new repertoires can be tested and refined and where gains can be secured and institutionalised? Equally important, how can organisations help translate the energy of the moment into strategic action that unifies the broader community of the rural poor around a broad set of issues?

If we assume that organisers and organisations can facilitate agency over time – even if this agency is not determinative *on its own* in the occurrence of further large-scale collective action – we must ask what kind of mobilising structures and organising approaches have the best chance to engage larger numbers of farm workers and to build leadership and struggle from below. The uprising in the Western Cape seems to suggest that approaches would include the following:

- *Take a community-based approach to organising rather than simply an employer-based, farm-by-farm approach.* This recommendation speaks to the importance of settlement communities as centres of activity and relationships, with fewer impediments to organising. This study indicates that a spatial dimension is key to building organisation, even if it suggests a different kind of approach and challenge to dealing with workplace issues.
- *Build organisation that speaks specifically to the new workforce, particularly seasonal and migrant workers.* This approach could mean exploring

different models of membership, particularly given that seasonal workers may be unemployed or working at alternative jobs during large parts of the year. It might also mean exploring a different set of services, facilitated through organisation, that address the different needs of these workers. Most importantly, organisations must be able to speak to both the workplace identity and the other identities of this changing workforce.

- *Organise and build organisations that speak to a broad set of issues and build a social base beyond farm workers.* Artificially separating the workplace issues faced by farm workers from the broader issues facing the rural poor narrows the relationship of farm workers and their communities to social movement organisations. A broader organisational approach also suggests adopting tactics and leadership development activities that allow broad participation – a 'horizontal expansion' – rather than being limited to a select number of worker leaders. This calls for organisations that are 'of' the community rather than simply allied with the community. It also means that participants must be given meaningful and consequential roles in activities, which in some ways can reduce centralised control and increase risk. Some elements of this horizontal expansion emerged in the participation of the unemployed, youth and other community members in the farm worker protests. As Du Toit and Ewert (2002: 98) explain, 'farm worker organisation, if it ever takes root on South Africa's farmed landscape, will much more closely resemble a broad-based "rural social movement" than a classical trade union'.
- *Recognise that influencing organisations can be important in building leadership outside moments of game-changing action.* Providing a supportive organisational context that is focused on building capacity and leadership outside the more immediate and direct action provides both confidence and connections among the rural poor.
- *Adopt an orientation towards collective problems and collective action rather than individual problems and legalistic action.* Many workers faced a massive backlash from farm owners after the uprising: some activists were fired; payroll deductions were taken for benefits that were previously free; production quotas were increased. The

challenges that organisations have had in supporting workers during this time prove some of the limits of using legal and institutional processes to resolve conflict in situations of such unequal power. More importantly, the focus on individual problems detracts from a larger movement narrative about the purpose of social movement organisations, reducing their aspirational nature to a more reactive and defensive 'job insurance' programme. The power of the uprising was its collective nature and its willingness to take the risk of operating outside of any proscribed legalistic mechanisms.
- *Undertake a strategic analysis, understanding and approach to the changing agricultural sector.* While this chapter has focused on the organising and power built around mass collective action, organisations hoping to continue to drive and sustain change from below might explore other sources of power, alliances or approaches based on a deep understanding of the global value chain and the needs and vulnerabilities of its respective actors.

Even under these approaches, perhaps the most challenging aspect of rural transformation still resides in the nuts and bolts of how organisations can speak to the power struggle *on the farm*. In many ways, even a strong organisation of the rural poor would face disaggregation of their power in the daily workings of the farm, where, mostly far removed from regulatory agencies or threats of mass collective action, individual farm owners still hold a decision-making authority over smaller groups of workers.

These challenges also highlight the distinction between *mobilising*, which is primarily about moving pre-existing structures and networks into collective action around specific issues, and *organising*, which is about building the individual and institutional leadership capacity to act. Of course, in the practice of building social movements, organising and mobilising often overlap and contribute to each other. But the distinction is important because organising generally happens over a longer period of time and through more sustained engagement, while mobilisation is more time-limited and often focused on specific events. Even a breakdown of the impediments to collective action, coupled with a set of stories, structures and strategies designed to mobilise the resources of the rural poor in 'spurts' of mass resistance, doesn't necessarily speak to the organisation and leadership needed to act consistently *over time* – the ability to both win and hold, and then win again, allowing for more than fleeting progress in meaningfully shifting power and wealth to the rural poor.

Given these challenges, it may be most critical for established organisations to create the space for 'organisational experimentation' and more 'learning by doing' in terms of resistance among farm workers and the rural poor. And when moments of madness erupt, they should be ready to amplify and support the moment in such a way as to build the leadership, networks and organisation for further action. These moments can indeed create opportunities to challenge over the longer term not only material conditions on the farms but the underlying power relationships holding back broader transformation. As one farm worker stated while reflecting on the uprising, 'I will never forget the way people stood together. It was amazing. And we could see the power of togetherness, and I will never forget that we could see that the farmer, for once, was really afraid of us' (interview, Erumas 2014).

Note
1. Influencing organisations are not necessarily directly involved in planning and organising the strike itself, but their activities leading up to the action may impact eventual participants, facilitate participation or shift the broader context (IIE 1974).

References
Barrientos, S. and A. Kritzinger. 2004. 'Squaring the Circle: Global Production and the Informalization of Work in South African Fruit Exports'. *Journal of International Development* 16(1): 81–92.
BFAP (Bureau for Food and Agricultural Policy). 2012. 'Farm Sectoral Determination: An Analysis of Agricultural Wages in South Africa'. Pretoria: BFAP.
Campbell, S. 2013. 'Solidarity Formations under Flexibilisation: Workplace Struggles of Precarious Migrants in Thailand'. *Global Labour Journal* 4(2): 134–51.
Du Toit, A. 1993. 'The Micro-Politics of Paternalism: The Discourses of Management and Resistance on South African Fruit and Wine Farms'. *Journal of Southern African Studies* 19(2): 314–36.
Du Toit, A. and J. Ewert. 2002. 'Myths of Globalisation: Private Regulation and Farm Worker Livelihoods on Western Cape Farms'. *Transformation: Critical Perspectives on Southern Africa* 50 (1): 77–104.

Ewert, J. and A. du Toit. 2005. 'A Deepening Divide in the Countryside: Restructuring and Rural Livelihoods in the South African Wine Industry'. *Journal of Southern African Studies* 31(2): 315-32.
Fisher, F. 1978. 'Workers: Class Consciousness among Colonized Workers in South Africa'. In *Change, Reform, and Economic Growth in South Africa*, edited by L. Schlemmer and E. Webster. Johannesburg: Ravan Press.
Ganz, M. 2010. *Organizing Notes: People, Power, Change*. Distributed at John F. Kennedy School of Government, Harvard University, January.
Human Rights Watch. 2011. 'Ripe with Abuse: Human Rights Conditions in South Africa's Fruit and Wine Industries'. New York: Human Rights Watch.
IIE (Institute for Industrial Education). 1974. *The Durban Strikes*. Johannesburg: Ravan Press.
Killian, L. 1984. 'Organization, Rationality, and Spontaneity in the Civil Rights Movement'. *American Sociological Review* 49(6): 770-83.
Kuzwayo, J. and E. Webster. 1978. 'A Research Note on Consciousness and the Problem of Organization'. In *Change, Reform, and Growth in South Africa*, edited by L. Schlemmer and E. Webster. Johannesburg: Ravan Press.
NALEDI (National Labour and Economic Development Institute). 2011. 'Identifying Obstacles to Union Organizing in Farms: Toward a Decent Work Strategy in the Farming Sector'. Johannesburg: NALEDI.
Polletta, F. 1998. '"It Was Like a Fever . . .": Narrative and Identity in Social Protest'. *Social Problems* 45(2): 137-59.
Pons-Vignon, N. and W. Anseeuw. 2009. 'Great Expectations: Working Conditions in South Africa since the End of Apartheid'. *Journal of Southern African Studies* 35(4): 883-99.
Tarrow, S. 1993. 'Cycles of Collective Action: Between Moments of Madness and the Repertoire of Contention'. *Social Science History* 17(2): 281-307.

Interviews
Brink, Petrus. 23 November 2013.
CSAAWU (Commercial Stevedoring Agricultural Allied Workers Union) activist members, group interview. 8 March 2014.
De Wet, Peter. 7 March 2014.
Dube, Deneco. 22 November and 7 March 2014.
Du Toit, Andres. 3 March 2014.
Erumas, Christina. 7 March 2014.
FAWU (Food and Allied Workers Union) members at 1st Farm, group interview. 9 March 2014.
Gouws, Joseph. 10 March 2014.
Jacobs, Ida. 29 November 2013 and 5 March 2014.
Jacobs, Simon. 24 November 2013.
Jansen, Denia. 22 November 2013 and 6 March 2014.

Kleinbooi, Karin. 26 November 2013.
Knill, Buche. 10 March 2014.
Marowmo, Owen. 10 March 2014.
Mouton, Donald. 5 March 2014.
Prins, Magrieta. 28 November 2013.
Shirleen (first name only). 6 March 2014.
Visser, Margareet. 3 March 2014.
Wesso, Ronald. 18 November 2013.
Witbooi, Eldrina. 28 November 2013.
Yanda, Shawn. 28 November 2013.

5

Organising Farm Workers in Gauteng
Economic Upgrading and Social Downgrading

uMbuso we Nkosi

In South Africa the horticultural value chain plays a very significant role in employment creation and exports (Barrientos and Visser 2012). There has been significant change in this sector given that 'traditionally fresh produce value chains linked African exports primarily to Europe, where dominant supermarket buyers set key commercial criteria and standards applied to producers and workers' (2). This relationship has always been a key focus in the literature of the global value chain analysis (Barientos, Dolan and Tallontire 2003; Tallontire et al. 2005; Barrientos and Visser 2012).

The conceptual framing by Stephanie Barientos, Gary Gereffi and Arianna Rossi (2011), focusing on the linkages between economic upgrading of firms and social upgrading of workers, is pivotal in that it questions who benefits when firms move up the global value chain. This analysis is most relevant to those who are interested in coming up with policy responses to the problems in labour markets and are keen on finding out what feasible solutions are available for the problems faced by labour in the epoch of neoliberal globalisation. Barrientos, Gereffi and Rossi (2011: 323) indicate that there are four types of economic upgrading: process upgrading, involving changes in the production process with the objective of making production more efficient; product upgrading, with a focus on a shift to a more advanced product; functional upgrading, when firms change the mix of activities they perform towards higher-value-added tasks; and chain upgrading, which involves shifting into more advanced production chains. Social upgrading entails adhering to measurable standards (decent work, working contracts, health and safety) and enhancing worker empowerment (for example, no discrimination and freedom of association) (Barrientos and Visser 2012).

South Africa has seen an increase in local retailers who have adopted standards similar to those of European retailers. With the rise of such standards, the literature has shifted to an exploration of issues related to economic and social upgrading and downgrading (Barrientos and Visser 2012). This chapter focuses on the local value chain in Gauteng – more specifically, on vegetable production, which is largely for the domestic market. The discussion draws on work by Benjamin Selwyn (2007, 2011, 2012) and his critique of the global commodity chain approach; this was revised by Gary Gereffi and Miguel Korzeniewicz (1994) to favour a much more interventionist policy approach, although their emphasis has been on showing the 'trickle-down' process of economic growth. The contention is that the process of economic upgrading will lead to spill-over effects for the wider economy, contributing to increased employment, better working conditions and local development (Selwyn 2012: 5–17). This view is also put forward by Barrientos, Gereffi and Rossi (2011). Selwyn (2012: 5) argues that in the global commodity chain analysis 'labour has no role in determining processes and outcomes of global integration and development'. Therefore, labour in this firm-centric argument is 'portrayed as subject to [the] firm's strategies of cost-price rationalization, which are in turn a function of the supplier's subordination to northern-led firms' (27). Selwyn's hypothesis is that

> the nature of capital-labour relations is a fundamental determinant of a region's (and by extension a state's and the entire globe's) developmental trajectory. If workers are able to organize successfully and, through class struggles, achieve meaningful concessions from capital, a region's developmental process will be very different to that where workers are unorganized and completely subordinated to the dictates of firms' accumulation strategies (Selwyn 2012: 1).

This chapter discusses the rising power of local retailers in the procurement of vegetables and the standards they set. It sets out the changing working conditions in the agricultural sector, presents the findings of a survey of farm workers in Gauteng, and describes the relations between the farm workers and the farmers who are supplying the local retailers. The findings indicate that the process of economic upgrading has not been accompanied by a process of social upgrading. The main conclusion drawn is that value chain analysis centred on economic upgrading and social upgrading is pivotal, but methodologically it lacks a conversation with the subjects studied. If the aim is to organise 'vulnerable workers', then perhaps scholars ought to enter into a dialogue with those that they study as a way of avoiding the pitfall of seeing trade unions (mostly from urban areas) as the main institutions that are organising and articulating the interests of those who are working in the 'countryside'.

The decline of the national fresh produce markets and the rise of the local retail sector

The fresh produce markets in South Africa were created to allow producers and consumers to trade under the control of a local government body (Chikazunga et al. 2008). However, in 1967 the Department of Agricultural Economics recommended the formation of national markets to separate markets of national and local interest; these included National Fresh Produce Markets (NFPMs) as well as privately owned markets (Chikazunga et al. 2008). In this section, the focus is on the NFPMs controlled by government by-laws (selling mostly fresh fruit and vegetables).

There are four major NFPMs in South Africa (Durban, Johannesburg, Cape Town, Pretoria); four medium markets (Bloemfontein, East London, Pietermaritzburg, Port Elizabeth); and six smaller markets (Kimberley, Klerksdorp, Springs, Uitenhage, Vereeniging, Welkom) (Chikazunga et al. 2008: 2; Euromonitor International 2010).[1] Respective local authorities manage most of these markets.

The NFPMs aim to establish equal trade opportunities for both large-scale and small-scale farmers. Therefore, they have created a space for small-scale farmers to find a market and sell their products easily 'as the barriers to entry into the market would otherwise be near impossible, as large corporate buyers and marketing agents are not interested in procuring small fluctuating quantities and/or varying quality fresh produce from these smallholders' (Chikazunga et al. 2008: 2). However, 'large scale commercial farmers still dominate the majority of the supply to the NFPMs with between 80 and 90 percent while small scale producers supply the remaining variable volumes'. This reflects the problems faced by small-scale farmers who lack suitable transportation (refrigerated trucks) and adequate equipment (tractors, irrigation).

How do the NFPMs function and how are they structured? They use a 'marketing floor' system whereby farmers or producers pay 5 per cent to the NFPM market management and 5–7.5 per cent to the agents who sell the produce on the market floor (interview, Consignment Control Process Manager [hereafter CCP Manager], 4 May 2012). The prices are set by a system of supply and demand: if there is an oversupply, farmers get a low price for their produce; but if there is undersupply, farmers get a good price for their produce (interviews: CCP Manager, 4 May 2012; Johan, 22 November 2012).[2]

The NFPMs sell produce in bulk but also cater for individual purchases (Chikazunga et al. 2008). The NFPMs cater for the following buyers: exporters (mostly from southern African countries), processors, hawkers, Woolworths, Spar, Pick n Pay, and Shoprite/Checkers (interview, CCP Manager, 4 May 2012). The flow of produce moves from the farmer to NFPMs via a marketing agent, and then on to the different buyers. Generally, the price fluctuates depending on the amount of produce the marketing agent has procured from different farmers (interviews: CCP Manager, 4 May 2012; Johan, 22 November 2012). The four dominant retailers – that is, Shoprite/Checkers, Pick n Pay, Spar and Woolworths – have been procuring less of their produce from the NFPMs over the years because of concerns related to a lack of cold chain maintenance in the NFPMs and the adoption of internationally recognised food quality standards (Bienabe and Vermeulen 2007). Hence, the retailers procure as little as 10 per cent from the NFPMs, mainly produce such as potatoes and onions (Bienabe and Vermeulen 2007). Essentially, this means that demand has been reduced on the market floor.

'South African food markets are estimated to be worth over R200 billion, with the fresh produce sector commanding a 15% share' (Chikazunga and Paradza 2012). The four retail chains are described as oligopolistic entities, with growing market power (Weatherspoon and Reardon 2003; Kirsten 2009; Chikazunga and Paradza 2012). 'Market power refers to the ability to raise selling prices and depress input prices, to deter entry, to redistribute profit to oneself from other firms and, more importantly, to sustain these benefits over time' (Kirsten 2009: 5). This market power reflects the changing procurement styles of these retailers from the apartheid years to the post-apartheid era (Weatherspoon and Reardon 2003; Stroebel 2010). Shoprite/Checkers is the leader of the four retailers, owning about 21 per cent of the formal food markets, followed by Pick n Pay (18 per cent), Spar (12 per cent) and Woolworths Food (8 per cent) (Euromonitor 2010; Naidoo 2011).

The four retailers have different procurement strategies; they use either their direct distribution centres or their direct contracts with farmers. This is a reflection of a centralised procurement scheme that has been adopted by most retailers around the world (Kirsten 2009). These retailers' procurement strategy is also based on the 'preferred suppliers' list, which places emphasis on quality fresh produce, consistency of supply, adherence to prices set by the retailers, and safety standards (Weatherspoon and Reardon 2003; Bienabe and Vermeulen 2007; Kirsten 2009). These preferred suppliers remain on the list only if they are able to upgrade their production, emphasising quality standards and meeting the rest of the standards stipulated above. Failure to adhere to these standard results in delisting of suppliers. Payment made to preferred suppliers can take up to 40 days, with no written contract signed (Beinabe and Vermeulen 2007). The preferred suppliers pack the produce in their packhouses and, using their refrigerated trucks, deliver to the retail distribution centres (Weatherspoon and Reardon 2003).

Most South African retailers require that their fresh produce suppliers adhere to internationally recognised food quality and safety systems such as EurepGAP at farm level and to guidelines for hazard analysis and critical control points (HACCP) at packhouse/processing level.[3] Most produce delivered by the farmers to the distribution centres is packaged and ready for supermarket shelves (Bienabe and Vermeulen 2007: 4).

Thus, the four dominant retailers have strategically chosen large-scale farmers in South Africa who export to the United Kingdom or the United States because they follow international food quality production standards (Weatherspoon and Reardon 2003). Research shows that such standards have meant that small-scale farmers are unable to consistently supply the retailers. Only a few small-scale farmers in the southern African region supply the four South African retailers; most of them are in the rural areas and are considered to be suppliers of the 'emerging markets' (Weatherspoon and Reardon 2003; Bienabe and Vermeulen 2007; Chikazunga and Paradza 2012).

'All Woolworths' stores receive their fresh produce through the central procurement system. The Spar group's central distribution system for fresh produce is mainly for their Freshline brand (a limited range of upmarket, expensive, value-added, superior quality fresh produce)' (Bienabe and Vermeulen 2007: 3-4). Shoprite/Checkers uses Freshmark, which procures 90 per cent of fruit and vegetables directly from the farmers through its distribution centres and ensures that its suppliers adhere to the aforementioned international production standards. For safety attributes such as pesticide use and hygiene, Freshmark uses a third-party laboratory called Swift Micro Laboratories (Weatherspoon and Reardon 2003). Pick n Pay uses its distribution centres to procure fresh produce from the farmers; these centres are located in Johannesburg, Durban and Port Elizabeth, in areas in which Pick n Pay has stores, thus minimising costs for the retailer (Weatherspoon and Reardon 2003). Pick n Pay also ensures that its producers adhere to international food production standards, and makes use of a third-party laboratory, PRIMUS, based in California, for health and safety matters (Weatherspoon and Reardon 2003). One can see similarities between the retail revolution in the North and the rise of the four local retailers in regards to the adherence of quality standards and in terms of their buying power given that 'retail firms obtain from suppliers more favourable terms than those available to other buyers, or to be expected under normal competitive conditions' (Kirsten 2009: 8).

Stephanie Barrientos and Margaret Visser (2012) contend that, with the exception of Woolworths, most of the retailers in South Africa emphasise product quality and have not focused on the social upgrade, with less emphasis on codes of decent labour practice in the packhouses and health and safety regulation. According to Barrientos and Visser (2012: 34), the importance of these standards is that they act as regulatory mechanisms in cases where the state fails to send labour inspectors to monitor health and safety issues. Their findings show that farmers who were sending their produce to Woolworths indicated that the retailer would check the living conditions of workers, whether the houses needed painting or whether workers had toilets. Barrientos and Visser

(2012) go on to show that because of a lack of compliance with social standards there has been an ethical trade initiative, led by Fruit South Africa, that has developed its own industry and ethical trade programme that complies with South African labour laws and International Labour Organization conventions.

How does the relationship between the farmers and the retailers operate? The preferred suppliers (i.e. farmers), who are personally selected by the retailers, send their produce to the retailer's distribution centres; because of its buying power, the retailer sets the price of the produce procured from the farmer (Weatherspoon and Reardon 2003; interviews with farmers, 2012). Therefore, the farmers in this case are 'price takers' – that is, they do not set the price, but take the price set by the retailers (interview, Thandi, 20 November 2012). A buyer-driven chain exists when the retailers make key decisions in the chain, even though they are not directly involved in manufacturing (Barrientos, Dolan and Tallontire 2003).

Johann Kirsten (2009) shows that this system can sometimes be coercive, as retailers search for producers who will sell to them cheaply, threatening to delist the farmers who do not want to give in to their demands. Such tactics give retailers greater selling power, which will ensure that they sell good-quality produce (procured at a price they have set) at a higher price. As Barrientos and Visser (2012: 11) have noted, 'data on supermarket retailing of fresh produce within the country is very difficult to obtain'. Although this chapter aims to show the structure of the domestic value chain in Gauteng, details on the amounts of vegetables that go directly to the distribution centres of different retailers are difficult to obtain, especially for areas such as Gauteng.

Changing working conditions in commercial agriculture in South Africa

When referring to the changing working conditions in the agricultural sector, most scholarly literature in South Africa argues that during segregation and apartheid the state intervened extensively in agriculture and food production (Naidoo 2011; Roberts 2011; Bernstein 2013). The marketing and prices for almost every agricultural product were controlled by marketing boards, and subsidised finance was allocated to farmers through the state-owned Land Bank (Roberts 2011). However, in the late 1960s the state had begun to decrease its support to commercial agriculture and marketing boards. During this period, employment in agriculture was declining (Naidoo 2011). In 1996, the government 'went about removing state regulations and continuing the liberalisation which had been started under the former regime' (Roberts 2011: 1). The marketing boards were relinquished through the passing of the Marketing of Agricultural Products Act, No. 47 of 1996 (Roberts 2011). Studies also indicate that, during the years of state intervention, employers in agriculture relied on permanent workers who lived on the farms. With the move away from state intervention, starting in the late 1960s, employers began relying on seasonal and temporary workers, changing the nature of the employment conditions in the sector (Clarke, Godfrey and Theron 2002: 39; Naidoo 2011). This means that the changes in the working conditions of farm workers were not sudden; they reflect the changes in agriculture from intervention to non-intervention (Pons-Vignon and Anseeuw 2009). But what is missing in this interpretation is an analysis of how workers' agency played a role in their working conditions (see Wilderman, Chapter 4, this volume).

Employment relations in South African commercial agriculture have undergone significant changes under trade liberalisation and with the withdrawal of the subsidies provided by the apartheid government. By 2007, permanent workers employed on a continuous full-time or part-time basis comprised 54.2 per cent of the agricultural workforce, while temporary workers employed for a specific period of time (seasonal workers) and casual workers (intermittent or 'standby' workers) comprised 45.8 per cent (NALEDI 2011). The government has also tried to pass labour laws that would protect farm workers and regulate employer–employee relations in this sector (Du Toit and Ally 2003; Pons-Vignon and Anseeuw 2009; Naidoo 2011).

From this history, the contradictions are clear. First, the government has liberalised; second, the farmers have been hiring casual and seasonal workers as well as mechanising; and third, the post-apartheid government insists on promulgating labour laws that will promote harmonious employer-and-employee-like industrial relations. It can also be argued that because of the aforementioned changes, the farmers have shifted the labour process from a permanent workforce to a seasonal workforce (sometimes living off the farm) and to mechanisation.

The effects of these changes are covered under the different themes of the findings in this chapter. In agriculture, we are not dealing with an industrial worker who is subject both to economic coercion mediated by the labour market and to extra forms of coercion mediated by historical and political factors (in the form of feudal paternalistic relations). There is an implicit assumption that the promotion of labour policies protecting farm workers will be a result of the benevolence of the employer (farmer) or the result of progressive state policy (BFAP 2012; Webster 2012). Yet this assumption does not take into consideration the rise of powerful corporate retailers and their relationship with farmers. The farmers are also expanding their production and investing in other African states (Bernstein 2013), which indicates a need to question what this means for labour and organising strategies.

The government has also promoted freedom of association for farm workers. In spite of an estimated 34 unions organising in an agricultural sector of nearly 800 000 workers nationwide, union density is only 3 per cent (NALEDI 2011). Some attribute this lack of success in organising farm workers to unequal power dynamics, suggesting that the rural farming sector in South Africa is characterised by paternalistic social and economic relations. These relations involve the farmers seeing themselves as the 'fathers' of the farm workers and the farm workers being their 'children' (the words that farmers usually use to describe the farm workers are 'boys' and 'girls'). The farmer, in turn, provides housing for the workers, which further supports the idea that they belong to him (Du Toit 1993).

Findings in Gauteng: A focus on farm workers

Beginning with this section, the chapter builds on an earlier work based on a survey of 600 farm workers in Gauteng (Webster and Nkosi 2013). Nine decent work indicators developed by the International Labour Organization were used to ascertain whether government policy interventions in this sector had been effective. Farm workers were interviewed within an informal environment (while waiting at taxi ranks or grocery shopping). The survey dealt with workers in livestock, field crops, horticulture and mixed farming. Nearly one out of five respondents (19 per cent) worked in the horticultural sector. Survey findings indicated that the agricultural sector in Gauteng had a 'decent work deficit', and that if workers attempted to address their working conditions they were shown the 'gate', a metaphor of the tight boundaries through which employers exercise their power over the entry and exit of employees to and from their private property. The survey was conducted in February 2012, when the minimum monthly wage, as stipulated in the sectoral determination of the Labour Relations Act, was R1 375.94.

This portion of the chapter gives an account of the voices of the workers only; the farmer's views are reported in later sections under various themes. The purpose of this separation of voices is to present a contestation grounded in the labour process, and reflects the assumption that it is workers themselves who can best tell us about their working conditions.

Table 5.1 presents a summary of the survey findings in relation to social upgrading/downgrading on horticultural farms; to avoid information overload, the table includes only the six decent work indicators discussed in this chapter.

Table 5.1 Social upgrading/downgrading: Summary of findings

Decent work indicator	Evidence from workers on horticulture farms
1. Stability and security	• 29% of workers surveyed had a written contract • 44% had no dismissal procedure
2. Earnings	• 50% earned below the minimum wage • Female workers earned 20% less than male workers in all sectors
3. Working hours	• More than 50% worked over 45 hours a week in all sectors
4. Work-family life balance	• 72% of all horticultural workers could not refuse overtime since they were threatened with dismissal if they did so. The long hours impacted negatively on work-family life balance.
5. Social protection	• 16% received paid maternity leave • 1% had medical aid • 11% belonged to a pension or provident fund
6. Social dialogue	• 4% were unionised in horticulture; total unionisation in all sectors was 3%

Source: Webster and Nkosi (2013: 24).

Before presenting the farmers' voices, a subsection is presented to report on selected conversations held with two union organisers from the Food and Allied Workers Union (FAWU), the largest union in the agricultural sector. The purpose of these conversations was to account for the union's limited ability to organise on the farms (only 4 per cent of surveyed horticultural workers were unionised) and to explain the methods used in union organising efforts.

Written working contract: 'No, I was just hired. I do not know my status'

Table 5.1 indicates that only 29 per cent of the surveyed horticultural workers had a written contract. Most workers who were interviewed indicated that they were 'permanent', which they understood to mean that they had a job on a continuous basis for an indefinite period without a written contract. The unclear and precarious nature of their employment status is illustrated in the comment below:

> No, I was just hired. I do not know my status [referring to the verbal contract], but I am full-time . . . because the boss wants to be able to fire any time he feels like it (interview, Nthabiseng, 11 March 2012).

The survey findings go against the argument that as the farmers supply the retailers, they require a permanent, skilled workforce; instead, all of the farms surveyed relied on workers who were not permanently employed and were mostly migrants from neighbouring countries. Table 5.1 presents a clear picture of what is happening in terms of the working conditions in the sector. In terms of the labour process itself, all of the farmers have come to emphasise the idea of discipline, and this means an increase in working hours, with 72 per cent of the workers not being able to refuse overtime.

Enhancing empowerment and workers' perceptions of the union

Table 5.1 indicates that only 4 per cent of horticultural workers who participated in the survey were unionised. The virtual failure of trade unions to organise farm workers stems partly from the fact that farmers refuse union representatives access to the farms, sometimes threatening to shoot them. Farmers oppose organising by unions, arguing that, in light of the rise in farm killings, they fear being killed (NALEDI 2011). As the conversations with the organisers from FAWU indicate, they have relied on 'the kindness and receptiveness [of the farmer] when it comes to organising' (interview, FAWU organiser 2, 8 May 2012) – which the organiser termed the traditional method of organising. What is this method?

> We first start by sending our team on the ground to identify a farm that employs large numbers of workers. We then check if that farm has a trade union by asking the workers. If they indicate that there is no union, then we go speak to the farmer, who would then grant us permission or deny us. Once permission is granted, we then speak to the workers, and tell them about the purpose of the union [to protect their rights] and then ask them if they would be interested in joining the union (interview, FAWU organiser 2, 8 May 2012).

This was highlighted as the main strategy the union had been using. As the organisers admitted, this strategy has its limitations because of its reliance on the farmer, and they needed to employ 'guerrilla' methods of organising (interviews: FAWU organiser 1, 4 May 2012; FAWU organiser 2, 8 May 2012). To get around the farmers, the union would target the workers when they went to buy food outside the farm or as they were going to church or taking a taxi. The method was identified as key since it meant that the union representatives had to start engaging in conversations with the workers, rather than assuming that the union would automatically take charge and that once the workers were unionised 'their problems would be solved' (interview, FAWU organiser 2, 8 May 2012).

Unions would also sometimes rush to the scene of a large strike and try to take over once the workers were outside the confines of the farm. This sort of response has limitations in that it ignores the need for a union to enter into dialogue with the workers to negotiate a role for the union or to try to understand the challenges confronting the workers and how they have dealt with them. Dialogue between unions and workers goes beyond the matter of what the unions can do to help the workers; rather, through such engagement workers can help the unions come up with strategies to deal with the problems the workers face. Thus the workers and the unions will be educating each other through this engagement.

Workers indicated that when unions organised strikes for increases in wages, many of their colleagues would be fired despite being members of the unions. As a result, many workers have decided against joining a union, as they fear losing their jobs. Others do not trust trade unions because they believe unions give workers a false sense of hope. Yet, although workers may lack formal associational power, this is not to say that they do not possess the power to thwart production (Selwyn 2012); indeed, workers in the sector have an understanding of the production calendar and how they can disturb production and distribution. Outside the trade unions, workers would strategically stage independent strikes. In the East Rand, for example, Monday was an important day for workers' action. One horticultural worker in Gauteng explained:

> [We] would protest on Mondays because this day is important to them [the farmers]; it is the day when trucks go to Pick n Pay and the boss does not want anything going wrong this day . . . We chose this day because we know that he will talk to us because he fears that his distribution will be disturbed (interview, Makhwezi, 11 March 2012).

Thus, on this worker's farm Monday was an important day for workers to present their position to the farmer. However, in this case the employer had more power: 'He fired those who were behind organising those protests' (interview, Makhwezi, 11 March 2012). The employer was able to do so because he had created institutional methods that reduce labour's bargaining power, as indicated above. The implication is not as simple as saying associational power should be promoted; even in cases where workers were organised under a trade union, they were still fired. But because of the importance of supplying retailers, any day when the produce is sent to the retailers became an important day for workers to present their grievances. Focusing on that day was how workers mobilised themselves. Because of the fear of being unionised or the inability of unions to operate on farms, workers organised themselves around this strategy. They were empowered by the fact that they understood the production calendar, and threatening to cause havoc was an expression of their agency and power. Such actions indicated to the farmer that the workers were not easily subdued or disposable.

Wilderman (Chapter 4, this volume) argues that another source of power for the farm workers in the Western Cape was that they were no longer living on the farm and were able to speak to each other outside the surveillance of the farmer. Thus, he contends that staying outside the farm gave workers power when it came to mobilising themselves. It can also be argued that staying on the farm could also be a source of power. For example, on the same East Rand farm where workers chose to strike on Mondays, all the workers who took part in the strikes were the ones who lived on the farm. As one worker indicated:

> We who stay on the farms have established bonds since some of us came from the same areas in Lesotho and others from Zimbabwe. We have been able to discuss the issues . . . We asked ourselves on which day we can show to the farmer that we have a problem . . . and Monday was identified (interview, Nthabiseng, 11 March 2012).

Findings in Gauteng: A focus on farmers
Production calendar

Farmers were interviewed to ascertain how production is structured: the farmer's production calendar and the movement of produce from the farmer to the buyers. This methodology was employed by Selwyn (2012), who noted that São Francisco Valley farmers in Brazil organised their production calendar so that they could be year-round producers of higher-quality grapes because they were consistently supplying to retailers in the United Kingdom. His argument is that because of this economic upgrading, there were also changes in the social relations and that these have helped in the development of the region. Because their skills were needed by employers, workers gained structural or marketplace bargaining power, and their diligence in the process gave them workplace bargaining power (Silver 2003; Selywn 2007, 2012). The workers' structural power meant they could disrupt production if they were not satisfied with the working conditions in this sector; employers could not afford to allow this given the strict delivery requirements from the retailers. Selwyn (2007, 2012) goes on to show that the structural power meant nothing if it was not linked with associational power, which is the power to join a union.

Selwyn (2012) focused on global retailers, while the survey discussed in this chapter focused on local retailers. It is also important to point out that, as shown by Dave Weatherspoon and Thomas Reardon (2003) and Barrientos and Visser (2012), the four dominant retailers in South Africa cannot be reduced to only being local, as they have adopted food production standards similar to those of the Northern retailers. They dominate the southern African region and have also invested in India and the Middle East. With the rise of local retailers, 'for the first time . . . producers also have a greater choice in whether they want to upgrade to European standards, or focus on South African or regional markets' (Barrientos and Visser 2012: 37).

An issue discussed with the farmers was the challenges they encountered in ensuring that their production calendar followed the demands of their buyers. Two of the interviewed farmers supplied to the four dominant retailers (Shoprite/Checkers, Pick n Pay, Spar, Woolworths), and it was important to consider the pressures they faced in supplying the retailers and whether they had upgraded their production over the years. The production patterns and pressures of small-scale farmers were also significant issues. Small-scale farmers spoke about the importance of the sizes of the vegetable cuts and the different sizes of the leaves. However, pressures or challenges faced by the farmers differed: those supplying to the NFPMs indicated that getting a good price on the market floor was what mattered, while those supplying the retailers spoke of food quality standards and issues of prices set by the retailers. It was also pointed out that the production calendar of the Gauteng farmers has been disturbed because of climate change, especially by cold weather in winter and hail storms in summer (interview, Johan, 22 November 2012).

One farmer (interview, Pete, 10 October 2012) reported that he supplied Woolworths indirectly, because if Shoprite/Checkers (Freshmark) or Pick n Pay were to learn he was supplying another retailer, he would be delisted. This confirms Kirsten's (2009) argument that as retailers search for competitive prices, they sometimes use coercive measures to procure products. These measures include threatening to delist farmers if they do not take the price set by the retailer or restricting farmers from supplying other retailers.

Discussions with farmers also revealed a key aspect of economic upgrading: the adherence to international food quality standards such as the GlobalGAP, HACCP and EurepGAP in order to meet the requirements of buyers. They were clearly aware that the emphasis was on supplying high-quality produce. This meant that farmers needed reliable workers who 'will always come to work consistently and give me the output that will meet what the retailer wants' (interview, Pete, 10 October 2012). However, in large commercial farming it was evident that most of the workers who were considered 'permanent' – that is, employed for an indefinite period of time – were the foreign migrants, and most of them worked in the packhouses handling repetitive tasks. For example, the tractor driver would collect carrots from the harvester; the carrots were then cleaned and kept fresh through the cold chain; in the packhouse, workers checked the quality and packed the carrots under the watch of a white supervisor or the farmer's son.

These large-scale farmers did not emphasise the importance of skilling the workforce but spoke of disciplining workers to perform their tasks. This points to the issue of whether the economic upgrading that occurred as the farmers shifted to supplying local retailers translated to social upgrading. With small-scale farming, where production is labour-intensive, the farmers spoke of the importance of employing people who knew how to handle vegetables. This suggests that, unlike in the large-scale farms where economic upgrading was accompanied by methods of disciplining labour (with workers indicating that they could be easily dismissed), small farmers emphasised the side of learning, although this may reflect the fact that they were trying to move up in the value chain. Thus, the small-scale farms were still focused on labour-intensive methods with less usage of machines (this could also be a result of a lack of capital).

Fluctuating prices: The retailers and the NFPMs
Some of the farmers had stopped supplying the retailers and had begun sending their produce to the NFPMs. Retailers, on the other hand, had threatened that they would procure produce from the NFPMs if the farmers did not accept the prices they had set. One farmer (interview, Joey, 19 April 2012) stated that because of problems related to the market-floor price system in the NFPMs and supplying the retailers, she

has found a 'niche in the micro greens . . . The only pressure is ensuring that the handpicked leaves are in good standard and supplied on time to the restaurants.'

However, an important incentive for supplying retailers is that once economic upgrading has taken place, the farmers have a guarantee of being preferred suppliers. This means they have to adopt new forms of technology that will increase their output. A deal with a retailer means following global food quality standards, promotion of efficient technology, and knowing that 'you have someone who will guarantee the procurement of your goods unlike the fluctuation in the NFPM' (interview, Pete, 10 October 2012). One farmer (interview, Johan, 22 November 2012) has deliberately opted not to deal with the retailers, because negotiating for the price is difficult. As he indicated, this does not mean he has economically downgraded since supplying to the NFPM; it means that he has to focus on branding and ensuring the fresh produce is delivered on time and is of quality standard.

Employment creation versus better working conditions

In a discussion of who the farmers sell their products to and their relationship with the buyers, the cost of labour came up. This issue may be posed as a question of social upgrading or downgrading (Barrientos and Visser 2012). The quote below sets the context:

> The costs keep escalating because the truck is costing over a million rand now . . . With the carrots you got R15 twenty years ago; today you're still getting R15, and the cabbage and the lettuce as well is killing us . . . Plus the demands of the retailers are killing us. *So it has forced us to bring more production, to have more youth per take, to use more machines and all that stuff to minimise your wages. Where can you cut in the farm? You cannot cut on your fertiliser, your pesticides and your herbicides, that sort of stuff, but you can cut down on your wages by mechanising the system* (interview, Pete, 10 October 2012, emphasis added).

This farmer clearly perceives labour as a cost, spurring on the idea of mechanisation of production. Interestingly, all farmers interviewed stated that they were interested in employment creation and in ensuring they had a skilled workforce, but they openly admitted to considering the mechanised route if the workforce complained about wages and working conditions. This contestation was linked to fears of unrest like that among horticultural workers in the Western Cape. One farmer argued:

> In the horticultural industry we can create work as long as we stay on a sustainable salary because what's going to happen if they push our salaries too high? We go very mechanical . . . The horticulture, agriculture employs a huge percentage of the labour in South Africa . . . But with this unrest we have got at the moment, in the Cape, it is starting to come to us already [in Gauteng], and in the vegetable industry the farmers can go very mechanical and we are going to have unemployment then . . . In my area we prefer employment creation and I also personally believe in this (Johan, interview, 22 November 2012).

There is a contradiction here: the farmers claimed that they were committed to employment creation, but only if it was not costly and did not involve benefits that would interfere with their profits. This contestation indicates the power of the employer in controlling labour and the inability of organised labour to push for concessions.

Unregistered foreign migrants helped farmers reduce their operational costs and maintain a profit. These migrants were also hired because they would not join unions (less associational power); even in cases where farmers were saying that they were interested in employment creation, they made it explicit that unions were a problem (interview, Johan, 22 November 2012).

This stance reflects a clear class tension that interfered with development on the farms. If employers wanted to upgrade their production, they preferred to create employment for the unregistered foreign migrants, who had less bargaining power. To the farmers, labourers were a cost that should always remain low and they must not be unionised. Only if these conditions were met would employers agree to employment creation. If such conditions were not met, then the employers articulated a political position centred on mechanising production and hiring unregistered foreign migrants who are difficult to organise.

Conclusion

Examining the local value chain in Gauteng reveals that the processes of economic and social upgrading are contested. As 'supermarkets negotiate hard on price . . . suppliers face rising costs' (Barrientos and Visser 2012: 18). As a result, the farmers who have entered the process of economic upgrading tend to exploit their workers, as the results of the decent work survey have indicated.

The findings of this chapter show that farm workers lack associational power as a result of the way the labour process is structured. That is, farmers have employed a number of unregistered immigrants who 'do not have rights' and who endure this exploitation, for they are constantly in fear of being deported and not being able to provide for their families back home. In terms of organising vulnerable workers, periods of ethnographic or participatory action research would force those interested in the subject matter to have a conversation with those they study and thus gain an understanding of their world. The purpose of this engagement is to shift to the question of what workers can teach organisers (trade unionists) about their lives. Once the problems facing agricultural workers are elucidated from the workers' point of view to the researcher or even the trade unionist (the goal of ethnographic fieldwork), the challenge will lie in how we respond to the information gained from an insider perspective.

Notes

1. Research by Euromonitor International (2010: 1) shows that 'the [four] main national fresh produce markets [FPMs] in South Africa . . . accounted for about 75% of the total turnover of all 18 national markets in 2006. The Johannesburg FPM was the largest, with a 35% market share in terms of turnover and a 32% market share in terms of volume handled. 6.1% of the market share is made up of eight much smaller national markets with very small contributions to the overall turnover of the fresh produce market.'
2. Pseudonyms have been used for many of the interviewees. See the list of interviews at the end of the chapter for details.
3. EurepGAP is an initiative by retailers belonging to the Euro-Retailer Produce Working Group.

References

Barrientos, S., C. Dolan and A. Tallontire. 2003. 'A Gendered Value Chain Approach to Codes of Conduct in African Horticulture'. *World Development* 31(9): 1511–26.

Barrientos, S., G. Gereffi and A. Rossi. 2011. 'Economic and Social Upgrading in Global Production Networks: A New Paradigm for a Changing World'. *International Labour Review* 150(3–4): 319–40.

Barrientos, S. and M. Visser. 2012. 'South African Horticulture: Opportunities and Challenges for Economic and Social Upgrading in Value Chains'. Capturing the Gains Working Paper 12, Global Summit, 3–5 December, Cape Town. http://www.capturingthegains.org/pdf/ctg-wp-2012-12.pdf (accessed 15 January 2013).

Bernstein, H. 2013. 'Commercial Agriculture in South Africa since 1994: "Natural, Simply Capitalism"'. *Journal of Agrarian Change* 13(1): 23–46.

BFAP (Bureau for Food and Agricultural Policy). 2012. 'Farm Sectoral Determination: An Analysis of Agricultural Wages in South Africa'. BFAP Report, December. http://www.bfap.co.za/documents/research%20reports/BFAP%20farm%20sector%20determination%20report%20draft%2017%20Dec.PDF (accessed 7 January 2013).

Bienabe, E. and H. Vermeulen. 2007. 'New Trends in Supermarket Procurement System in South Africa: The Case of Local Procurement Schemes from Small-Scale Farmers by Rural-Based Retail Chain Stores'. Paper presented to European Association of Agricultural Economists, 103rd Seminar, 23–25 April, Barcelona.

Chikazunga, D., S. Deall, A. Louw and J. van Deventer. 2008. 'The Role of Fresh Produce Markets in South Africa'. Regoverning Markets Policy Brief 4, September. http://www.up.ac.za/media/shared/Legacy/sitefiles/file/48/2052/5_roleoffreshproducemarkets.pdf (accessed 5 December 2012).

Chikazunga, D. and G. Paradza. 2012. 'Can Smallholder Farmers Find a Home in South Africa's Food-System? Lessons from Limpopo Province'. Institute for Poverty, Land and Agrarian Studies (PLASS), 22 June. http://www.plaas.org.za/blog/can-smallholder-farmers-find-home-south-africa%E2%80%99s-food-system-lessons-limpopo-province (accessed 10 November 2012).

Clarke, M., S. Godfrey and J. Theron. 2002. 'Workers' Protection: An Update on the Situation in South Africa'. Study undertaken by the International Labour Organization in preparation for the discussion at the International Labour Conference in 2006. Geneva: ILO.

Du Toit, A. 1993. 'The Micro-politics of Paternalism: The Discourse of Management and Resistance on South African Fruit and Wine Farms'. *Journal of Southern African Studies* 19(2): 314–36.

Du Toit, A. and F. Ally. 2003. 'The Externalisation and Casualization of Farm Labour in Western Cape Horticulture'. Research Report 16, Centre for Rural Legal Studies, Stellenbosch.

Euromonitor International. 2010. 'National Fresh Produce Markets (NFPMs) Important, but Losing Relevance'. Research report for Produce Marketing Association (PMA), September.

Gereffi, G. and M. Korzeniewicz. 1994. *Commodity Chains and Global Capitalism*. Westport, CT: Praeger.

Kirsten, J. 2009. 'The Impact of Market Power and Dominance of Supermarkets on Agricultural Producers in South Africa: A Case Study of the South African Diary Industry'. Report commissioned by the National Agricultural Marketing Council (NAMC), Pretoria.

Naidoo, S. 2011. 'Big Five Fight for Food Market Share'. *Mail & Guardian Online*, 4 November. http://mg.co.za/article/2011-11-04-big-five-fight-for-food-market-share (accessed 15 November 2012).

NALEDI (National Labour and Economic Development Institute). 2011. 'Identifying Obstacles to Union Organizing in Farms: Towards a Decent Work Strategy in the Farming Sector'. Final research report. Johannesburg: NALEDI.

Pons-Vignon, N. and W. Anseeuw. 2009. 'Great Expectations: Working Conditions in South Africa since the End of Apartheid'. *Journal of Southern African Studies* 35(4): 883–99.

Roberts, S. 2011. 'Competition Policy, Food and Agricultural Markets, and the State in South Africa'. Unpublished paper, University of Johannesburg.

Selwyn, B. 2007. 'Labour Process and Workers' Bargaining Power in Export Grape Production, North East Brazil'. *Journal of Agrarian Change* 7(4): 526–53.

———. 2011. 'Beyond Firm-Centrism: Re-integrating Labour and Capitalism into Global Commodity Chain Analysis'. *Journal of Economic Geography* 12(1): 205–26.

———. 2012. *Workers, State and Development in Brazil: Powers of Labour, Chains of Value*. Manchester and New York: Manchester University Press.

Silver, B. 2003. *Forces of Labour: Workers Movements and Globalization since 1870*. Cambridge: Cambridge University Press.

Stroebel, L. 2010. 'Food Retailing and Agricultural Development in South Africa'. In *Unlocking Markets to Smallholders: Lessons from South Africa*, edited by H.D. van Schalkwyk, J.A. Groenewald, G.C.G. Fraser, A. Obi and A. van Tilburg. Wageningen, Netherlands: Wageningen Academic.

Tallontire, A., C. Dolan, S. Smith and S. Barrientos. 2005. 'Reaching the Marginalised? Gender Value Chains and Ethical Trade in African Horticulture'. *Development in Practice* 15(3–4): 559–71.

Weatherspoon, D.D. and T. Reardon. 2003. 'The Rise of Supermarkets in Africa: Implications for Agrifood Systems and the Rural Poor'. *Development Policy Review* 21(3): 333–55.

Webster, E. 2012. 'Decent Work and Development: The South African Challenge'. Unpublished paper, University of the Witwatersrand, Johannesburg.

Webster, E. and M. Nkosi. 2013. '"You Entered through that Gate and You Will Leave through that Gate": The Decent Work Deficit amongst Farm Workers'. In *The Food Crisis and the Labour Movement*, edited by C. Scherrer. Kassel, Germany: Kassel University Press.

Interviews
*pseudonym

Farmers
*Joey, South African (female), Dainfern (Johannesburg), 19 April 2012.
*Johan, South African (male), Germiston (East Rand), 22 November 2012.
*Pete, South African (male), West Rand, 10 October 2012.
*Thandi, South African (female), Sedibeng Region, 20 November 2012.

Farm workers
*Makhwezi, Lesotho (female), Germiston (East Rand), 11 March 2012.
*Nthabiseng, Lesotho (female), Germiston (East Rand), 11 March 2012.

Food and Allied Workers Union (FAWU) organisers
FAWU organiser 1, male, Johannesburg, conversation, 4 May 2012.
FAWU organiser 2, female, Johannesburg, conversation, 8 May 2012.

National Fresh Produce Market (NFPM)
Consignment Control Process (CCP) Manager, Johannesburg, 4 May 2012.

PART II

Urban Considerations

6

Implications of Private Participation in Solid Waste Management for Collective Organisation in Accra, Ghana

Owusu Boampong and Benjamin Y. Tachie

The management of municipal solid waste is complex and includes activities such as source separation, storage, collection, transportation and disposal. In many developing countries, city authorities have traditionally been responsible for managing urban solid waste as part of their public health service provisioning. In Ghana, the local governments tasked to perform this basic function are, like many others in Africa, faced with the challenge of managing tons of waste generated daily, especially in urban centres. The weak institutional capacity on the part of city authorities in sub-Saharan Africa to manage solid waste, coupled with the neoliberal restructuring in the waste management sector, has compelled city authorities to seek new partnerships with private contractors in delivering waste management services (Ahmed and Ali 2003; Boadi et al. 2005; Oteng-Ababio 2010). Clyde Mitchell-Weaver and Brenda Manning (1991) argue that developing countries adopted public-private partnerships (PPPs) in response to pressure from the World Bank, the International Monetary Fund and donors within the context of economic restructuring to allow private businesses to participate in the economic development process. In the waste management sector, private participation takes the form of a PPP arrangement in which the municipal authority contracts out the actual collection, transportation and disposal of solid waste to formal private contractors and concentrates its own efforts on the regulation of solid waste management. The local authority and private waste contractors assume co-responsibility and co-ownership for the delivery of solid waste management services. In effect, the local authority privatises the actual collection, transportation and disposal of solid waste, while regulation remains a public good. However, private participation in city waste management has implications for the livelihoods and working conditions of waste workers who collect and dispose of municipal solid waste (Samson 2009).

Empirical evidence suggests that private contractors participate in the collection, transportation and disposal of municipal solid waste in Accra, Ghana (Oteng-Ababio 2010), Dar es Salaam, Tanzania (Kassim and Ali 2006), and Kampala, Uganda (Katusiimeh, Mol and Burger 2012). Participants in urban solid waste collection, transportation, recovery of recyclables and disposal may include private formal and informal actors. Waste workers are not a uniform group of workers (Wilson, Velis and Cheeseman 2006). The urban informal waste management workers are basically self-employed individuals, including itinerant waste buyers, informal waste pickers and door-to-door waste collectors, who see opportunities in waste collection, disposal and material recovery to make a living (Ahmed and Ali 2003). Waste pickers, who are regarded as being at the bottom of the larger municipal waste management chain, are 'people who reclaim reusable and recyclable materials from waste' and trade them for money (Samson 2009: 2). The informal solid waste workers undertake these activities for survival reasons (Van de Klundert and Lardinois 1995). There are also large-scale private contractors who employ street sweepers and waste pickers. In addition, the contractors employ municipal waste collection crews who collect and dispose of solid waste from households and communal containers (Wilson, Velis and Cheeseman 2006; Gugssa 2012).

The workers who manually collect and dispose of urban solid waste to maintain a healthy urban environment are frequently exposed to risks of diseases and work-related hazards (Abou-ElWafa et al. 2012); these health risks are greater for informal waste workers due to their unprotected exposure to hazardous materials, faecal matter, chemical residues and heavy metals. The exposure of waste workers to toxic fumes predisposes them to respiratory diseases. Waste workers persistently endure musculoskeletal disorders resulting from static posture, repetitive work and moving heavy loads. They may be run over by waste trucks at dump sites and suffer physical injuries. Despite these hazards, the plight of waste workers rarely receives attention in public policy processes in many developing countries (Samson 2009). Moreover, waste workers are disrespected and their work described in derogatory terms by the public, and they usually suffer low self-esteem. They work for long hours and yet their incomes are insecure, especially for female waste workers. Thus there is a need to explore their conditions of work and identify organisational avenues that could be used to empower them to influence their working conditions for the better.

PPPs in municipal solid waste management have received a great deal of treatment in the literature. Authors such as Arnold van de Klundert and Inge Lardinois (1995) and Sandra Cointreau-Levine (1995) have examined the institutional dimension and the economic rationale for the adoption of PPPs in developing countries. Within the context of sub-Saharan Africa, Martin Oteng-Ababio (2010) reviewed the nature of PPPs in solid waste management in Accra. Salha Kassim and Mansoor Ali (2006) and M.W. Katusiimeh, A.P.J. Mol and C.P.J. Burger (2012) carried out studies on households' perceptions of the operations and effectiveness of private sector actors in municipal solid waste management in Dar es Salaam and Kampala respectively. These studies highlight the effectiveness and efficiency of private participation as germane to urban solid waste management, but fail to recognise that effective waste management is also predicated on a healthy and contented workforce. What appears to be missing in research on private participation in municipal solid waste management in sub-Saharan Africa is an examination of the working conditions of solid waste workers and how they collectively organise to promote their common interests.

This chapter explores the working conditions of waste workers in Accra and their organisational efforts at protection as a result of the privatisation of municipal solid waste management. It begins with a brief literature discussion on the politics of informality, emphasising the individual and collective agencies of informal workers in their quest for survival. Also discussed within the literature review section is the design adopted for this study. The policy framework that gives direction to waste management is discussed in the next section, with particular focus on the gradual roll-back of public sources of funding for waste management and the increasing participation of private actors. This is followed by sections describing the categories of waste workers and their working conditions, the tensions and competition between informal waste workers and private contractors, and the organisational forms that are emerging in the sector. The findings presented in the chapter are summarised in the conclusion.

The politics of informality: Individual and collective agency

The study is based on the assumption that waste workers may be vulnerable, yet they can exercise agency to influence their working conditions (Lindell 2010a). The chapter thus draws on recent literature on individual and collective agency of informal workers in the South. Individual agency emphasises quiet forms of resistance among informal workers, which are non-confrontational and characterised by quiet daily struggles taking the form of individual practices and actions (Scott 1985, 1991). Such daily struggles, though deliberate, are covert rather than overt public actions. Similarly, the notion of a 'quiet encroachment of the ordinary' propounded by Asef Bayat (2010) stresses how informal workers, through their daily individual practices, appropriate new space from dominant and powerful actors for survival. He defined this notion as

> silent, protracted, but pervasive advancement of the ordinary people on the propertied, powerful, or the public, in order to survive and improve their lives. They are marked by quiet, largely atomised and prolonged mobilization with episodic collective action – open and fleeting struggles without clear leadership, ideology or structured organisation (Bayat 2010: 56).

Quiet encroachment is about the politics not of open protest but of redress – agency that avoids overt collective demands and large-scale mobilisation (Lindell 2010b). The driving force of this individual agency, according to Bayat, is the necessity to survive. The informal workers may choose individual circumventing practices and silent struggles instead of collective demand or action because they 'lack organizational power of disruption – the possibility of going on strike, for example' (Bayat 2010: 58). This notwithstanding, Bayat adds that informal actors may engage in collective politics to defend their gains when these are threatened by other powerful actors.

Other recent studies on the politics of informality point to the multiplicity of collective organising initiatives emerging among informal workers in the South. These collective initiatives provide a platform for informal workers to voice their grievances and articulate their interests by engaging, negotiating and allying with state agencies. A collection of studies on the emerging politics and agency of informal people in sub-Saharan Africa highlights the growing number of collective interest-seeking groups among informal workers (Lindell 2010a). Some of the informal workers engage in contentious politics and open protests to defend their rights. In Pune, India, waste collectors have organised themselves into unions and worker-based cooperatives to defend and advance their interests (Chikarmane 2012; Gadgil and Samson, Chapter 7, this volume). The Kagad Kach Patra Kashtakari Panchayat (KKPKP) waste workers' union and the Solid Waste Collection and Handling (SWaCH) cooperative associations are examples of informal collective organisations that have supported waste workers to define 'a legitimate workspace for themselves in municipal solid waste management, in ways that improved their working conditions' (Chikarmane 2012: 1). Notably, the KKPKP campaigned for waste workers to be recognised as workers and also protested against abuse and discrimination of waste pickers.

The politics and agency of informal work need not be seen as *either* individual *or* collective forms of agency but should rather be conceived as a continuum: 'at one end, individual circumventing practices dominate; at the other end, one finds collective interest groups with articulate visions; in between, there is a vast field of intermediate forms (diffuse social networks, different forms of collaboration and cooperative work, etc.)' (Lindell 2010b: 7). This chapter reflects the position that the kind of informal politics pertaining to the waste sector in Accra takes the form of subtle manoeuvrings by the informal workers to appropriate waste collection space – akin to Bayat's notion of quiet encroachment – which do bring them into episodic clashes with state agencies and waste contractors. Membership-based associations and cooperatives formed around migrant ethnic groups have also emerged in the sector for the purposes of addressing collective interests and grievances of informal waste workers.

The design of this study was explorative and data was collected using in-depth interviews. Interviewees included:

- the managers of eight licensed private waste contractors operating in the Greater Accra Area;
- two officials of the Environmental Service Providers Association (ESPA), an umbrella organisation of formal and informal waste management service providers;
- the gender desk officer of the Ghana Trades Union Congress (TUC);
- the deputy general secretary of the Local Government Workers Union (LGWU);
- two officials of the Accra Metropolitan Assembly (AMA); and
- the executives of eight informal-based waste worker groups.

In addition to the interviews, two focus group discussions were conducted with the waste workers employed by the AMA.

The data collection focused on work forms, both formal and informal, in the waste management process, general working conditions, occupational health and safety, and situations of collective action among waste workers for interest protection.

Privatisation of solid waste management services in Accra

The Environmental Sanitation Policy of 1999 and the revised version of 2010 provide the policy framework for private sector participation in solid waste collection in Ghana. A greater role is assigned to the private sector in the delivery of environmental sanitation services, while the public sector is consigned to delivering at least 20 per cent of environmental sanitation services. This implies that the private sector providers are in charge of delivering 80 per cent of environmental sanitation services; they are to recover costs by charging user fees set by metropolitan, municipal and district assemblies (MMDAs). Direct cost recovery is considered a major factor in achieving financial sustainability in the delivery of waste management services, and where it is possible service providers are to charge a full commercial price to cover costs. The 1999 and 2010 policy documents have much in common in that both emphasise the major role of private sector providers in waste management and cost recovery to ensure financial sustainability. The two policy statements differ, however, in the area of public sector funding for waste management. The 1999 version explicitly spelled out public sources of funding and the financial obligations of district assemblies and the central government towards waste management:

> District Assemblies shall allocate the additional funds needed for the provision of environmental sanitation programmes and services from their general revenues. They may also decide to fix a proportion of all District Assembly revenues to be reserved for this purpose . . . Central government shall provide funding for environmental sanitation to the Assemblies through a number of channels (including District Assemblies' Common Fund, grants and credits to cover investments in environmental sanitation equipment and infrastructure and revenues from fines for environmental offences and taxes on pollution and polluters).

None of these sources of public funding is mentioned in the 2010 version of the policy, which suggests that these funding sources are no longer available to waste management services. Instead, MMDAs have the responsibility to fix user fees and to provide subsidies where full cost recovery is not possible. This typifies the gradual roll-back of direct government funding and the intensification of cost recovery for waste management services. When an AMA official was asked how he views the future of private participation in solid waste management, he pointed to the financial relief the 2010 policy regime has brought to the assembly:

> Well, it's very . . . good. It has taken a huge burden off our shoulders. Like I said, hitherto we were paying so much, huge sums of money to collect the waste. But with this PPP, from 2010 when we rolled in the policy, we don't pay them [private contractors]. We were able to clear our last arrears, I think about GH₵600 000, last month. Before 2010, we owed the contractors so much. But now, from 2010, we don't owe . . . That financial burden has been lifted off our shoulders. So that is . . . a relief for us. And then you can see that [the] number [of private contractors] has increased and therefore Accra is becoming neater day by day. Hitherto, it was very difficult to do it; but when we brought in the contractors, we are realising that we are performing better than we used to do.

The Greater Accra Metropolitan Area (GAMA), the largest urban agglomeration in Ghana (Oteng-Ababio 2010), has sixteen metropoles, municipalities and districts. Accra Metropolitan and Tema Metropolitan are the two metropoles in the GAMA. There are a number of formal waste companies that have the responsibility of providing solid waste management services in these areas. For instance, nine formal private waste contractors have been registered by the AMA to carry out solid waste management services in eleven sub-metropolitan assemblies under franchise agreement (Gugssa 2012). The private contractors have jurisdiction over the management of solid waste in zones allotted to them and they view these public spaces as their bona fide areas of operation; therefore, other agents found operating in these areas are treated as trespassers. This can be called the privatisation of the municipal waste management space to formal waste contractors. The sole authority given to the private contractors to collect waste in specific zones has become a source of tension between some formal private waste contractors and informal waste workers. The latter, who once could move freely across the municipal space to collect and dispose of waste, are treated as illegal operators if found in the concessions of the private contractors.

Solid waste workers and precariousness of work

The solid waste workers in Greater Accra can be categorised into formal and informal waste workers, although in terms of working conditions the boundary between them is blurred. Both groups face similar precarious working conditions. Formal waste workers include both public and private workers. Relative to public sector waste workers, private formal waste workers appear to be assuming a dominant role in solid waste management following private participation in the sector.

Informal waste workers

The informal waste workers include the *Kaya Bola*,[1] *Taxi Bola*, and plastic and scrap metal dealers. While the *Kaya Bola* and *Taxi Bola* provide direct waste collection services to their clients in low- and middle-income areas for a fee, the plastic and scrap metal dealers buy scrap metals and trade them to middlemen. Some of the *Kaya Bola* and *Taxi Bola* recover valuable plastics and metal from the waste stream and sell them to the plastic and metal dealers. There is a paucity of information on the total number of informal waste workers in the Greater Accra area. According to ESPA records, the total membership of fourteen associations of *Taxi Bola* operators and scrap dealers is 540. This figure obviously excludes those informal workers who are not members of these informal groups.

The *Kaya Bola* use sacks and pushcarts to collect household and commercial waste for disposal (Oteng-Ababio 2010). The *Taxi Bola* appear to be a recent phenomenon and they are more organised than the *Kaya Bola*. The *Taxi Bola* have a driver and one or two janitors who load and offload the vehicle. The 'taxis' are motorised four-wheel or three-wheel vehicles (Motor Kings). The *Bola* and *Taxi* workers could be any of the following:

- Owner drivers of *Taxi Bola*.
- Those operating on a 'work and pay' (a form of hire purchase) arrangement. The vehicle driver pays a certain amount daily, weekly or monthly, depending on the terms of the arrangement, until the total cost of the vehicle is defrayed. The advantage of this arrangement is that the vehicle becomes the driver's personal property once the cost is paid off.
- An individual who rents a vehicle from an owner, with daily fixed rates ranging from GH₵20 to GH₵50. After making allowances for food and payment for the dump site, which ranges from GH₵20 to GH₵25, the excess becomes the income earned. This translates into GH₵480–GH₵600 per 24 working days.
- Janitors treated as apprentices who could be recommended to vehicle owners as drivers. The drivers give them food and a daily income of about GH₵5 for their services.

The informal waste workers do face work-related insecurity. First, they are harassed by waste contractors and state agencies for 'illegally' collecting waste within the concessions of the private contractors. The police very often arrest the scrap dealers for buying stolen property. Their carts may be seized by the city authorities and the police for being used on ceremonial roads. Second, the workers must travel long distances to dump sites to dispose of waste, which increases their operational costs.

Formal waste workers

The municipal authorities employ waste workers, mostly women, to undertake street sweeping and cleaning of public places. For instance, the AMA employs about 1 200 waste workers; the majority of them are females, and there are a few male supervisors. The monthly wage of the public municipal waste workers ranges from GH₵100 to GH₵250, the lowest among the different categories of waste workers identified in the study. The waste work in the formal public sector rarely begets full-time employment. One official of the municipal authority could not contain his frustration with the casualisation of the waste workers:

> ... some of us are always aggrieved but we cannot go beyond a certain point. If you employ a labourer for a certain period, he's no more a casual labourer, you understand. But believe you me, we are treating our labourers as casual labourers. Some of them have these appointment letters – what does that mean? It doesn't mean much, so you understand. So you cannot dwell on that to fight for any increment or anything. I wish I can find you some appointment letters; it's vague (interview with AMA official).

With the exception of a few core staff such as administrators and revenue collectors who are permanent, the majority of the janitors engaged by the private contractors are casual workers. In many cases, the employment contract between waste contractors and waste workers is a verbal agreement, and the process of recruitment is informal and ad hoc. In the words of one contractor, the workers he is working with simply

> walked in and jobs were offered ... everything is oral. Even sometimes, the workers on the truck recruit the people and recommend them to me [saying] that they are hard-working and so I should employ them ... Some can even come to work this morning, go to the field and do not return ... It is very casual (interview with waste contractor).

In terms of wages, all the waste contractors pay the janitors fixed monthly wages ranging from GH₵250 to GH₵450. The lower end of this range is just barely above the national monthly minimum wage. With regard to occupational health and safety, workers complained about using protective gadgets such as a nose guard because they cannot breathe if they wear them, and they say they have to drink alcohol to deal with the stench emanating from the garbage. The use of alcohol has been the cause of work-related accidents among the workers, suggesting weak enforcement of safety standards by the contractors. The disrespect towards waste work by a section of the society also affects workers' self-esteem:

> We feel good about the job except that sometimes the public ridicule us. We want the public to treat us with respect. Residents in the estate areas give us respect, but those in the Zongo areas disrespect us (focus group discussion with Ablekuma North Motor Waste Union members).[2]

Informal waste workers and formal waste contractors: Competition, collision and complementarities

Although municipal waste management in Greater Accra has been legally allocated to private waste contractors, the informal waste workers, especially the *Kaya Bola* and the *Taxi Bola*, have identified a niche in the municipal space where they have competitive strength. They provide a cost-effective mechanism and operational flexibility to fill the gaps resulting from the weaknesses of formal private waste contractors. In her study of the waste recovery system in Accra, Beamlak Gugssa (2012: 25) observed that when the private waste contractors fail to keep to their waste collection schedule for their registered households, informal waste workers step in to provide the service; and 'households whether registered or not prefer informal waste collectors as they pay less for the service compared with [the services of private contractors]'. The private contractors with their heavy vehicles are unable to access the unplanned and underprivileged areas within their contracted zones. The informal waste workers, with light feet, sacks, pushcarts and motorised three-wheel vehicles, are able to access households in underprivileged areas to collect waste:

> . . . there are certain places that they [contractors] cannot reach because of the way we have planned our city, certain parts of the city, you know, like Chorkor, Sukura [low-income areas]. So it's very difficult for the contractors to get to the households . . . this

gives way for these informal people to come in because somebody will store the waste and is willing to dispose of it. Now this accredited contractor cannot get access to these places . . . so these informal people are even ready to carry waste from these premises so that they can get something (interview, AMA official).

The competitiveness of the informal waste workers has set them on a collision course with the formal waste contractors. Informal workers found operating within the jurisdiction of waste contractors are treated as illegal operators, and the contractors can take action against them, including arrest and seizure of carts. 'The companies consider the waste within their contracted areas as their own property even if they do not manage to provide adequate service to their clients' (Gugssa 2012: 55). One informal worker reported on the comments made by a waste contractor:

Bola is gold, and if the *Taxi Bola* operators try to tamper with [the contractor's] work he will not spare them; you know, a hungry man is an angry man. The big companies like Zoomlion and Rural Waste do not worry us much, but the small private companies do harass us (interview, *Taxi Bola* operator).

It is not surprising that some of the private contractors fiercely guard their allocated zones against interference by the informal waste workers. The *Taxi Bola* operators interviewed complained about harassment from the contractors, sometimes merely for transporting waste through their jurisdictions. They are often accused of dumping waste indiscriminately, leaving it for the contractors to clear. It also appears that the large waste contractors are accommodative of the *Taxi Bola* operators, unlike the relatively small formal contractors, who view the informal waste workers as competitors and therefore feel threatened by their activities.

There is a degree of willingness by some formal contractors to integrate the informal waste workers, particularly the *Taxi Bola* operators, into their operations. Zoomlion Ghana Ltd, the leading private waste company in Ghana, is reported to have begun an initiative to organise and integrate the activities of the informal waste workers in the low-income areas where the company has access problems. In an interview, the director of research at Zoomlion alluded to the complementary role of the informal waste workers and the effort his company and the ESPA is making to organise these workers in order to regulate their activities. He indicated that in Ghana anything to do with waste is often associated with the name Zoomlion. For example, when informal waste workers dump waste in unauthorised places, the action is often associated with Zoomlion – thus the company's reputation suffers. The attempt to organise and regulate the activities of the informal waste workers is thus in the interest of the company. The two quotations below, by contractors, exemplify how formal waste contractors are already reaching out to informal waste workers:

> They do not have dump sites and so they just dump anywhere and they bring the problem back to us [contractors in general]. But now, we are picking them and adding them as agents to our company, except the stubborn ones.

> We have not had a clash with the informal waste workers. It does happen. When we see them on our site, we warn them and they get scared. If they claim to go to areas where our trucks cannot go, then they should register with my company so that they work as our agents.

Another contractor, Asadu Royal Waste, once organised the informal workers into an association in the district of Ablekuma North and entered into an arrangement with them to collect waste from inaccessible areas within its concession. The arrangement was later stopped because the waste workers operated beyond their assigned areas. This was confirmed by an official of the ESPA in an interview:

> These *Bola Taxi* guys are very aggressive, they want to make money . . . Currently we have serious issues to settle. For instance, the Kaneshi Association [of informal waste workers] had an arrangement with the contractor, Asadu, to work within certain areas, but according to Asadu the *Taxi Bolas* went beyond their allocated areas. Asadu claim they are picking waste from his commercial customers at a lower fee. Asadu is now arresting them for such behaviour.

The operational flexibility, the tensions and the nuisance activities of the informal waste workers have brought them into the limelight and forced other industry players to initiate a process to organise and regulate their activities:

> [In terms of our engagement with the informal waste workers] we have thought of it because if you can't beat them you have to join them, and these people, the service that they are providing is quite important. So we are arranging, we are thinking of bringing them together so that we can license all of them. You see, the whole thing is that these accredited contractors always complain that these guys are taking their jobs and we have realised that we have to bring them together; all of us should be on board so that they are recognised. They are also part of us and they do what we are doing, and therefore we want them to do it in a proper manner. So very soon, we will bring them under our umbrella (interview, AMA official).

The discourse about organising and integrating informal waste workers into the formal waste management system is significant in that it marks a shift from seeing informal waste workers as a nuisance to recognising them as important players who must be accommodated in municipal waste management. Just like the waste pickers in Pune, India, the informal waste workers in Accra have carved a niche in the solid waste management process, which provides the basis for their recognition and relevance. The attempt by the private contractors, the ESPA and the municipality to organise and integrate the informal waste workers raises the curious question of motive. It could be inferred that the players in the industry who are dominant actors relative to the workers seek to mobilise these workers so as to 'discipline' them. The ESPA officials and the waste contractors regard the informal waste workers as stubborn and aggressive, and accuse them of indiscriminately dumping waste in unauthorised places; organising them may give these dominant actors the opportunity to tame the workers. Again, integrating the informal workers as agents of the formal contractors would enable the contractors to deal with the 'unhealthy competition' of the informal waste workers. In Addis Ababa, Axel Baudouin et al. (2010) observed that a partnership strategy by the municipality to formalise and integrate informal waste workers with the stated objective of improving the efficiency of waste collection tended to facilitate the 'political dominance and local surveillance' of once independent informal waste collectors. The unstated objective was to 'marginalise the pre-existing solid waste collecting enterprises and to disrupt the existing system' (37).

Organisational forms among the waste workers

Public municipal waste workers have a relationship with two rival national trade unions: the LGWU and the Civil and Local Government Staff Association (CLOGSA). Despite the rivalry between LGWU and CLOGSA for control over municipal waste workers, the usefulness of these unions, particularly of the LGWU, is rarely felt by the waste workers. Evidence of unionisation of formal private waste workers is non-existent, while informal waste workers characteristically self-organise into associations, sometimes along ethnic lines, to address their common challenges with virtually no interaction with traditional trade unions.

The public municipal waste workers of the AMA are segmented into those who belong to the LGWU and those who belong to CLOGSA. CLOGSA workers enjoy relatively better working conditions from the central government, while LGWU workers are directly employed and paid by the AMA. Even though the LGWU has traditionally been organising the municipal workers, there appears to be a general preference for CLOGSA, which raises questions about the relevance of the LGWU to the waste workers:

> CLOGSA used to be the Civil Servants Association but now it is the Civil and Local Government Staff Association . . . they [CLOGSA and the TUC] are now trying together, but before then the TUC had the bargaining power . . . But now we are all trying to come together to use the CLOGSA. You know, the TUC has been of old so it is now a bit difficult trying to merge the two. But we are trying to do that so that we get the CLOGSA and then [get] the TUC away (interview, AMA official).

There is a yawning gap between the waste workers and the LGWU, which lacks structures to receive and address the concerns of the waste workers.

The LGWU has local representatives who should be working to protect the interests of the waste workers, but there is a lack of awareness among LGWU leadership about how the workers are being served by the union officers:

> We belong to the Local Government Workers Union but we only know [that] as a result of the deductions made on our salaries; apart from that we have not seen any activity by the union. In fact, we were not consulted before they started the deductions from our salary. We do not have membership cards or any means of identification as members. We also do not know any union representative at the local level. Therefore we do not know how to channel our grievances through the union (focus group discussion, AMA waste workers).

Like the union, the welfare association of which the public municipal waste workers are members is also unresponsive to their needs. One of the focus group discussants said that she contributes monthly to the welfare fund, but when she underwent medical surgery she did not receive any financial assistance from the fund. Strike actions to press for improvements in their working conditions are not something the workers are prepared to undertake, because of threats of dismissal. One of the sweepers narrated a scenario where sweepers at Korle-Gonno and Mamprobi, suburbs in Accra, decided to team up with sweepers at Kaneshi to address issues concerning their personal protective equipment; those at Kaneshi pulled out at the last minute because they feared being fired if they had gone ahead to meet the officials. The sweeper said that 'people are afraid to openly address their concerns for fear of being sacked'.

Organising among the formal private waste crews is a tall order. The very characteristics of the workers and resistance from the management of the private contractors account for this situation. One private waste contractor indicated that he does not discourage union formation, but that the short-term and casual nature of the workforce makes union formation a difficult exercise. For this particular contractor, the janitors he engages in his waste business are mostly migrant workers from Northern Ghana; they travel to Accra to sell yams, take up janitorial work for additional income, and return to their hometowns after their yam sales:

These workers work for shorter periods and so are not keen in organising themselves. The turnover rate is high among the janitors, who mostly come from the north to sell yams in Accra and while selling they take up the job. These janitors hardly stay beyond one year. They see the job as a transitional one.

Another private waste contractor corroborated this:

The labour turnover is quite high, especially for the janitors. This is because most of the workers come from the rural areas, so they work for about two, three or six months and leave for home. Those especially from Kpandai [a town in northern Ghana] come to sell yams and get in involved in the janitorial roles for some few months and leave for home when done with the yam business.

LGWU officials attempted to organise the 65 000 Zoomlion workers but had difficulties because of the resistance of the company's management to unionisation; the officials were refused an audience by the company's management. The union officials were reported to have met with about 25 workers who expressed interest in joining the union, but these workers were later sacked for approaching the union. The organisation of Zoomlion workers is also stifled by leadership inertia, which is holding back the LGWU from organising this category of workers.

The informal waste workers have organised themselves into informal groups to help address their common concerns, and where necessary they align with state and non-state actors other than the traditional unions. The associations are named based either on their geographical area of operations or on the ethnic origins of their members. Some of these associations include Kaneshi Amaalataba Association, Ablekuma North Motor Waste Union, Mamprobi Scrap and Plastic Waste Association, Asongtaba Waste Collectors Association, and Agbogbloshie Scrap Dealers Association, which has subgroups such as Alfa Alhussain/Korean Boys and Nyankpala Best. Members of some of these informal associations – such as Mamprobi Plastic, Agbogbloshie Scrap Dealers, Asongtaba Waste Collectors and Nyankpala Best – come from ethnic groups in Northern Ghana and are largely Muslims. Table 6.1 gives some basic facts about some associations of informal waste workers.

Table 6.1 Some associations of informal waste workers

Association	Year established	Geographical area of operation	Ethnic origin of members	Size of membership
La Nkwantanan Waste Management Association	2013	Madina, Adenta and Abokobi	?	20 *Kaya Bola* 10 *Taxi Bola*
Okai-Koi North Tricycle Association	2013	–	?	35 *Taxi Bola*
Ayawaso Central Association	2014	–	?	25 *Taxi Bola*
Kaneshi Amaalataba Association	2010	Kaneshi	?	35 *Taxi Bola*
Ablekuma North Motor Waste Union	2013	Ablekuma North sub-metro	?	150 *Taxi Bola*
Asongtaba Waste Collectors Association	2006	Ablekuma Central and Ablekuma South sub-metros	Grunusi	3 *Taxi Bola* 17 *Kaya Bola*
Agbogbloshie Scrap Dealers	1997	Agbogbloshie Yard		3 000 'boys' and 'masters'
a) Alfa Alhussain	2004		a) Dagoma (Yendi, Tamale and Zabzungu)	
b) Nyankpala Best	2004		b) Nyankpala district	
Mamprobi Scrap and Plastic Waste Association	1990	Mamprobi	Bolgatanga	30

Source: Gugssa (2012) and field data, 2014.

Motor-based waste workers' associations are recent formations and either emerged from the initiatives of the waste workers or were encouraged by some of the private contractors. The ESPA, which is the umbrella association of both formal waste contractors and informal waste workers, seeks to provide a common platform to regulate the activities of members, and in particular to resolve conflicts between private waste contractors and *Taxi Bola* operators. About 325 *Taxi Bola* and scrap dealers have been registered by the ESPA. Membership of the ESPA gives the informal waste workers recognition.

According to the informal waste workers, they have organised themselves into associations in order to present a common front to the municipal authorities in their demand to be allocated areas where they can operate. The Kaneshi Amaalataba Association, according to its president, approached AMA officials to regularise the areas in which they are operating, but this was not successful because the waste workers were unwilling to pay the fees the city officials proposed to charge them. Another reason adduced for organising was to help members who rent motor vehicles to acquire their own motor vehicles. Some of the associations have given registration numbers to their members; these numbers are boldly written on their vehicles for easy identification to reduce indiscriminate dumping and pilferage.

The land on which the members of Agbogbloshie Scrap Dealers are operating belongs to the National Youth Authority. In the earlier years of their operations, the dealers had problems with the authority, which persistently harassed them with ejections. Later the authority changed its stand. Recognising that the scrap business was providing employment to the youth, the authority asked the dealers to form an association if they wished to work on the land. So the dealers hired a lawyer to help them draft a constitution, which was sent to the registrar general's office for registration. The Youth Authority remains the landlord of the yard to which the association pays royalties. The non-governmental organisation (NGO) Green Advocacy has been educating the dealers on the harmful effects of burning e-waste and occasionally advises them to wear protective gear. The NGO is also in the process of providing the dealers with an environmentally friendly plant for extracting copper and other metals. If members are arrested and their carts seized, the NGO executives, who have strong political connections with the major political parties, use their influence to get the members and their carts released.

Conclusion

Formal private participation has not necessarily formalised the conditions of work of waste workers in Accra. Similarly, the working conditions of the waste workers employed by the municipal authorities have all the signs of risks associated with informality and precarity. The waste workers, whether formal or informal, face similar employment vulnerabilities. On the other hand, informal groups of waste workers are forming alliances with state and non-state actors to gain recognition in order to protect their interests. Within the same sector, there are multiple waste workers and different organisational forms. Many of the motor waste workers have organised themselves with the intent of negotiating with municipal authorities and private companies for a concession to operate within the municipal space. Despite this, informal waste workers have carved a niche in low-income areas, where they operate efficiently and effectively, and appear more competitive than the formal waste contractors in these areas. It behoves the private contractors and municipal authorities to enter into some licensing agreement with the informal waste workers to legitimise and regularise their activities. However, any strategy for integrating the informal waste workers should be developed with caution as these workers may be locked into exploitative relationships that could worsen their plight.

The presence of trade unions in the waste management sector is generally weak, and union leaders have been taken completely unaware by the intensified privatisation of municipal waste management under the cloak of public-private partnership and the attendant informalisation of municipal waste management work. The workers, particularly those who are members of the LGWU, demand value for their dues. The unions should therefore reactivate their structures and become more responsive to the concerns of the waste workers.

Notes

1. *Bola* means 'waste'; *Kaya* means 'head porter'.
2. 'Zongo' refers to a multi-ethnic enclave common in many Ghanaian towns and cities. A Zongo is usually a low-income area.

References

Abou-ElWafa, H.S., S.F. El-Besta, A.H. El-Gilany and E.E. Awad. 2012. 'Musculoskeletal Disorders among Municipal Solid Waste Collectors in Mansoura, Egypt: A Cross-sectional Study'. *BMJ Open*. https://dx.doi.org/10.1136%2Fbmjopen-2012-001338 (accessed 15 January 2014).

Ahmed, A.S. and M. Ali. 2003. 'Partnership for Solid Waste Management in Developing Countries: Linking Theories to Realities'. *Habitat International* 28: 467-79.

Baudouin, A., C. Bjerkli, Y. Habtemariam and Z.F. Chekole. 2010. 'Between Neglect and Control: Questioning Partnerships and the Integration of Informal Actors in Public Solid Waste Management in Addis Ababa, Ethiopia'. *African Studies Quarterly* 11(2-3): 29-42.

Bayat, A. 2010. *Life as Politics: How Ordinary People Change the Middle East.* Amsterdam: Amsterdam University Press.

Boadi, K., M. Kuitunen, K. Raheem and K. Hanninen. 2005. 'Urbanization without Development: Environmental and Health Implications in African Cities'. *Environment, Development and Sustainability* 7: 465-500.

Chikarmane, P. 2012. 'Integrating Waste Pickers into Municipal Solid Waste Management in Pune, India'. WIEGO Policy Brief 8 (Urban Policies). Cambridge, MA: WIEGO.

Cointreau-Levine, S. 1995. *Private Sector Participation in Municipal Solid Waste Services in Developing Countries, Volume 1.* Washington, D.C.: World Bank.

Gugssa, B.T. 2012. 'The Cycle of Solid Waste: A Case Study on the Informal Plastic and Metal Recovery System in Accra'. Master's dissertation, Department of Earth Sciences, Uppsala University, Sweden.

Kassim, S.M. and M. Ali. 2006. 'Solid Waste Collection by the Private Sector: Households' Perspective – Findings from a Study in Dar es Salam City, Tanzania'. *Habitat International* 30: 769-80.

Katusiimeh, M.W., A.P.J. Mol and C.P.J. Burger. 2012. 'The Operations and Effectiveness of Public and Private Provision of Solid Waste Collection Services in Kampala'. *Habitat International* 36: 247-52.

Lindell, I. (ed.). 2010a. *Africa's Informal Workers: Collective Agency, Alliances and Transnational Organizing in Urban Africa.* London: Zed.

Lindell, I. 2010b. 'Between Exit and Voice: Informality and the Spaces of Popular Agency'. *African Studies Quarterly* 11(2-3): 1-11.

Mitchell-Weaver, C. and B. Manning. 1991. *Public-Private Partnership in Third World Development. A Conceptual Overview.* Reading, UK: University of Reading.

Oteng-Abibio, M. 2010. 'Private Sector Participation in Solid Waste Management in the Greater Accra Metropolitan Area in Ghana'. *Waste Management and Research* 28: 322-9.

Samson, M. 2009. 'Confronting and Engaging Privatization'. In *Refusing to Be Cast Aside: Waste Pickers Organising around the World*, edited by M. Samson. Cambridge, MA: WIEGO.

Scott, J. 1985. *Weapons of the Weak: Everyday Forms of Peasant Resistance*. New Haven, CT: Yale University Press.

———. 1991. *Domination and the Arts of Resistance: Hidden Transcripts*. London: Yale University Press.

Van de Klundert, A. and I. Lardinois. 1995. 'Community and Private (Formal and Informal) Sector Involvement in Municipal Solid Waste Management in Developing Countries'. Background paper for the Urban Management Programme Workshop in Ittingen, Switzerland, 10-12 April.

Wilson, D.C., C. Velis and C. Cheeseman. 2006. 'Role of Informal Sector Recycling in Waste Management in Developing Countries'. *Habitat International* 30: 797-808.

7

Hybrid Organisations, Complex Politics
When Unions Form Cooperatives

Malati Gadgil and Melanie Samson

In recent years a growing body of literature has emerged exploring organising by informal workers. Long dismissed as 'unorganisable' by academics and traditional trade unionists alike (as many of the chapters in this book attest), informal workers are now upheld as innovators of new forms of organising and as a source of hope for labour movements struggling to sustain themselves in the face of neoliberalisation and globalisation. Perhaps because academics have only recently 'discovered' organising by informal workers, research to date has focused primarily on how they recruit members, as well as on specific mobilisations and campaigns. Scant attention has been paid to the challenges informal worker organisations face in sustaining themselves, as well as in maintaining their relationships with and democratic accountability to members. Yet, although academic interest in informal worker organising is relatively new, the organisations themselves are not. It is therefore important to analyse how informal worker unions transform over time as they expand and develop more complex organisational forms, as well as how this affects their internal politics, their relationships with members and the very nature of the unions themselves.

This chapter opens up this discussion through a case study of the Kagad Kach Patra Kashtakari Panchayat (KKPKP) trade union of waste pickers in Pune, India. Formed in 1993, KKPKP has 10 000 members, 90 per cent of whom are women. As it has developed, the union has combined mass struggle with the formation of cooperatives to meet a variety of membership needs, including the Solid Waste

Collection and Handling (SWaCH) cooperative contracted by the municipality to collect waste from residents, a savings cooperative, and a cooperative scrap shop that purchases recyclables from waste pickers. Other studies note that some informal economy unions are developing hybrid organisational forms that include cooperatives (Samson 2009a; Webster 2011; Chikarmane 2012). This chapter advances discussion on hybrid organisational forms by arguing that it is crucially important to interrogate the political implications of such organisational innovations. It therefore explores the dynamic interplay between the cooperatives and the union; the extent to which the cooperatives deepened, extended and/or undermined the union's political practice; and how the union has addressed these challenges. The contention is that in addition to addressing specific economic or work-related needs, forming cooperatives can engender new forms of organising and strengthen broader political campaigns within the founding union. These gains are easier to obtain when the structures, principles and processes of the union and the cooperative are closely aligned; when membership overlaps; and when the cooperative is accountable only to its members. Cooperatives can, however, also generate internal cultures at odds with those of their founding unions – cultures that can have ripple effects within the unions themselves. These challenges appear more prone to arise in situations where the membership base of the cooperative and the union diverges, and where the cooperative provides a service and is in some way accountable to an external party that introduces its own pressures and political dynamics. Within such contexts it is crucial for the union to carefully strategise how to ensure that the cooperative remains consistent with and enhances the political orientation and struggles of the union. KKPKP's experience provides important insights into how this can be done.

The chapter draws on four main sources of information. First, it is grounded in the personal experience of co-author Malati Gadgil. Malati was the chief executive officer of the SWaCH cooperative from 2010 to 2013 and was actively involved in many of the processes discussed here. She maintains a strong link to SWaCH and KKPKP through her role as coordinator of the Asia waste picker networking process, housed within KKPKP. Second, the chapter draws on articles written by two founders of KKPKP, Lakshmi Narayan (KKPKP's founding general secretary) and

Poornima Chikarmane (a lecturer at SNDT Women's University who provides ongoing support to KKPKP). Somewhat unusually, throughout the history of the union these two active participants in the organisation have written a number of articles in which they critically reflect on the union's strategies and experiences, providing crucial insight into the organisational life of KKPKP. Third, the chapter incorporates responses to a set of questions discussed with members as well as non-waste-picker activists in the union and the cooperatives. Malati facilitated a two-hour focus group of 43 union members (38 women and 5 men) after a meeting of the credit cooperative on 16 December 2014, and interviews were conducted with key leaders in the cooperatives and the union to gain additional insights and obtain feedback on a draft of the chapter. Lastly, the findings presented here are informed by a number of popular and academic articles on KKPKP and SWaCH written by chapter co-author Melanie Samson, who has worked with KKPKP since 2008 in her role as the Africa waste sector specialist for Women in Informal Employment: Globalizing and Organizing (WIEGO).

The remainder of this chapter is organised in three sections. The first section presents a brief history of how and why KKPKP was formed and describes its approach to organising waste pickers and running the union. The second section explores why KKPKP created aligned cooperatives, interrogating the political culture and practice of each cooperative and the implications for the union. The concluding section highlights key ways the cooperatives affected the union's approach to membership and organising, and draws out broader implications for other informal worker organisations and for how these organisations are theorised.

Building a democratic membership-based union
Origins of the KKPKP

Unlike explicit attempts to 'organise informal workers' discussed in other chapters in this book, KKPKP arose organically out of a Freirian educational initiative (Freire 2000) of feminists at the SNDT University in Pune, including Poornima Chikarmane and Lakshmi Narayan. While conducting the National Adult Education Programme, these activist academics met girls working as waste pickers. They realised that if they could assist the girls to access segregated waste, then they would be able to work more efficiently and have time to attend school. The girls' mothers, who also worked as waste pickers, argued that if they could access segregated waste, then the girls could stop working completely and focus on their education (Chikarmane and Narayan 2005: 1). Mobilising together, the activist academics and waste pickers achieved this goal in one neighbourhood, dramatically increasing the women's incomes, decreasing their working time and allowing the girls to go to school. However, as is often the case internationally, formal business tried to capture this sphere of accumulation once it had been created informally by waste pickers (Samson 2009b). In this instance, an entrepreneur began offering door-to-door collection with a motorised vehicle. The waste pickers challenged both the entrepreneur and the residents, arguing that the entrepreneur had many other business opportunities but their own options were extremely limited beause of their caste, class and gender, and they had conducted this work for generations. Drawing inspiration from the Chipko movement (in which women chained themselves to trees to prevent them from being cut down), the waste pickers launched a *bin chipko andolan*, holding onto the waste bins to prevent the entrepreneur from removing them (Chikarmane and Narayan 2005: 1; Narayan and Chikarmane 2013: 221).

Although successful in getting rid of that particular entrepreneur, the waste pickers and activists realised they would continue to face this type of threat and that the only way to counter it would be to organise collectively. In doing so they received crucial inspiration and support from Dr Baba Adhav, the president of the Hamal Panchayat, the trade union of headloaders. While organising of informal workers is often framed as a new phenomenon, the Hamal Panchayat was already 50 years old, and Dr Adhav drew on a wealth of experience in guiding the waste pickers. Of key importance was his emphasis on having a 'critical mass', as numerical strength would be essential to transforming power relations in the sector (Chikarmane and Narayan 2005: 2; Narayan and Chikarmane 2013: 213–14).

The activists began to organise waste pickers in a manner that emphasised empowering processes and methodologies. As Chikarmane and Narayan elaborate:

> The process of organising waste-pickers pre-dated the actual formation of the Union. Waste-pickers and *their perceptions of*

issues were central in the organising process. Since the activists accompanied the waste-pickers on their beats the *reality of the present*, and the ongoing process of *reflection and analysis* enabled them to crystallise the *critical issues* that are so important in process of organising. This also offered the opportunity of establishing *close and enduring reciprocal relationships* with waste-pickers (Chikarmane and Narayan 2005: 2; emphasis in original).

Through the process of holding meetings in their own homes and the places where they lived, the waste pickers for the first time began to see themselves as 'workers' who made important contributions to the city and the environment. They also acknowledged that waste picking was preferable to other jobs available to them, and decided to unite to struggle to improve their terms and conditions of employment instead of trying to leave the sector. This conscientisation and development of a new identity as workers became central to both the organising process and the decision to form a union (Chikarmane and Narayan 2005: 2-3, 5).

In May 1993 the SNDT activists joined with Dr Adhav from the headloaders' union and Mohan Nanavre (a leader in the Dalit movement who is the son of a waste picker) to call the first convention of waste pickers, where KKPKP was founded.[1] Chikarmane and Narayan highlight the importance of the fact that these links were present from the beginning: due to his extensive and respected experience organising headloaders, Dr Adhav commanded great respect from the urban poor and lent the convention credibility, and the involvement of both he and Mr Nanavre ensured that the new union was forged in relation to, and in solidarity with, other movements struggling to transform society. At the founding convention, KKPKP committed itself to being part of these larger struggles; accepting all members regardless of gender, caste, region or religion; being a membership-based union of scrap collectors; collecting annual membership fees to support the union; and adopting non-violent methods of resistance and satyagraha (Chikarmane and Narayan 2005: 3-4).

Rather than assuming unity, KKPKP acknowledges that deep power relations exist between waste pickers, rooted in gender, caste, religion and nationality; the organisation adopts a range of innovative methods (such as collective cross-caste weddings) to help waste pickers to understand and accept each other and proactively forge a common identity (Narayan and Chikarmane 2013). Given that the overwhelming majority of KKPKP members are women, the union prioritises addressing gender inequality. For example, in recognition of the centrality of women in the union and of their poor conditions in the sector, the KKPKP logo depicts a woman waste picker. Some men initially opposed this as they felt it compromised their dignity to have a woman on their identification cards. But the women held firm in debate and discussion and the logo was adopted. Although some men initially refused to take the cards, most eventually saw the benefits of belonging to the union and possessing an identity card (Chikarmane and Narayan 2005: 24; Narayan and Chikarmane 2013: 225).

Approaches to organising and internal functioning

In keeping with Freirian concepts and methods (Freire 2000), a commitment to empowerment underpins KKPKP's approaches to organising as well as the internal functioning of the union. Within KKPKP, 'empowerment is understood to be a process in which the poor critically reflect upon their life situation, analyse it and experience a sense of confidence and self-worth through the building of a collective identity, and then exercise the power to make, influence or control decisions that affect their lives' (Chikarmane and Narayan 2005: 10). Chikarmane and Narayan (41) further note that empowerment 'is an ongoing process of *"becoming"* increasingly empowered from a beginning state of powerlessness. It is therefore not an end state but an enabling process' (emphasis in original).

KKPKP campaigns and demands are developed through a 'process-oriented, organic approach prioritizing participation of waste pickers who constitute the organisation' (Narayan and Chikarmane 2013: 216). For example, targeting police harassment emerged organically as the obvious issue around which to launch the first campaign because it was a hardship confronted by all waste pickers on a daily basis as they worked in the city's streets. Successfully uniting to take on the police increased the waste pickers' security and emboldened them to take up other struggles (Chikarmane and Narayan 2005: 27).

The early campaigns that were born through this process related to securing recognition of waste pickers as workers who contribute to the city and the environment and then using this recognition to obtain social benefits for waste pickers. In these struggles the union combined conventional trade union strategies such as 'rallies, struggle, mobilization and widespread profile' with strategies that had mass appeal such as street theatre, song and oral traditions (Narayan and Chikarmane 2013: 214-15). KKPKP also adapted traditional rituals and practices to conscientise members and make claims on other parties. Finally, in 2000 KKPKP drew on its relationship with academics to produce research that determined that at the time waste pickers were saving the municipality US$330 000 a year in transportation costs, and that each individual waste picker provided US$5 worth of free labour to the municipality each month (Chikarmane and Narayan 2005: 23-6; Narayan and Chikarmane 2013: 221-2). Throughout its history KKPKP has continued to innovate on the union form, eclectically and strategically drawing on and developing a range of methods of mobilisation that include but move beyond standard union approaches.

Through this mix of strategies KKPKP sustained member commitment to the campaigns and achieved a number of groundbreaking victories that significantly transformed the status, conditions and incomes of members, including gaining municipal endorsement of members' identity cards, securing access to a state scholarship programme for children of waste pickers, obtaining a medical insurance scheme for registered waste pickers, and securing social security for KKPKP members (Chikarmane and Narayan 2005: 14-16; Chikarmane 2012: 8). KKPKP continues to struggle for social rights and protections, with members prioritising active participation in the state-wide struggle for pensions for informal workers.

Governance of a democratic union: Building leadership vs building leaders

The governance structure, decision-making processes and approach to building leadership within KKPKP focus on building mass participation and democratic practice. Unlike many non-governmental organisations (NGOs) that work with waste pickers, the union does not provide services or soft loans for members, making clear that it is not a welfare organisation. The principles that members must pay membership fees, that these fees must fund the core union activities, and that waste pickers cannot receive the benefits and protection of membership unless they have paid their dues are firmly engrained within the union (Chikarmane and Narayan 2005: 28–9).

There are thirteen members of the statutory governing body, including five office bearers who are non-waste-picker activists. However, the main decision-making body is the representative council, made up of 80 waste picker representatives elected by geographical area (five of whom were men in 2013). Like all decision-making processes in the union, the representative council works by consensus (Narayan and Chikarmane 2013: 228). The representatives are responsible for communicating with members in their communities and addressing their issues. When the union was first formed, these tasks were performed by paid fieldworkers. However, from 1996 there was a focus on building the capacity of representatives to act as organisers, and by 2003 this shift had taken place (Chikarmane and Narayan 2005: 22).

In addition to shifting power and responsibility between staff and members, KKPKP has consciously worked to ensure that divisions are not created between 'leaders' and 'members'. It has focused on 'building leadership as opposed to leaders' (Samson 2014) by involving a wide range of members in leadership activities in order to avoid concentrations of power (Chikarmane and Narayan 2005: 22; Narayan and Chikarmane 2013: 229). In the focus group one member declared, 'We are all leaders as we all know what is going on, so taking over from someone is not hard. Also, if someone doesn't show up we can still have a meeting.' Others noted that when Baby Mohite, the treasurer of SWaCH, said that she needed to take a break, other members agreed to step into the roles she had been playing.

Forming cooperatives
In addition to mobilising to win demands from the state, KKPKP members also engage in 'development activities':

> KKPKP engages in mass struggle as it understands that this is crucial to challenging existing power structures. However, the union recognises that such struggle entails high costs for members, and has also always engaged in 'development activities' in order to meet the needs of members and sustain their involvement (Chikarmane and Narayan 2005: 5).

These development activities include education, a 'gold loan scheme' (which bought back gold given as surety to lenders and now provides women with loans at more reasonable interest against their gold), a group life insurance scheme and work to eliminate child labour. These are differentiated from the welfare activities of NGOs as they are worker-controlled and democratic. Of key interest here is the formation of a number of worker cooperatives linked to the union. Each cooperative was formed to address a specific economic or work-related issue faced by KKPKP's members which the union felt could not be addressed through existing organisational structures. As Narayan and Chikarmane (2013: 206) note:

> Flexibility and adaptability has been a necessity for an organization like this. Informal sector workers have no employers to stabilize or regulate the conditions of their livelihoods. Instead they rely on a resource, and as the external environment changes the conditions, systems and terms of access to that resource, so too the work of those dependent on it must change. This is an important reason why KKPKP has developed in the ways it has.

The formation of each cooperative was preceded by a 'pilot' to test whether the initiative met the union's two main criteria of satisfying the needs of a large member base and being financially sustainable. Once the cooperatives were established, it became clear that they had important implications for the union's approach to organising, empowerment and internal democracy. The remainder of this section provides an overview of three main cooperatives formed by KKPKP and explores the political implications for the union of this shift to a more complex, hybrid organisational form.

Kagad Kach Patra Kashtakari Nagri Sahakari Pat Sanstha

The Kagad Kach Patra Kashtakari Nagri Sahakari Pat Sanstha (KKPKNSPS) savings-linked credit cooperative was registered as a financial institution for KKPKP members in 1997. By 2015 it had approximately 3 000 members and employed two staff. All eleven members of the governing board were waste picker members of the cooperative. Members of KKPKNSPS can each borrow up to four times the amount they have saved. Loans are approved by a monthly meeting of *vasti* (slum) representatives. Borrowers pay 12 per cent annual interest plus 12 per cent annually into a social security scheme for members. This is far lower than the exorbitant rates charged by moneylenders, which can be as high as 2 per cent per day. Members take responsibility for all repayments through *vasti* representatives and the cooperative is fully self-financing. Focus group participants were unanimous on the positive effects and importance of KKPKNSPS. Union member Mangal Bai said, 'I rebuilt my house with a loan I got from the cooperative.' Other members have done the same. Some purchased small trucks, which allowed them to service scattered neighbourhoods, thus providing additional income.

While the credit cooperative was conceived purely to fulfil members' need for loans, it extended far beyond social development. Although legally a separate entity from KKPKP, the cooperative is only open to members of KKPKP, functions according to the same principles as the union, and provides an additional space where union members can deepen their democratic practice. The meeting held on the day of the focus group is a case in point. The 50 members in attendance spent less than a quarter of the meeting time sanctioning loans. The bulk of the meeting focused on discussing a range of issues such as a strategy for continuing union advocacy for old-age pensions and forming a consensus on repayment rates and sustainability of the cooperative. The discussion on sustainability was initiated when one newer member asserted that 'only 20–30 per cent [of borrowers] are honest and return the money. How will it [the cooperative] survive?' A few others bemoaned how repayment rates had been better in the past. However, the conversation transformed as specifics of repayment were discussed. *Vasti* representatives noted that they had not encountered such high default rates and that they avoided defaults by building a rapport with members and visiting them in their homes. By drawing on the union's approach to reaching consensus through discussion, the members eventually agreed on both the objective reality of a default rate of only around 10 per cent and the importance of an organising approach focused on building and maintaining relations with members to secure repayment.

The cooperative also has become a space for organising itself. For example, one of the early experiences of the credit society was in Chaitraban, where many of the 'waste pickers' were actually domestic workers only infrequently moonlighting as pickers. As they wanted access to the credit society, they steadily increased their waste picking in order to meet the union's requirement of trade. Other members of the union questioned their legitimacy, but eventually women from Chaitraban produced receipts from scrap dealers to prove their occupation. These members were extremely regular in repayment and saving and provided stability to the credit society. As a result the 'traditional' waste pickers became willing to expand their definition of a waste picker to include these newcomers to the trade. Today the former domestic workers exclusively pick waste and are members of the union, the credit society and SWaCH.

Kashtachi Kamai

Waste pickers sell their collected recyclables to local small junk dealers or scrap shops. Although in 2011 there were at least 600 scrap shops in Pune, each waste picker usually sells consistently to only one. The relationship between waste pickers and scrap shop owners is simultaneously exploitative and symbiotic: while the scrap shop owners underpay waste pickers for their materials, over years deep relations are forged as scrap owners advance waste pickers money in times of need. In a recent participatory study, KKPKP members identified scrap shop owners as both a positive and a negative driving force in the sector (Chikarmane 2014a).

These relations make it difficult for waste pickers to mobilise directly against scrap shop owners. In response to the exploitative aspects of their relationships with scrap shop owners, members decided to create their own scrap shop in order to increase transparency around prices and develop a new profit-sharing model in the sector. In 1998 members of the union created the cooperative scrap shop Kashtachi Kamai, which means 'earnings from labour'. Membership is open to all members of KKPKP. Seventeen years later Kashtachi Kamai cooperative has two employees and 40 members who sell their materials at the cooperative shop. Kashtachi Kamai purchases materials at a competitive and transparent rate. Profits are paid to members based on the amount of sales to the shop. In 2014 members received a 30 per cent bonus, with one member earning US$3 000. The shop has run at a profit since it was opened. In addition to receiving competitive prices for recyclables and sharing profits, members of Kashtachi Kamai contribute to a public provident fund.

While the immediate benefits of the cooperative accrue to its members, the cooperative has generated broader positive outcomes for the union as well as waste pickers in Pune more generally. Waste pickers who sell at some other shops have used the example of Kashtachi Kamai to successfully demand that owners display prices and pay regular clients annual monetary bonuses. For example, union member Tipavva Shivnur said, 'These shopkeepers used to give us some vessel or jug. I told him, "I don't need yet another jug. You give us money which is useful to me during Diwali [festival season]."' Noting how the union helped women to transform relations with scrap shop owners, Sumanbai (one of the union's oldest members) noted:

> My shopkeeper is quite good now. But not all of them are like that. Even mine wasn't for a long time. Once I became part of the union, then he shaped up. Women depend on them so they take advantage. However, they know very well we are their bread and butter. The union taught us that.

The experience of running Kashtachi Kamai has also strengthened KKPKP's advocacy work by providing the union with insight into the workings of the historically closed and secretive scrap trade and allowing KKPKP to quantify the economic contribution of waste pickers. KKPKP members used the fact that Kashtachi Kamai does not buy scrap from children to launch a massive campaign in 2013 to demand that other shops follow suit. Although the union recognises that it will likely never be able to replace all scrap shops in the city with cooperatives, the close linkage between the cooperative and the union ensures that the union can draw on this experience to wage struggles and campaigns to bring about broader transformation in the sector.

Solid Waste Collection and Handling (SWaCH) cooperative

The third cooperative associated with KKPKP is SWaCH, which in 2008 signed a memorandum of understanding (MoU) with the Pune Municipal Corporation (PMC) to collect segregated waste and recyclables from households in the city. As discussed above, the struggle to access segregated waste from households played a critical role in the formation of KKPKP and remained a key priority for union members. Although they succeeded in reaching paid service agreements with residents in some parts of Pune, for the most part waste pickers still salvaged materials from mixed waste and were not paid for their services. The signing of the MoU was therefore a historic achievement for the union. However, because of the history and nature of both the cooperative and the MoU, SWaCH raised a number of issues for the union not encountered in the other cooperatives.

The formation of SWaCH and the signing of the MoU were catalysed by the adoption of new municipal solid waste rules by the national government in 2000, which for the first time required municipalities to ensure waste segregation, door-to-door collection and the processing of recyclable materials. KKPKP feared the municipality would contract a private company to collect waste from households, which would reduce waste picker incomes and reverse the gains made through existing segregated collection initiatives. The union therefore used the passage of the legislation as a strategic opportunity to reach a formal agreement with the municipality for waste pickers to provide the service.

KKPKP began by securing authorisation from the Pune municipal commissioner in 2005 to conduct a pilot door-to-door collection service with support from the municipality and SNDT Women's University. Waste pickers received equipment, space and training to collect waste from homes; retrieve and sell the recyclables; and deposit the remaining waste in municipal containers or compost pits. They were paid directly by the residents, which facilitated the development of a direct relationship with the people they were servicing.

The pilot proved that waste pickers were capable of delivering the service. After unprecedented lobbying and political mobilisation by the union, in February 2007 the PMC approved the formation of a cooperative of waste pickers to perform door-to-door collection. However, after municipal elections the new council rescinded this decision. The supportive new municipal commissioner succeeded in having the resolution reinstated. However, in the process one key modification was introduced: membership of the cooperative was opened to waste pickers who were not members of the union and to poor urban residents who had not previously worked as waste pickers but were interested in doing collection work. This was to have important political implications for both the cooperative and KKPKP.

SWaCH was formed in August 2007 and in 2008 entered into the MoU with the PMC to conduct door-to-door collection of waste and recyclables. SwaCH members earned income from the sale of recyclables plus a service fee paid by residents. As in the pilot, SWaCH members collected fees directly from residents and were accountable to local citizens' groups. Within the first year SWaCH members' incomes increased by 40 per cent, their daily working hours decreased, and they gained a weekly rest period (SNDT Women's University and Chintan 2008: 106).

In the MoU the PMC committed to providing SWaCH with administrative funds for the first five years. As informal waste pickers must usually provide their own protective and work equipment, it was significant that the PMC also agreed to provide SWaCH members with uniforms, gloves, handcarts, maintenance for the handcarts and insurance (SNDT Women's University and Chintan 2008: 51-2, 106; Chikarmane 2012: 7-8). However, in February 2011 the municipality ceased paying the administrative funds, long before the end of the five-year term. Since the MoU expired in 2013, SWaCH no longer receives support from the municipality, but services continue to be provided to and paid for by residents (Chikarmane 2014b: 14). As of April 2014, SWaCH's 2 300 members collected 600 tons of waste a day (90 tons of which was recyclable) from 375 000 non-slum households and 28 716 slum households (Chikarmane 2014b: 11, 14).

SWaCH has achieved undeniable success in improving the livelihoods and working conditions of its members, in the process providing an important service to Pune's residents and improving the social status of waste pickers. It is important, however, to interrogate how the opening of the cooperative both to waste pickers who were not members of KKPKP and to the urban poor who had not historically worked as waste pickers, as well as the MoU with the municipality, introduced political complexities that KKPKP had not encountered in the other cooperatives and to explore how the union addressed these issues.

The formal relationship with the municipality brought both benefits and challenges. The PMC had two representatives on the SWaCH governing board (which also included two representatives from KKPKP as well as eleven members of the cooperative), which gave the PMC a certain amount of direct influence in the cooperative. The municipal payment provided for the first few years meant the cooperative could hire additional staff and overcome the problems of financial viability usually encountered by start-up cooperatives. By 2010 SWaCH had more than 120 staff members, far more than the skeletal staff of the union. Although the cooperative was committed to the same principles of democratic control and wide participation of members that infused KKPKP, the dramatic increase in the number of staff as well as the relationship with the PMC and residents shifted dynamics within the cooperative. Accountability to residents' committees deepened relationships between SWaCH members and residents in many areas, but in other parts of the city residents reported problems to the municipality instead of to SWaCH members. A small local NGO of middle-class residents that had opposed the MoU and believed waste pickers should be 'rehabilitated' into other professions exacerbated this pressure on the municipality by continuing to agitate against the model.

The PMC was not accustomed to working with waste pickers or cooperatives, and municipal officials expected SWaCH staff not just to provide data and address complaints from citizens but to 'discipline' waste pickers. In meetings at the ward level, ward officers often demanded that a staff member 'replace this waste picker' if it was perceived that she was not doing her job. According to SWaCH's rules, a waste picker could be replaced only through a collective decision at a members' meeting. However, due to the power and authority of the municipal corporation, SWaCH staff felt tremendous pressure to act at the behest of the PMC. Further complicating matters, it also became clear that SWaCH would not be able to take hard-line positions with the PMC if terms and conditions of the contract were violated. The unequal power relations between the PMC and the cooperative, combined with the PMC's misconception that SWaCH staff had the power to discipline members, began to undermine the carefully constructed democratic practice of the union and led some staff to start treating members like employees. Even seasoned KKPKP activists in the SWaCH administration struggled to train staff and give them a clear perspective on their role in relation to members.

Many members' understandings of their relationships with the PMC and SWaCH staff also began to change. Ironically, the victory in the contract negotiations that required the municipality to provide SWaCH members with equipment undermined ongoing member mobilisation.

Whereas in the past KKPKP members knew they needed to struggle for pushcarts, buckets and sorting sheds, many members began to argue that staff were responsible for securing equipment and access to more homes. Some staff talked about members working in their jurisdictions as 'my women' and boasted about accessing pushcarts from a local elected representative without the active participation of members. While staff in KKPKP were always seen as activists and referred to as '*tai*' (older sister), in SWaCH they were becoming supervisors, often addressed as 'madam'.

Changes in the relationships between staff and members were compounded by the emergence of new divisions between members of SWaCH, as well as between KKPKP members who chose to join SWaCH and those who elected to continue to work independently. Membership of the scrap shop and savings cooperatives was limited to KKPKP members, making it relatively easy to ensure continuity in political culture and practice between the cooperatives and the union. However, many members of SWaCH had not previously worked as waste pickers, let alone been members of KKPKP. Virtually all eventually joined KKPKP, often in order to join the credit cooperative and benefit from the loan scheme in addition to the general advantages of being members of the union. Thus, the various cooperatives helped the union to recruit and retain new members. It is important to note, however, that it took time to inculcate the new members into the democratic practice of the union, and that the presence in the union of such a large number of people without a history of struggle exacerbated the tendencies to expect SWaCH staff to secure victories on their behalf. As one long-standing member noted during the focus group:

> For us the union is everything and our struggles have been long and hard. But for new members this has come too easy and it's taken for granted. But I suppose we also need new members, as some of us are too old to work. It's hard for the new ones to fully understand and appreciate the present.

The creation of SWaCH also produced new divisions between KKPKP members in a context where the union was already proactively attempting to engage and overcome pre-existing social divisions between members rooted in caste, gender, religion and migration (Narayan and Chikarmane

2013). All KKPKP members were eligible to join SWaCH. However, in early 2015 only 60 per cent of KKPKP members were also members of SWaCH. Reasons for not joining SWaCH ranged from not wanting to be accountable for delivering a service, preferring to continue to work independently, and feeling that door-to-door collection was too physically strenuous. The KKPKP members who did not join SWaCH generally fell into two broad groups. The majority were older women who worked on the landfill. A smaller group collected scrap in lucrative commercial areas and did not think that they would benefit from moving to door-to-door collection. This latter group were more agnostic regarding SWaCH. However, older women at the landfill argued that as a result of SWaCH's door-to-door collection, they accessed fewer materials. They also felt that KKPKP was focusing too much on doorstep collectors. Nevertheless, they remained in the union because of the benefits, many of which came from the credit cooperative, the cooperative scrap shop and the union's other 'development' activities, in addition to the broader social welfare gains and general improvements in their status and working conditions gained through struggle. In the focus group some noted they were particularly encouraged by and supportive of the union's campaign to secure pensions for waste pickers and other informal workers. KKPKP has been able to draw on its deep historical commitment and well-established practice of identifying, speaking openly about and grappling with social divisions in the union to develop ways of working through the new divisions associated with the formation of SWaCH (Narayan and Chikarmane 2013).

Since mid-2010 there has been a concentrated effort to revisit the building blocks of the cooperative to re-entrench collective, democratic control by members. Key to this was renewed commitment by members to paying 5 per cent of the user fees collected as dues to run the organisation and maintain an administrative staff. This became even more crucial in February 2011, when the municipality reneged on the MoU and stopped paying the agreed amount to SWaCH, creating more pressure for the organisation to become financially sustainable. During the first few years of euphoria and era of expansion in SWaCH, members barely paid these dues. This was a great diversion of character for a KKPKP member who was required to pay all union dues in order to get a loan or to become eligible for the insurance policy. In SWaCH, on the other hand, paying and non-paying members had the same privileges. It was not just unfair towards paying members; it also did not make long-term economic sense. Non-payment of dues began to percolate into the union, albeit to a much smaller extent. After a series of discussions, members realised that this needed to be changed immediately. Members agreed to tie most activities, distribution of PMC-given equipment, access to shorting sheds and repair of equipment to payment of dues. This helped members take stronger ownership of the systems and get involved, not just in crucial decisions, but also in everyday operations of the cooperative, including checking 5 per cent contributions and knowing the amounts being collected. Most SWaCH members are now clear on the importance of the cooperative being financially independent and self-sustaining. When one focus group participant suggested that SWaCH should secure donor funding to assist with financial sustainability, most members countered that independence was what would ensure the long-term existence of the cooperative. Critical reflection on the negative effects of interference by the municipality and the subsequent transformations within SWaCH to realign it with KKPKP's empowerment approach meant that members now understood organisational sustainability in more political terms.

In a further effort to bring the working culture of the KKPKP into the cooperative and to fully utilise the large SWaCH staff and their almost daily contact with members, the cooperative staff began to undertake union activities. For example, SWaCH staff were charged with supporting KKPKP members in their struggles for better rates from scrap dealers and ensuring children of waste pickers were admitted to school under the Right to Education Act quota.

The politics of hybrid organisations: Some conclusions and further questions

This chapter demonstrates that the politics of developing hybrid organisations is complex. The willingness and ability of informal economy unions to recognise that the union form can be simultaneously crucial and insufficient for meeting the needs of their members is an important organisational innovation that can help to recruit and retain members and advance collective struggle. Rather than drawing a clear distinction between development activities conducted by cooperatives and political campaigns of the union, the example of the Kashtachi Kamai cooperative scrap shop demonstrates how knowledge generated in the cooperative can be used to strengthen broader campaigns. Because the memberships of Kashtachi Kamai and KKPKNSPS are drawn from KKPKP, membership of the cooperatives is seen as a benefit of belonging to the union and helps to retain union membership. This overlap in membership also facilitates a fluidity between the union and the cooperatives, which allows cooperative meetings to become additional spaces for debate and discussion about broader union issues, deepening democratisation in the union.

While participants in the focus group felt that SWaCH should be seen as part of a continuum with the union as opposed to a completely distinct organisation, several factors mean that it occupies a different relationship with the union and has had a different impact on it. First, because the municipality required SWaCH to be open to all members of the urban poor who wanted to become involved in door-to-door collection, not all SWaCH members had worked as waste pickers in the past or been members of KKPKP. They were not steeped in KKPKP's politics grounded in empowerment, had no connection to the historical struggles of KKPKP, and therefore brought a different political culture into SWaCH.

The formation of SWaCH and the signing of the MoU with the municipality represented a groundbreaking advance in the struggle for secure access to segregated waste that had been central to the very formation of the union. Significant benefits accrue to members in terms of improved incomes, working conditions and work security. However, many of the victories in the agreement with the municipality were doubled-edged swords. The requirement that for the first five years the PMC pay SWaCH an amount in addition to fees collected from residents was rooted in the important recognition that it is hard to make separation at source economically viable in the first few years. But the infusion of funds from the municipality meant that perhaps too many staff were hired too quickly to allow for adequate training, and too great a dependence on paid staff was generated in a context where the union prioritised members fulfilling organising functions. It also meant that the cooperative could afford to be lax in collecting dues in the first few years, resulting in high levels of non-payment that began to seep into the union.

The signing of an official MoU with the municipality to be the sole provider of door-to-door collection services provided the waste pickers with secure access to materials and protection against dispossession by private companies that has been the envy of waste picker movements around the world (Samson 2016). Yet, the power imbalances meant that the municipality exerted undue influence on the cooperative. And because the municipal staff did not understand that the staff in a cooperative is accountable to members and not vice versa, they put pressure on the cooperative staff to discipline members, creating a dramatic transformation in the political culture and dynamics within the cooperative that diverged greatly from that inside KKPKP.

By drawing on the union's praxis of empowerment, rooted in the dynamic movement between critical reflection and action, SWaCH members and staff were able to identify the source of the problems encountered and to develop strategies to address them and to transform the organisation. Ironically, the fact that the municipality reneged on the agreement facilitated the process. The internal political culture of SWaCH is now more closely aligned with that of KKPKP and the two organisations are more integrated, as most SWaCH members are now also members of KKPKP, with SWaCH staff playing a more active role in union work. The union must, however, add the new divisions created between KKPKP members who belong to SWaCH and those who do not to the challenges it faces in forging a common identity among members.

Due to the nature of the work performed by informal workers, increasing numbers of informal worker organisations are developing hybrid forms to address a range of needs far wider than those of formally employed wage workers. Because waste pickers provide a municipal service, within this sector there is also growing interest in negotiating agreements between waste picker cooperatives and municipalities to secure formal recognition of their role, access to materials and payment for their services. In addition to Pune, innovative agreements have been developed in Bogotá in Colombia and Belo Horizonte and Diadema in Brazil (Dias and Cidrin 2008; Gutberlet 2008). But while much has been written on the nature of these agreements and the material benefits for waste pickers, residents and municipalities, scant attention has been paid to the political and organisational implications of the agreements for the cooperatives and unions involved. Waste picker organisations (as well as organisations of other informal workers seeking agreements with the state) can learn a great deal from the challenges that the agreement with the municipality raised for both SWaCH and KKPKP, as well as how the cooperative and the union are addressing these challenges. Thus, although the insights in this chapter into the political implications of the formation of cooperatives by an informal worker union are drawn from KKPKP's experience, they raise issues and generate questions that should be explored in other contexts. While KKPKP is still grappling with how to navigate the political complexities of its hybrid form, and in particular how this form affects the union's internal political culture, it is in fact this very culture that focuses on processes of critical reflection, dialogue, debate and empowerment that can guide both KKPKP and other informal economy unions through this difficult terrain.

Note

1. Most waste picker workers in this region in India belong to the Matang caste, one of the many Dalit castes that are historically stigmatised, socially excluded and isolated. The Dalit movement has waged a long, historical struggle to transform the position of Dalit castes within Indian society.

References

Chikarmane, P. 2012. 'Integrating Waste Pickers into Municipal Solid Waste Management in Pune, India'. WIEGO Policy Brief (Urban Policies) No. 8. http://wiego.org/sites/wiego.org/files/publications/files/Chikarmane_WIEGO_PB8.pdf (accessed 1 December 2016).

Chikarmane, P. 2014a. 'Informal Economy Monitoring Study: Waste Pickers in Pune, India'. Manchester: WIEGO.

———. 2014b. 'Of Users, Providers and the State: Solid Waste Management in Pune, India'. Paper presented at the Putting Public in Public Services: Research, Action and Equity in the Global South Municipal Services Project Conference, 13–16 April, Cape Town.

Chikarmane, P. and L. Narayan 2005. 'Organising the Unorganised: A Case Study of the Kagad Kach Patra Kashtakari Panchayat (Trade Union of Waste-Pickers)'. http://wiego.org/sites/wiego.org/files/resources/files/Chikarmane_Narayan_case-kkpkp.pdf (accessed 1 December 2016).

Dias, S. and F. Cidrin 2008. 'Integration of the Informal Recycling Sector in Solid Waste Management in Brazil'. Study prepared for the Sector Project Promotion of

Concepts for Pro-poor and Environmentally Friendly Closed-Loop Approaches in Solid Waste Management (SWM). PN 03.2144.8. GTZ. http://www.gtz.de/de/dokumente/gtz2008-informal-recycling-brazil.pdf (accessed 5 September 2011).

Freire, P. 2000. *Pedagogy of the Oppressed: 30th Anniversary Edition*. London: Bloomsbury Academic.

Gutberlet, J. 2008. *Recovering Resources, Recycling Citizenship: Urban Poverty Reduction in Latin America*. Burlington, VT: Ashgate.

Narayan, L. and P. Chikarmane 2013. 'Power at the Bottom of the Heap: Organizing Waste Pickers in Pune'. In *Organizing Women Workers in the Informal Economy: Beyond the Weapons of the Weak*, edited by N. Kabeer, R. Sudarshan and K. Milward. London: Zed.

Samson, M. 2009a. 'Refusing to Be Cast Aside: Waste Pickers Organising around the World'. Cambridge, MA: WIEGO. http://wiego.org/sites/wiego.org/files/publications/files/Samson-Refusing-to-be-Cast-Aside-Wastepickers-Wiego-publication-English.pdf (accessed 1 December 2016).

———. 2009b. 'Wasted Citizenship? Reclaimers and the Privatized Expansion of the Public Sphere'. *Africa Development* 34(3-4): 1-25.

———. 2014. 'Gender, Empowerment, and Women's Leadership in the Informal Economy'. Paper presented at the WIEGO General Assembly, 11 November, Yogyakarta, Indonesia.

———. 2016. 'Old Trash, New Ideas: Re-conceptualizing the Public in Waste Management'. In *Making Public in a Privatized World*, edited by D. McDonald. London: Zed.

SNDT Women's University and Chintan. 2008. 'Recycling Livelihoods: Integration of the Informal Recycling Sector in Solid Waste Management in India'. GTZ. http://swachcoop.com/pdf/Recycling_Livelihoods_2008.pdf (accessed 1 December 2016).

Webster, E. 2011. 'Organizing in the Informal Economy: Ela Bhatt and the Self-employed Women's Association of India'. *Labour, Capital & Society* 44(1): 98-125.

8

Sword of Justice or Defender of Vested Interest?
The Struggles of Johannesburg's Municipal Workers

Edward Webster and Carmen Ludwig

At the centre of trade union strategy is a tension between the extent to which trade unions focus on the immediate interests of their members against a broader commitment to the interests of working people. This tension between inclusion and exclusion is captured evocatively in Allan Flanders's (1970: 15) idea of the two faces of unionism: the idea of the union as a 'sword of justice' or as a 'defender of vested interest'. Put differently, trade unions can be seen in conventional terms as membership-based organisations or they can be understood as social movements of working people with a transformative agenda. This tension within trade unions was captured in the 1980s in South Africa through the concept of social movement unionism (Webster 1988).

In this chapter we draw on social movement theory and the power resources approach to place the struggles of municipal workers against contract or precarious work at the centre of our analysis. We employ social movement theory to examine how workers acquire a sense of injustice or grievance and how these grievances become collective. As John Kelly (1998: 126) suggests, social movement theory introduces the notion of injustice into the heart of industrial relations research.

We locate these struggles of municipal workers in the context of the changing world of work and the challenges facing the South African Municipal Workers Union (SAMWU) and its predecessors in Johannesburg, is the economic centre of South Africa. It is also the union's stronghold, with 13 per cent of SAMWU's 160 000 members concentrated in the Johannesburg region (SAMWU 2012: 18). We chose this region because it has a history of struggle over conditions of work. It is also the site of a successful campaign of resistance to the process of informalisation through innovative strategies and new sources of power that deepen and expand traditional sources of workers' power.

We identify three cycles of labour contention, framed around the repertoires of inclusion and exclusion. We suggest that the increasing fragmentation of the workforce in post-apartheid South Africa has brought the tension between the two faces of unionism sharply to the fore. The question raised by our analysis of these cycles of contention is whether municipal workers' struggles are discrete and disconnected instances of resistance or whether they have the potential to build long-term unity between workers. How far do municipal workers frame and pursue their interest in ways that include those of other constituencies and movements from below?

In the first cycle, 1980 to 1995, municipal workers' struggle is framed against racial discrimination by the demand for an inclusive, democratic citizenship. The cycle culminated in a brief honeymoon period and the promise of a participatory labour regime. The second cycle covers the shift to privatisation, 1996 to 2000, when intense ideological contention focused on the opposition to privatisation, with workers demanding public goods. In the third cycle, 2001 to 2011, the union confronted the consequences of flexibilisation and the return of contract work. The union responded to employers' strategies by embarking on a campaign against corruption and demanding job security. This culminated in the 2011 strike against the quasi-private waste removal company Pikitup, an action that brought together 'casual' and 'permanent' workers in a successful demand for permanent jobs and an investigation into corruption.

Our study reveals a deepening of traditional sources of worker power through 'new' forms of logistical and societal power. Municipal workers were able to mobilise new sources of power in the second and third cycles, framed in terms of anti-corruption and broader coalitions that go beyond union–party alliances. Those power resources remain embryonic and sporadic as a decline in internal solidarity has weakened SAMWU's capacity to address the dilemma presented to trade unions by the two faces of unionism.

Mobilising union power

For Sidney Tarrow (2011: 101), at the core of contention is the power to disrupt. From which source(s) do workers draw power in order to influence the structural imbalance of power relations between capital and labour? Traditional forms of power, such as *associational* or *organisational power*, derive from the formation of collective workers' organisations such as trade unions or political parties. *Structural power* develops from the status of specific groups in the economic system or in the labour market and can be exerted spontaneously (Wright 2000). Therefore, workers' structural power is particularly shaped by the 'social relations of production' and the political-economic context (Barker et al. 2013: 13). *Marketplace bargaining power* refers to power to negotiate arising from tight labour markets, while *workplace bargaining power* results from a specific strategic position of a group of workers within the value chain and therefore workers' ability to effectively interrupt production processes though collective action (Silver 2003: 13–14). In another form of structural power, *logistical power*, disruptive politics are drawn from the workplace into the public arena (Webster, Lambert and Bezuidenhout 2008: 13). For example, in the case of the farm worker strikes in De Doorns, Western Cape, in November 2012, workers' collective action was mainly expressed through blockading roads and highways.

As a secondary source of power, *institutional power* derives from previous workers' struggles. Thus, structural and organisational power can be incorporated into societal institutions through social compromises (for example, in labour law) for further economic and political cycles. As institutional power creates the frame, it can pre-structure future processes of negotiations and trade union strategies (Dörre, Holst and Nachtwey 2009).

In contrast, *societal power* depends on unions' ability to frame their struggle in ways that aim at organising a counter-hegemonic force, based on *cooperative power* through coalition building with social movements or on *discourse power* through influencing public discourses around issues of justice. All these forms of power, and the relationship between them, are illustrated in Figure 1.1 in Chapter 1 of this volume (see also Arbeitskreis Strategic Unionism 2013: 364).

As studies on social movements show, 'material conditions do not necessarily and automatically generate mobilizing grievances' (Lévesque and Murray 2013: 779). Actors must therefore assign meaning to these conditions in order to transform grievances into successful mobilisation. For example, precarious workers can compensate for the lack of associational power 'by drawing upon the contested arena of culture and public debates about values' (Chun 2009: 7) and by winning public recognition and legitimacy for workers' struggles. Christian Lévesque and Gregor Murray (2010: 342) argue that framing is a strategic capability that allows for trade unions to define an autonomous agenda and to shape workers' grievances into broader and more resonant claims. As Lévesque and Murray convincingly conclude, power resources are a necessary but insufficient condition to respond to the changing conditions affecting unions. The capacity of trade unions to represent workers' interests and to effect social change depends on the dynamic relationship between power resources and strategic capabilities. So far, only a few studies have focused on the link between power resources and strategic capabilities, identifying different sets of strategic capabilities (Lévesque and Murray 2010; Arbeitskreis Strategic Unionism 2013). However, as Lévesque and Murray (2010: 346) argue, 'an understanding of union resources and capabilities is critical to an understanding of efforts to enhance union power because they provide keys to detect emergent patterns which, once integrated, might alter path dependencies'.

Contesting the labour regime

Johannesburg has a long history of struggle over municipal services since its establishment as a gold mining town in the late nineteenth century (Barchiesi 2007). By early 1918 there were signs of great discontent among both white and black workers on the Rand, especially in Johannesburg (Hyslop 2004: 280). Indeed, in March 1918 syndicalists appealed to white workers of Johannesburg to implement their own version of the Russian Revolution by occupying the power station (286). In May, the Johannesburg Council's refusal to improve black workers' working conditions led to the 'bucket boys' strike, which city authorities suppressed by arresting sanitary workers. Although at this stage black workers were not able to translate their struggle into organisational power, they started seeing their power though collective resistance (Callinicos 1987: 89). However, black workers remained vulnerable to deportation to the rural areas as they were allowed only temporary entrance to what was seen as the white man's city and they were tightly controlled by the pass system.

The first cycle of municipal workers' resistance, 1980 to 1995, was framed against racial discrimination and demanded an inclusive, democratic citizenship. This was a period of municipal workers' militancy and of building associational power as illustrated by a mass strike of municipal employees in Johannesburg in July 1980. The strike started in the Orlando Power Station over the demand for a minimum wage and quickly spread to other departments; after two days about 10 000 black workers had joined the strike. The strike that 'shook Johannesburg' lasted one week and was finally crushed through massive police intervention. More than 1 000 workers were deported to the rural Bantustans (Keenan 1981: 4).

The disruptive collective action of municipal workers centred on demands for higher wages and trade union recognition, but the strike was also an attack on the exploitative social relations of the migrant labour system. Contract labour was a central pillar of the apartheid system and was used as a means of 'influx control' and of forcing workers into the lowest-paid sectors. Marketplace bargaining power of municipal workers was weak as the majority of them had hardly any chance of taking up other jobs. For recruitment, the Johannesburg City Council (JCC) relied primarily on the most remote districts of the Transkei, the oldest of apartheid's Bantustans, where poverty was high and workers were forced to take the most unpleasant jobs, particularly as sanitation workers.

The JCC employed more than 12 000 migrant workers out of a total workforce of 14 000 black workers in 1980 (Keenan 1981: 10). The migrant workers from the Bantustans usually received one-year contracts and call-in cards for contract renewal. The majority were classified as unskilled workers and were trapped in that position. Two-thirds of the municipal workforce lived in tightly controlled and overcrowded compounds located close to their workplaces (Keenan 1981; LRC 1981: 68).

Although the state had begun to widen the area of legality by providing for trade union recognition of black workers as a result of the 1979 Wiehahn Commission, institutional power remained weak for municipal employees, who faced employer resistance to unionisation. As a consequence, worker resistance relied primarily on their workplace bargaining power.[1] The Black Municipal Workers' Union (BMWU), created to counteract management efforts to establish a sweetheart union, had been in existence for one month when the strike erupted. Mobilisation was fuelled by long-standing grievances in depots and compounds, uniting skilled and unskilled workers, contract and non-contract workers. Despite being premature in its organisational capacity, the BMWU played an important role in support of the strike. First, the leadership of the BMWU consisted of workers who had challenged management before and had gained experience in trade union organising (Keenan 1981: 7-10). Second, the union and its already organised sections proved to be crucial for fostering solidarity between contract and non-contract workers (LRC 1981). Third, the controlled compounds were turned into the central site of trade union recruitment of contract workers, laying the basis for workers' militant actions (Keenan 1981: 15).

Until the formation of SAMWU in 1987 through a merger of five unions, municipal workers' associational power remained limited due to massive state repression as well as trade union fragmentation.[2] From the largest municipal union at the time, the Cape Town Municipal Workers' Association, SAMWU inherited the 'peculiar blend of workplace-based and community-orientated activism rooted in an image of itself as a representative of citizens as well as workers' (Barchiesi 2011: 152). SAMWU's efforts focused on building its organisation around the dismantling of the apartheid and contract labour systems. The union had already contested attempts by the apartheid government to encourage private participation in municipal services in the late 1980s, stating that 'the privatisation of basic services will weaken the ability of a post-apartheid government to meet the needs of the majority of the people of this country' (SAMWU 1991: n.p.).

The end of apartheid led to a brief honeymoon period of institutionalisation, which saw an increase of institutional power and the rise of SAMWU's associational power. As they had played a significant role in the fight against apartheid, trade unions gained in the form of 'policy dividends' and 'institutional dividends' (Buhlungu 2010: 164).

The former came in the form of progressive labour laws – in particular the Labour Relations Act – aimed at eliminating discrimination in the labour market. The latter refers to the establishment of corporatist institutions, in particular the National Economic Development and Labour Council (NEDLAC),[3] which gave unions a say over social and economic issues. For the first time black municipal workers negotiated wages and social benefits in a bargaining council. SAMWU became one of the fastest-growing unions in the Congress of South African Trade Unions (COSATU) (Barchiesi 2011: 152), and the dominant union in the municipal sector.

Contesting the commodification of public goods

The second cycle covers the shift to privatisation, 1996 to 2000, when intense ideological contention was focused on the opposition to privatisation, with workers demanding public goods. As Jo Beall, Owen Crankshaw and Susan Parnell (2002: 99) argue:

> [The] conflict became the base of the most organized campaign by labour against the ANC [African National Congress] government since the Alliance in support of the 1994 electoral victory. The underlying positions that were adopted reflect diametrically opposed approaches to the entire project of post-apartheid reconstruction and development; these were larger disputes that came to be played out on the Johannesburg stage.

The restructuring of municipalities in post-apartheid South Africa followed contradictory imperatives. On the one hand, the government was committed to the deracialisation of the South African state and to the promotion of redress and development. On the other hand, the state was promoting neoliberal globalisation (Samson 2008: 25). The ANC's macroeconomic policy shifted in 1996 from a commitment towards state intervention and redistribution, as formulated in the Reconstruction and Development Programme (RDP), to the highly contested Growth, Employment and Redistribution (GEAR) programme, which entailed a market-oriented strategy including trade liberalisation, privatisation, tax reduction and fiscal deficit reduction (Webster, Lambert and Bezuidenhout 2008: 165–7).

In line with this policy shift, in 1999 the JCC adopted a plan, iGoli 2002, to transform and restructure the municipality. This led to the most far-reaching model of 'contracting out' as municipal departments were turned into utilities, agencies or corporatised entities (Van Niekerk and Ronnie 2009: 31). The iGoli 2002 project was embedded into a wider neoliberal agenda, thereby facilitating what Rosa Luxemburg called capitalist *Landnahme*, or processes of commodification and the expansion of capital into areas that were previously withdrawn from profit maximisation (Dörre 2010). GEAR resulted in severe cuts in intergovernmental grants from national to lower levels, thereby reducing the transfers for the Greater Johannesburg Metropolitan Council (GJMC) from R500 million in 1993 to R24 million in 1999 (Gordhan 2000) and applying pressure on local government.[4] At the same time, incentives were set by the World Bank and the Department of Finance in order to support the realisation of the iGoli project.[5] Advocates of the iGoli 2002 process, including the ANC-led GJMC and business, framed the implementation as an optimisation of services through cost recovery and by creating 'commercial imperatives for improved performance and efficiency' (GJMC 1999: 15), with the underlying assumption of market efficiency in contrast to state bureaucracy. Correspondingly, citizens were regarded as customers of the outsourced services. 'The challenge is to transform the current bureaucracy into a business approach because the city is a "big business"' (6).

In contrast, SAMWU's post-apartheid strategy was to pursue a double track of opposing the privatisation of municipal services and engaging in the reorganisation of municipal services on the basis of the social rights entrenched in South Africa's democratic Constitution (Wainwright 2012: 78). In the 'propaganda war' (*Financial Mail*, 7 July 2000) around iGoli 2002, SAMWU highlighted that privatisation would lead to rate increases, job losses and limited access of the unemployed to basic services such as water and electricity. SAMWU emphasised labour–community links and social citizenship, realised through a democratically controlled public service. Accordingly, the union also criticised the lack of participation of labour and the community in the process as, similar to the adoption of GEAR, iGoli 2002 was the result of an internal government process with the involvement of private consultants. SAMWU commented:

In South Africa the workers' movement has never confined struggles to narrow interests of organised workers only. The SA Municipal Workers Union (SAMWU) is committed to an affordable and efficient public service; and that includes democratic community and worker participation (SAMWU pamphlet 6 April 1999).

Although SAMWU revived its strategy of social movement unionism to fight against privatisation, as David Lier and Kristian Stokke (2006) argue, social movement unionism was limited by COSATU's alliance with the ruling party, the ANC, which made it difficult for SAMWU to fundamentally oppose privatisation in Johannesburg. SAMWU's campaign was constrained by an 'underlying tension between loyalty to the ANC and loyalty to the labour movement'.[6] The unwillingness of COSATU to seriously challenge its alliance partner on the issue of privatisation further impacted negatively on SAMWU's campaign and led to the failure to exploit political opportunities, such as the local government election in 1999.

In 2000 SAMWU was involved in the foundation of the Anti-Privatisation Forum – a coalition of anti-privatisation movements and organisations, including sections of COSATU – but the union increasingly withdrew its support from the Forum due to 'strategic differences' between social movements and the COSATU affiliates centred on their relationship with the ruling party.[7]

As Trevor Ngwane (2012: 130) concludes, the campaign lost drive as the government offered some concessions and the unions compromised. Overall, SAMWU's campaign focus shifted from a strategy of inclusive solidarity fundamentally opposed to privatisation to a more exclusive approach focusing on its immediate membership interests and job protection. As a former SAMWU officer concluded, 'The fight was not lost outside, it was lost within. The members, staff – we were not as one. Although we had one resolution, the implementation of it became a problem.'[8]

This also impacted on the set of repertoires used by the union. SAMWU's campaign strategy was based on 'a combination of mass action and strategic engagement',[9] including the struggle for public opinion, worker mobilisation, negotiations with the GJMC and political negotiations with the ANC (Van Driel 2003: 75). On the one hand, the union made use of disruptive forms of contention, including mass mobilisation, strike action, sit-ins and the disruption of road traffic, thereby making use of workers' structural power (Musi 2010: 89). Combining workplace bargaining and logistical power, municipal workers took to the street in a wildcat strike in July 2000, trashing the streets of Johannesburg's central business district (CBD). On the other hand, by focusing on negotiations SAMWU gave preference to containing forms of protest, even agreeing to temporarily abstain from protest action.[10] In contrast, crisis committees and citizen forums preferred direct action to institutionalised processes (Barchiesi 2011: 158).

Despite its limitations, SAMWU was able to exert societal power in its anti-privatisation campaign. As Dale McKinley (2014: 14) reflects, SAMWU's campaign against iGoli 2002 formed part of the union's broader national anti-privatisation campaign, which involved sustained efforts to forge alliances with community organisations. The union was at times able to mobilise *cooperative power* by organising and uniting societal forces such as new social movements and parts of the alliance (Musi 2010: 89) and, linked to this, mobilised *discourse power* in the 'contest over meaning' (Tarrow 2011: 12).

Facing the divide: Increasing fragmentation of workforce in solid waste

In the third cycle, 2001 to 2011, the union confronted the consequences of flexibilisation and the return of contract labour. Figure 8.1 illustrates the process of fragmentation in the solid waste sector in Johannesburg, with each successive zone being located further from the core municipal workers and the core employer, the City of Johannesburg – further, in other words, from the zone of work stability and job security. The further the distance from the core, in both legal and geographical terms, the greater the vulnerability of workers and therefore the greater difficulty in organising them (Von Holdt and Webster 2008: 338). In the outer zone, the periphery, the notion changes from *earning a living* to *making a living* through creating one's own income-generating or subsistence activities. In solid waste this group is made up of waste pickers who collect litter at landfill sites or in the streets to sell for recycling (Samson 2004; Webster et al. 2008).

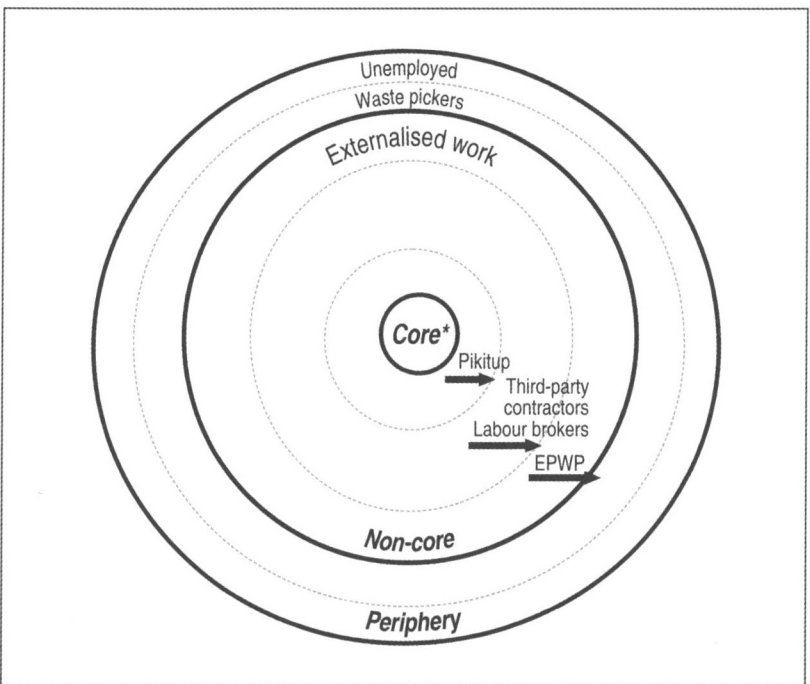

Figure 8.1 Increasing fragmentation of workforce in solid waste in Johannesburg

* The 'core' refers to the remaining municipal workforce, which has been drastically reduced through the externalising of the city's municipal services into fourteen municipal-owned entities, including Pikitup, City Power and Johannesburg Water.

EPWP Expanded Public Works Programme.

The distinct zones of the flexible world of work are not separate spheres but intertwined in many respects. First, the different types of workers often operate in the same physical space – that is to say, they are working alongside each other in the workplace. Second, as shown by Edward Webster et al. (2008: 47), formal and informal economic activities are asymmetrically interdependent through value chains.

In terms of the flexible world of municipal work, Figure 8.1 illustrates that work in solid waste has moved away from being located in the core of municipal work. This is due, firstly, to the creation of Pikitup itself. As a result of the lost fight against iGoli 2002, the City of Johannesburg's waste removal company Pikitup was created as a utility in 2001. It is owned by the City of Johannesburg but run like a private company. Permanent and temporary municipal employees were absorbed into the new entity, although it took three years until the former temporary workers were on the same wage level as their colleagues who had been working for the municipality on a permanent basis (Samson 2003). Despite promises made to workers when Pikitup was created, conditions rapidly deteriorated. Pikitup started reducing its workforce through 'natural attrition' by not replacing workers who left, were dismissed or had passed away. As a result, Pikitup increased the workload and pressure on the remaining workforce to get the same amount of work done as before (Samson 2003: 68).

Secondly, over time Pikitup made increasing use of outsourcing and labour broking in non-revenue areas, especially in the labour-intensive task of street cleaning. As S. van Niekerk and R. Ronnie (2009: 31) note, municipalities often have contracts with many small companies, which makes it difficult to keep track of outsourcing activities. A shop steward estimated that in 2011 Pikitup was working with about 24 contractors.[11] The externalisation of work is characterised by a process of triangulation and represents 'a shift away from the employment relationship altogether where the workplace ceases to be the physical and social space in which the relationship between workers and their employer is located' (Von Holdt and Webster 2008: 339).

As the client, Pikitup is on top of the triangular power relationship and in control of all terms of contracts with labour brokers and subcontractors, without having to bear any of the risks associated with being the employer (Theron 2005: 619). Contracts between Pikitup and subcontractors did not entail regulations about workers' rights, and Pikitup also did not make sure that companies abided by labour laws. Consequently, many third-party contractors denied their workers basic rights (Samson 2003: 64–5). Workers from third-party contractors and labour brokers were performing the same work as general workers in Pikitup. Wage disparities appeared between contractors and Pikitup, with permanent employees earning R6 122 per month (see Table 8.1). In addition, third-party contractors were paying contributions to the Unemployment Insurance Fund but denying their workers all other benefits, such as medical aid or pension fund.

Table 8.1 Wage disparities among contract workers working for Pikitup in 2013

Contractor	Workforce	Area in Johannesburg	Working days per week	Monthly salary
Chippa	89	Sandton CBD	5	R2 800
Zee	156	Johannesburg South (Booysens, Turffontein, Rosettenville, Mulbarton)	6	R3 900
Zenzeleni	166	Johannesburg South (informal settlements, Orange Farm, Avalon Depot)	3	R1 520
Vahluri	52	Greater Johannesburg (Roodepoort, Florida, Honeydew, Maraisburg, Princess)	5	R3 000
Dikala	60	Johannesburg CBD	5	R3 000 (approx.)

Source: Based on interviews with workers from Chippa, Zee and Zenzeleni (1 August 2013) and from Vahluri and Dikala (6 August 2013).

Pikitup (as well as the City of Johannesburg) also made use of the Expanded Public Works Programme (EPWP), which forms part of a public employment initiative of the national government aimed at poverty alleviation. Pikitup (2010: 47) employed 2 034 EPWP workers in the financial year 2009/10. EPWP workers are usually employed on short-term contracts and are paid at a much lower rate than regular employees.

Ten years after its creation, Pikitup employees found themselves in the minority in the workplace. By 2011 externalisation had increased to such an extent that about 60 per cent of the workforce was externalised, with the majority of workers provided by labour brokers. Hajo Holst, Oliver Nachtwey and Klaus Dörre (2009) distinguish between different forms of labour broking. For example, it can be used by companies temporarily when there is a need to respond to peak workloads in the form of ad hoc replacements. The authors argue that labour broking has experienced a fundamental change of function, however, as it is increasingly used by companies as a strategic instrument of profit maximisation, based on a flexible workforce of agency workers that supplements or replaces permanent employment. The increasingly high percentage of labour brokers indicates that labour broking in the municipal-owned Pikitup was used not as a 'flexibility buffer' (Holst, Nachtwey and Dörre 2009) in order to handle peak workloads but rather in a strategic manner with agency workers working on site for extended periods of time.

The increase of contract work in Pikitup diminished SAMWU's workplace bargaining power as well as its associational power. This was reinforced through Pikitup being a separate company. Even before Pikitup's creation, the GJMC employed a high number of contract workers in solid waste. However, casualisation impacted even more on the union's strength as the loss of associational power in the workplace could hardly be compensated through an involvement of other municipal sectors (for example, during strike action).

Bridging the divide: Mobilising contract workers and rebuilding union power in the workplace

In the third cycle, 2000 to 2011, workplace bargaining power as well as the associational power of SAMWU came under pressure as a result of privatisation. In 2011 SAMWU embarked on a campaign to turn this situation around and to make all casual workers permanent employees of Pikitup. SAMWU intensified organising among outsourced workers, thereby strengthening its bargaining and associational power. Shop stewards at Pikitup started recruiting externalised workers for the union, making use of the joint workplace at depots and in the streets. SAMWU's strategy aimed at building a relationship between the union and externalised workers on the one hand and between workers from Pikitup and third-party contractors on the other. These relationships were created though general meetings at the workplace that included all employees working directly or indirectly for Pikitup. In addition, SAMWU tried to sustain the relationship that it had built with organised workers of third-party contractors by maintaining their employment. When a contract between Pikitup and a service provider expired and a new company received the tender, SAMWU applied pressure to ensure that the new contractor provided trucks and tools and absorbed the employees that had been working for the old contractor in that particular area. SAMWU managed to reach a recognition agreement with some third-party contractors, where it established shop-steward structures that worked closely together with shop stewards in Pikitup.

The union also started to engage with Pikitup management. SAMWU's key demands were for Pikitup to take over all externalised workers on a permanent basis and to end corruption in the entity.[12] When negotiations deadlocked in the Local Labour Forum, workers embarked on a one-week go-slow on 1 April 2011 and a two-week protected strike on 7 April 2011. Pikitup management tried to interdict the strike through the Johannesburg Labour Court, but was not successful.[13] A broad majority of the workforce of Pikitup, which in 2010 consisted of about 2 800 employees (Pikitup 2010: 10), participated in the strike, as did employees of third-party contractors. An innovative feature of the Pikitup strike was that temporary and permanent workers went out on strike together. Solidarity of permanent and contract workers was necessary to ensure that the strike had an effect on the employer and therefore that SAMWU could exercise its workplace bargaining power.

During the strike no refuse collection took place, which put Pikitup's management as well as the City of Johannesburg under a great deal of pressure. Strikers closed down depots and halted waste collection with the effect that Johannesburg began to stink. That also put pressure on the JCC to say, 'Resolve this labour dispute because we want to walk in a clean city as we used to do'.[14]

During the strike, Pikitup workers increased the effect of the strike by 'trashing the street' – that is, emptying bins and strewing the rubbish in the streets – which in municipal strikes forms part of workers' repertoire of contention. Street trashing is a disruptive practice that serves different purposes. For workers in solid waste, it is seen as a means to 'undo the work we do' and therefore make visible the work they usually perform. It is also a means to turn the street as the workplace into a public site of contestation, thereby exercising logistical power. In addition, it demonstrates workers' determination and militancy in the conflict with the employer. At the same time, trashing increases the impact of the strike:

> [If] we were just marching, after that the next person that comes can't see anything; he won't recognize that there was something which was taking place. If it's clean there is no need for them to say that this strike should come to an end, but if it's not clean they will see the need of those people, that these people are important. [They will say:] Let us listen to them so then they must go and do their job.[15]

An important strategy leading to shifting the balance of power in favour of workers was SAMWU's ability to gain public recognition through discourse power. In entities like Pikitup, where the public is intensely affected by a strike, influencing public opinion plays an important role. Shop stewards had the impression that communities were sympathetic and in support of the workers' strike because the union was blowing the whistle on corruption in Pikitup. The process of contracting out and issuing tenders had fostered corruption in Pikitup. Although the Pikitup board initially denied that there was a problem with tenders and corruption, the managing director and all but one member of the board subsequently resigned (Pikitup 2011). The exposure of corruption added to the existing pressure on Pikitup and gave public legitimacy to the SAMWU strike. The union was also able to highlight the importance of accountability and public control.

The outcome of the strike was a victory for SAMWU, as the parties agreed to absorb contract workers involved in the core cleaning service (Pikitup 2011: 145).[16] As a result of the strike, Pikitup (2013) absorbed about 2 900 workers, increasing its total workforce to approximately 5 400.[17] Pikitup also agreed not to enter into new outsourced core cleaning services without embarking on a meaningful joint consensus-seeking process with SAMWU and to a forensic investigation into the allegations of corruption.[18]

To sum up, mobilising societal and logistical power provided Pikitup workers with an important additional resource that was crucial for the success of the strike. Municipal workers used logistical power to draw their struggle into the public arena and to increase its impact. SAMWU gained public support through framing its strike in terms of an anti-corruption struggle. Through this strategy workers' grievances were not confined to the workplace but extended their influence into society. The iGoli 2002 project had been framed by the JCC as an increase in public efficiency. In the Pikitup strike SAMWU exposed privatisation and 'tenderisation' as a source of corruption and self-enrichment.

Conclusion

Recent research among South African post office workers has shown how the established union failed to organise casual workers. Instead, casual workers developed their own organisation and, using a variety of disruptive tactics, were able to successfully transform temporary jobs into permanent employment (Dickinson 2015). By way of contrast, our study suggests that by deepening and extending traditional sources of power – structural, associational and institutional – through the use of logistical and societal power, it is possible to successfully challenge informalisation. In the second cycle – municipal workers' resistance to privatisation and iGoli 2002 – societal power was mobilised in order to challenge the shift to privatisation. In the Pikitup strike, SAMWU followed a strategy of inclusive solidarity in the workplace by organising and uniting a fragmented workforce. Although SAMWU was able to enhance the union's power resources, these new sources of power remained embryonic and fragile.

When fighting iGoli 2002, SAMWU was not able to uphold its strategy of inclusive solidarity and social movement unionism, because the union was torn between loyalty to its alliance partner and support for social movements that were contesting neoliberal policies. Today, SAMWU is similar to other unions in COSATU in that it is riven by internal conflicts in defining its relationship to the ruling party. Furthermore, the union has been weakened by allegations of corruption and a significant decline in worker control. Union officials and shop stewards, who were demanding financial accountability from the leadership, have been suspended or expelled from the union, including many from the Johannesburg region. Pikitup shop stewards have been in the forefront of demanding accountability from the national leadership and have been sidelined as a result.

The dilemma came to a head in December 2013, when COSATU's largest affiliate, the National Union of Metalworkers of South Africa, decided not to support the ANC in the April 2014 elections. Instead, it announced that it would be forming a United Front, where unions would move beyond organising around traditional workplace concerns to address community struggles as well. This initiative triggered a debate on how rank-and-file dynamism and democracy could be revived, how unity could be built across the formal–informal divide, and how worker unity could be built across political lines.

The tensions between these two forms of organisation – defender of vested interest and sword of justice – now exist deep inside SAMWU. At the time of writing (November 2016), the situation was fluid and difficult to predict. While it could be argued that open competition and debate within the union movement is desirable, what has become clear is that a very distinct culture of 'us' and 'them' has developed, whereby people are accepted as 'one of us' (a comrade or a veteran) on the basis of their commitment to the dominant faction in COSATU. Those who oppose become 'the enemy' or even 'counter-revolutionaries'. In other words, the margins of tolerance are low and can easily spill over into physical violence.

The developments over time illustrate the dilemma that labour is facing. Does it focus on defending its narrow interests through a strategy of exclusive solidarity or does it pursue its interests in ways that include those of other constituencies and movements from below – the union as a sword of justice? First, the different cycles of municipal workers' struggles against contract work in Johannesburg demonstrate that building inclusive solidarity is a contested process within unions. Second, as our analysis indicates, framing is a strategic capability that has been used successfully by SAMWU by linking workers' struggle to societal issues. Another key capability for building and maintaining associational power is related to the union's internal processes. The process of building solidarity is linked to the capacity of the union to arbitrate between conflicting demands within it. To maintain and build internal solidarity, 'deliberative vitality' is crucial: 'This processual nature of solidarity highlights the importance of participation in debates about union strategies. Internal solidarity is therefore a set of relationships, underpinned in important ways by the extent of deliberative vitality' (Lévesque and Murray 2010: 338).

Although SAMWU was able to strengthen its associational power in Johannesburg, the lack of accountability within the union has undermined these gains and has left the union significantly weakened. This indicates that trade unions are not able to consolidate their power without internal solidarity. Power resources are not enough; unions must be capable of using them. As Lévesque and Murray (2010: 346) conclude, 'Much experimentation, analysis, learning and research will be required, from both unionists and researchers, in order to elucidate the development of and interactions between these different union resources and capabilities and to match them to particular contexts and opportunities.' This relationship between power resources and strategic capabilities under varying conditions is the subject of our ongoing research.

Notes

1. On the one hand, workplace bargaining power was limited due to the existence of an industrial reserve army in the Bantustans. On the other hand, the municipal strike included strategic sectors such as electricity, sanitation and transport, giving structural power to workers. The JCC found it difficult to replace all striking workers due to the sheer number of workers involved as well as the skills required in particular jobs (LRC 1981: 82).
2. The Transport and General Workers Union, born out of the Durban strikes in 1973, was the main union in the municipal sector in Johannesburg at that time. Nonetheless, in 1986 it organised only one-tenth of the City's employees (Barchiesi 2011: 152).
3. NEDLAC is an institution of social dialogue, consisting of government, business, labour and community groupings on a national level consulting on economic, industrial relations and labour market policy with the aim of reaching consensus. It considers all proposed labour legislation before it is introduced in Parliament.
4. The GJMC was expected to generate 90 per cent of its revenue; the rest would come from national government.
5. The World Bank donated R20 million and the Department of Finance granted R550 million to help implement the process (*Business Report*, 10 October 1999; *Financial Mail*, 1 September 2000).
6. Interview, SAMWU national official, Cape Town, 9 November 2002. The interviews with SAMWU officials, shop stewards and third-party contract workers, conducted by Carmen Ludwig and Lawrence Ntuli, form part of a PhD project and a SAMWU research project.
7. Interview, SAMWU national official, Cape Town, 9 November 2012.
8. Interview, former SAMWU national office bearer, Mangaung, 8 August 2012 (together with Hilary Wainwright).
9. Interview, SAMWU national official, Cape Town, 9 November 2012.

10. The JCC, however, did not agree to a moratorium on the implementation of iGoli 2002 for the period of negotiations, which put SAMWU at a further disadvantage.
11. Focus group, Pikitup shop stewards, Johannesburg, 10 July 2013.
12. In addition, workers demanded a look at existing wage disparities in the department, thereby combining demands that benefited all employees (SAMWU press statement, 6 April 2011).
13. Pikitup Johannesburg (Pty) Ltd vs SAMWU, Judgement Labour Court Johannesburg, Case No 584/2011.
14. Interview, SAMWU regional official, Johannesburg, 1 October 2012.
15. Interview, Pikitup shop steward, Johannesburg, 24 February 2014.
16. To avoid Pikitup breaching its contracts with subcontractors, externalised workers were absorbed into Pikitup when their contracts expired. A concession SAMWU made was that the salaries of absorbed externalised workers started at R3 000 per month in June 2011 but were to be increased by July 2012 to the minimum wage level of R4 900. Contrary to SAMWU's demand for equalisation, a two-tier wage level still exists in Pikitup.
17. Although Pikitup started implementing the bargaining agreement and absorbing externalised workers in 2011, the process stalled in 2012 and about 500 former contract workers are still fighting to be absorbed by Pikitup. At the time of writing, SAMWU had taken the matter to the Labour Court.
18. The company hired auditors to investigate eleven of its contracts, worth nearly R366 million. The auditors' draft report found irregularities in all but one of them (*Times Live*, 7 August 2013).

References

Arbeitskreis Strategic Unionism. 2013. 'Jenaer Machtressourcenansatz 2.0'. In *Comeback der Gewerkschaften. Machtressourcen, innovative Praktiken, internationale Perspektiven*, edited by S. Schmalz and K. Dörre. Frankfurt and New York: Campus.

Barchiesi, F. 2007. 'Privatization and the Historical Trajectory of "Social Movement Unionism": A Case Study of Municipal Workers in Johannesburg, South Africa'. *International Labor and Working Class History* 71: 50–69.

———. 2011. *Precarious Liberation: Workers, the State, and Contested Social Citizenship in Postapartheid South Africa*. Pietermaritzburg: University of KwaZulu-Natal Press.

Barker, C., L. Cox, J. Krinsky and A.G. Nilsen (eds.). 2013. *Marxism and Social Movements*. Leiden and Boston: Brill.

Beall, J., O. Crankshaw and S. Parnell. 2002. *Uniting a Divided City: Governance and Social Exclusion in Johannesburg*. London and Sterling: Earthscan.

Buhlungu, S. 2010. *A Paradox of Victory: COSATU and the Democratic Transformation in South Africa*. Pietermaritzburg: University of KwaZulu-Natal Press.

Callinicos, L. 1987. *Working Life, Factories, Townships and Popular Culture on the Rand 1886–1940*. Johannesburg: Ravan Press.

Chun, J.J. 2009. *Organizing at the Margins: The Symbolic Politics of Labor in South Korea and the United States*. Ithaca, NY: Cornell University Press.

Dickinson, D. 2015. 'Fighting Their Own Battles: The Mabarete and the End of Labour Broking in the South African Post Office'. Society, Work and Development Institute Working Paper 2. Johannesburg: SWOP.

Dörre, K. 2010. 'Social Classes in the Process of Capitalist *Landnahme*: On the Relevance of Secondary Exploitation'. *Socialist Studies* 6(2): 43–74.

Dörre, K., H. Holst and O. Nachtwey. 2009. 'Organizing: A Strategic Option for Trade Union Renewal?' *International Journal of Action Research* 5(1): 33–67.

Flanders, A. 1970. *Management and Unions*. London: Faber.

GJMC (Greater Johannesburg Metropolitan Council. 1999. 'iGoli 2002: Making the City Work – It Cannot Be Business as Usual'. Johannesburg: GJMC.

Gordhan, K. 2000. 'Moving towards a Restructured Johannesburg'. 1 April.

Holst, H., O. Nachtwey and K. Dörre. 2009. *Funktionswandel von Leiharbeit. Neue Nutzungsstrategien und ihre arbeits- und mitbestimmungspolitischen Folgen*. Frankfurt am Main: OBS-Arbeitsheft 61.

Hyslop, J. 2004. *The Notorious Syndicalist: J.T. Bain – a Scottish Rebel in Colonial South Africa*. Johannesburg: Jacana.

Keenan, J. 1981. 'Migrants Awake: The 1980 Johannesburg Municipality Strike'. *South African Labour Bulletin* 6(7): 4–60.

Kelly, J. 1998. *Rethinking Industrial Relations: Mobilization, Collectivism and Long Waves*. London: Routledge.

Lévesque, C. and G. Murray. 2010. 'Understanding Union Power: Resources and Capabilities for Renewing Union Capacity'. *Transfer: European Review of Labour and Research* 16(3): 333–50.

———. 2013. 'Renewing Union Narrative Resources: How Union Capabilities Make a Difference'. *British Journal of Industrial Relations* 51(4): 777–96.

Lier, D.C. and K. Stokke. 2006. 'Maximum Working Class Unity? Challenges to Local Social Movement Unionism in Cape Town'. *Antipode* 38: 802–24.

LRC (Labour Research Committee). 1981. 'State Strategy and the Johannesburg Municipal Workers Strike'. *South African Labour Bulletin* 6(7): 61–86.

McKinley, D.T. 2014. 'Labour and Community in Transition: Alliances for Public Services in South Africa'. Municipal Services Project Occasional Paper No. 24. Johannesburg: Municipal Services Project.

Musi, M.M. 2010. 'Evaluating IMATU and SAMWU Policy Responses to iGoli 2002'. Master's dissertation, University of the Witwatersrand, Johannesburg.

Ngwane, T. 2012. 'Labour Strikes and Community Protests: Is There a Basis for Unity in Post-apartheid South Africa?' In *Contesting Transformation: Popular Resistance in Twenty-first Century South Africa*, edited by M.C. Dawson and L. Sinwell. London: Pluto.

Pikitup. 2010. 'Annual Report 2009/10'. Johannesburg.

———. 2011. 'Annual Report 2010/11'. Johannesburg.
———. 2013. 'Annual Report 2012/13'. Johannesburg.
Samson, M. 2003. 'Dumping on Women: Gender and Privatisation of Waste Management'. http://www.gdrc.info/docs/waste/005.pdf (accessed 12 September 2014).
———. 2004. 'Organizing in the Informal Economy: A Case Study of the Municipal Waste Management Industry in South Africa'. Geneva: International Labour Office.
———. 2008. 'Rescaling the State, Restructuring Social Relations'. *International Feminist Journal of Politics* 10(1): 19–39.
SAMWU (South African Municipal Workers Union). 1991. 'Privatisation'. Resolution adopted at SAMWU 3rd National Congress.
———. 2012. 'Secretariat Report'. 10th National Congress, Book 2.
Silver, B. 2003. *Forces of Labor: Workers' Movements and Globalization since 1870*. Cambridge: Cambridge University Press.
Tarrow, S.G. 2011. *Power in Movement: Social Movements and Contentious Politics*. 3rd ed. Cambridge: Cambridge University Press.
Theron, J. 2005. 'Intermediary or Employer? Labour Brokers and the Triangular Employment Relationship'. *Industrial Law Journal* 26: 618–49.
Van Driel, M. 2003. 'Unions and Privatisation in South Africa, 1990–2001'. In *Rethinking the Labour Movement in the 'New South Africa'*, edited by T. Bramble and F. Barchiesi. Aldershot: Ashgate.
Van Niekerk, S. and R. Ronnie. 2009. 'The SAMWU Experience'. In *New Forms of Organisation*, edited by V. Cornell. Papers from the Annual ILRIG - Rosa Luxemburg Cape Partners Conference 2009. Cape Town: RLS.
Von Holdt, K. and E. Webster. 2008. 'Organising on the Periphery: New Sources of Power in the South African Workplace'. *Employee Relations* 30(4): 333–54.
Wainwright, H. 2012. 'Transformative Resistance: The Role of Labour and Trade Unions in Alternatives to Privatisation'. In *Alternatives to Privatisation: Public Options for Essential Services in the Global South*, edited by D.A. McDonald and G. Ruiters. Cape Town: HSRC Press.
Webster, E. 1988. 'The Rise of Social Movement Unionism: The Two Faces of the Black Trade Union Movement'. In *State, Resistance and Change in South Africa*, edited by P. Franke, N. Pines and M. Swilling. London: Croom Helm.
Webster, E., A. Benya, X. Dilata, K. Joynt, K. Ngoepe and M. Tsoeu. 2008. 'Making Visible the Invisible: Confronting South Africa's Decent Work Deficit'. Research report for the Department of Labour, Johannesburg.
Webster, E., R. Lambert and A. Bezuidenhout. 2008. *Grounding Globalization: Labour in the Age of Insecurity*. Oxford: Blackwell.
Wright, E.O. 2000. 'Working-Class Power, Capitalist-Class Interests, and Class Compromise'. *American Journal of Sociology* 105(4): 957–1002.

9

Dickensian England in Twenty-first-century Delhi – Without Great Expectations

Informal Labour Organising in the Manufacturing Sector

Mouleshri Vyas

Informalisation of the manufacturing process, strikingly evident in present times across various industries in India, makes labour pay the heaviest price. Micro, small and medium enterprises in India contribute nearly 8 per cent of the country's gross domestic product (GDP), 45 per cent of manufacturing output and 40 per cent of exports. They provide the largest share of employment after agriculture.[1] However, the state of labour in unregulated manufacturing units is deplorable. These workplaces are registered under the Factories Act of 1948 and hence bound by rules governing work, working conditions and social security for the labourers. However, the nature of the state machinery that largely responds sporadically and selectively to labour-related grievances adds to the overall indifference and low importance accorded to informal labour in the country. The flexible labour market has resulted in a swelling of the ranks of informal workers in formal factory set-ups.

Mobilising and organising these workers is an arduous task. Yet there are individuals who are building collectives to activate workers' agency. These efforts need to be studied in order to draw lessons for further action. The diversity of the informal economy and the sheer number of workers involved mean that a contextual understanding of the nature of particular work and the issues with which labour is confronted is a necessary backdrop against which collectivising must be studied and appreciated.

This chapter details the manufacturing process in the steel utensil manufacturing industry located in the Wazirpur Industrial Area (WIA)[2] of the National Capital Region (NCR) of India – that is, Delhi – and discusses the condition of workers, their problems and the challenges of organising them. The Garam Rolla Mazdoor Ekta Samiti (GRMES), a recently formed collective of workers in this industry, is attempting to take up and seek redress for the problems of the workers. As the collective's strategies are still evolving, it would be premature to predict the group's likely future or to assess its level of success. Instead this chapter highlights the struggles of a labour organisation at the initial stage; the study reported on here underscores the fact that the WIA, with its tough physical and social conditions, as well as the extremely difficult nature of work and poor working conditions in unregulated workspaces, poses an immense challenge to any initiative aimed at collectivising labour. GRMES is going through a challenging phase, and it is unclear whether it will emerge stronger or weaker as a workers' organisation.

GRMES activists facilitated access into the WIA for me and a research assistant. While intermittent conversations with the leader of GRMES spanned a period of several months, interviews with workers were conducted over a period of two months in 2013. Primary data about work and lives in the utensil manufacturing industry was obtained through individual and group interviews, while the community profile was prepared through discussions with key informants. During the course of the study, the research assistant supported the ongoing work of GRMES; we were able to lend some support to a strike launched by them. We introduced GRMES to the New Trade Union Initiative (NTUI), a federation of several hundred worker organisations in the informal economy from across the country; it is a relationship that is developing. At the time of writing (March 2015), information about the collective was updated.

The chapter begins with a description of the WIA, which provides a physical context for the work and lives of those labouring in the utensil manufacturing industry. The second section outlines the nature of the manufacturing process; section three details the profile of some of the workers; and the last section examines the challenges of organising this section of the informal workforce.

Wazirpur Industrial Area

Time stands still in the WIA. After several decades of urban development, little seems to have changed in the area – at least not for the better. The following description of the WIA, written in the late 1980s, could have been written yesterday:

> The imposing roadside mansions, including a luxury restaurant, on the stretch of Delhi's ever-busy Ring Road around the Shalimar Bagh bus stop give the impression of prosperity. Turn to the road towards the railway crossing and you will see shop after shop of glittering steel utensils. This is Wazirpur, a big centre of steel utensil manufacture. Move into one of the roadside lanes, however, and you will come face-to-face with the stark reality of a huge, sprawling industrial slum.
>
> Here there are huge piles of iron and steel scrap (or scrap-like sheets) and cart-pullers carrying these sheets on their ramshackle carts. And there are the sheds where these sheets undergo numerous industrial processes before emerging as the glittering steel utensils that decorate the shops. There are children with their bodies and faces blackened in the process of polishing the utensils. Women inhale toxic fumes as they work with acidic solutions. And if it is one of those bad days which are becoming quite frequent, one may also see a profusely bleeding worker, the victim of an industrial accident, being rushed to one of the medical shops that pass as nursing homes (Dogra 1989: 1801).

The history of the area can be constructed through secondary sources and the narratives of some residents. The WIA, a hub of small industries, is one of 32 industrial areas in the region and is located in the north of the Delhi NCR (see Figure 9.1). It was developed in 1966 under the second master plan for Delhi and is spread over an area of 210 acres. Although the WIA was initially designed for the plastics, hosiery and electronics industries, today steel utensil manufacturing units overwhelmingly dominate the area. Other industries such as wool dyeing and copper wire

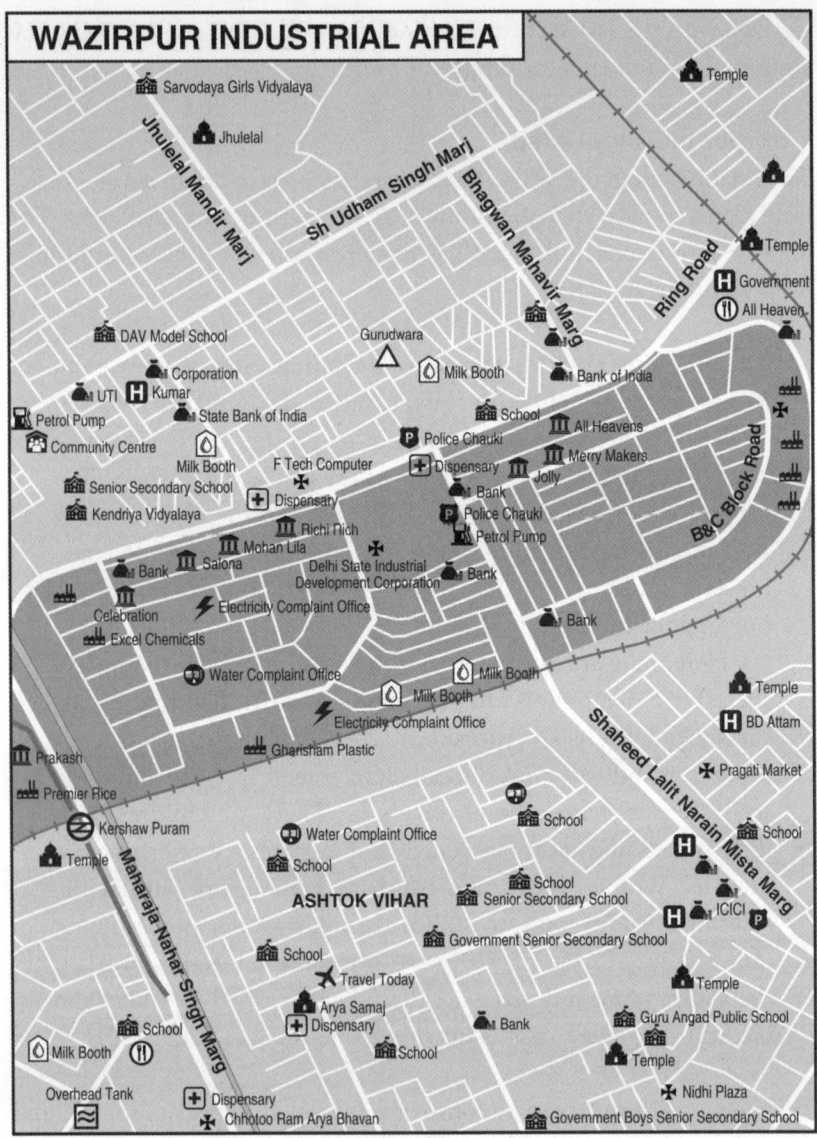

Figure 9.1 Wazirpur Industrial Area
Source: http://www.mapsofindia.com/delhi/wazirpur-industrial-area.html#.

drawing have also sprung up. In 2001, there were about 2 000 factory units in total, although 80 per cent of them were nameless, existing only as plot numbers. Barely 20 per cent were registered. These ghost units thrive on the most vulnerable migrant labourers, mostly from the very poor areas of northern India. The units are generally small and the owner also acts as the manager. Sometimes a single building houses eight to twelve units. About 60 000 workers labour in these factories, either living within the factory premises or as squatters within the WIA (Singh 2001: 1944). Maintaining such areas as a 'degenerated periphery' serves the interests of capitalists (Kundu 2003: 3530).

Residents recount the trajectory of growth and significant changes that have taken place in the WIA. Anand, the leader of GRMES, points out that much of the present labour force in the area comes from the families that settled here in the 1970s when the factories were being set up and was augmented by later migrants. When owners of industrial plots sold some portions of their property, the size of the industrial units was reduced; this fragmentation of plots resulted in an increase in the number of industries in the area. During the riots of 1984, in which Sikhs were targeted, some of the owners migrated to other places in Delhi and some abandoned their units completely. After this phase the industries in the WIA saw new ownership and a shift from hosiery making to steel utensil manufacturing.

Yakub, who has lived in the WIA for 30 years, adds that when steel utensil manufacturing came to this area, many workers who found it difficult to work in the new industry moved away; trained workers from other parts of the country came to work in their place. Those who were trained workers or machine operators (*karigar*) in hosiery manufacturing and decided to stay on in the area were demoted and became helpers in the new industry. For some workers, the decision about moving out of the area was linked to the status of their housing. Those who had purchased and settled down in small shanties in Wazirpur stayed and adjusted to the change or searched for work in other industrial areas. Those who had no base in Delhi travelled where the hosiery manufacturing industry took them.

It was only in the late 1980s that the situation improved for the WIA as an area of residence. More secure shelters were constructed, although the inadequacy of sanitation facilities persists even today. About the year 2000, the study circle started by Anand triggered a positive change in people's attitude to their children's education. In 2007, one of the residents of the area was elected to the municipal corporation; with his election, the harassment of local shopkeepers by the authorities stopped.

Today the WIA is known for the manufacture of stainless steel utensils. According to Anand, of the area's 1 000 small factory units, some 600 to 650 manufacture steel utensils. Each unit has at least 40 to 50 workers, but in some units there are more than 100 workers. Over a hundred units do syringe moulding and plastic-related work, while others engage in chain making, hosiery manufacturing, or work for hotels, restaurants and car showrooms. Most of the labourers are migrants from various states in the country. Outside of manufacturing work, men in the area are employed as security guards, drivers, rickshaw pullers, handcart pullers and headloaders.

Most of the workers are tenants here and share a room and the rent of about INR1 500-2 000 per month. Water and electricity facilities are available, but sanitation and solid waste management facilities are inadequate, resulting in water overflowing into the streets. Health conditions of workers are poor because of twelve-hour working days, congested surroundings, a polluted environment and lack of health facilities. Two or three major and eight to ten minor accidents occur each day, and four or five workers die every year due to accidents. The impact of the work and the surroundings on the health of the workers has also been detailed by Richa Singh (2001), who paints a bleak picture.

The steel utensil manufacturing process: Decent work?

As one walks through the pocket of the WIA where the steel manufacturing units are concentrated, it is possible to spot the beginning and end of the manufacturing process. Steel slabs are wheeled into the area on wooden carts that are pushed by men; finished utensils are visible in semi-open spaces, being packed and readied for sending out of the area. All the stages of the process take place inside small factory-like units that are poorly lit and unpainted, and may have one to five visible workers operating the machines or standing near the furnace. Their faces are blackened by dust and heat, and they wear an apron for protection from the machinery. The utensil manufacturing process includes grinding, hot and cold rolling, squeezing, cooling, acid circle cutting, pressing, polishing, packaging, and transporting via handcarts to the market. Hot rolling and cold rolling are the most risky phases of the process, and can result in fatal injuries. A brief outline of this part of the manufacturing process is indicative of the underlying risks.

Hot and cold rolling are key steps in the manufacturing process. A steel sheet 10 inches wide is converted into a 70-inch sheet after being pressed in a hot rolling machine. After the hot rolling, the sheet goes through cold rolling. The cold rolling process is even more hazardous because the steel becomes brittle in the lower temperature and the worker may be injured if the sheet breaks while it passes through the rollers. Hot rolling machines operate day and night without a break because of the high cost of increasing the temperature in the furnace; restarting the machine after cooling would add to the cost. Hence the workers in the hot rolling unit are forced to work overtime to prevent losses and wage cuts. In cold rolling, on a hot furnace powered by gas, two helpers work a six-hour shift each. The helpers rest for half an hour and then do a second shift of six hours. They are paid less than the machine operators. In cold rolling, machine *mistris* (mechanics) work four-hour shifts. They have a choice of whether or not to do overtime, and the factory does not necessarily work without a break. The helpers in cold and hot rolling have similar jobs and they keep standing through the day, but hot rolling is more difficult as workers must complete twelve-hour shifts. Helpers earn about INR8 500 per month, and furnace operators about INR9 000. In cold as well as hot rolling the workers age prematurely; after reaching the peak of his career when he is about 45 years old, a roller machine operator (with a monthly salary of INR10 000) gets demoted to the level of a helper as he no longer has the strength to do heavy work. The resultant lower salary impacts on his family at a time when the worker's children are either striving for higher education or thinking of getting married. This is the scenario for most workers who work beyond 20 or 25 years in this industry.

The next section profiles the lives of nine workers interviewed for this study.

Aspects of workers' lives

Interviews revealed that most of the workers in the area migrated to the city. The women came to Delhi with their parents or husbands. Lack of livelihoods in the villages, as well as the ineffectiveness of the National Rural Employment Guarantee Scheme, emerged as factors that prompted migration.

Some of the migrants found jobs in the utensil manufacturing industry through a friend from the village or a distant relative. In one instance, an uncle was a contractor in a polishing unit and brought his nephew into this work. He provided him with food and a place to stay (at the workplace) for an initial period of five months. In some instances, people found work for themselves. It emerges that in certain units a worker who started as a helper could learn specific skills on the job and move to the next level as a *mistri*. At least two of the women talked about the utensil factories as safe places for women to work. Shobha gave up waste picking to work at the factory, as it 'was not considered good' for a woman to be out on the streets picking up scrap. The ready availability of metal scrap in the area seems to have brought children and adults into waste picking to augment the family income. Zubeda indicated that her husband was suspicious of her whereabouts; however, he approved of the workplace where she sits with other women to apply chalk to the utensils.

All stages of the manufacturing process are fraught with risk for the worker. Aniket, who works at sheet cutting, pointed out the absence of safety gear. Mahesh said that acid spraying results in stomach ailments; he finds that his stomach is bloated every evening. However, workers do not absent themselves from work for long even if they are injured, as they fear losing their jobs. Yasin, who works at the polishing unit, said that his hands and palms were swollen; however, he is not complaining as he knows he is not alone in this. Shobha, who works at a polishing unit, said that polishers' hands get cut from the sharp edges of the uncut utensils.

There is a social division of work: women do not work at machines. Shobha was reprimanded when she once tried to operate a machine. Zubeda narrated an incident of sexual harassment at her workplace, where a man made a video of one of the women while she was working and circulated it among other workers, including her son. The woman was asked to stay at home and not allowed to go to work. After a month, economic necessity prevailed and she was allowed to go back to work. Preeti, who works at the packaging unit, was the only interviewed worker who said that the workplace is safe, as is the work. The highest risk seems to be at the rolling machines, where a sheet being put into a furnace can slide back rapidly and cut the worker in the abdomen. Physical and social risks seem to be commonplace in this industry; for the women, it is more the latter that they have to deal with on an everyday basis.

Wages vary with the nature of work, the working hours, and the weight and size of the utensils. One of the workers said there is 'no concept of minimum wages' as the market rate for steel determines the processing charges for the utensils. Most workers across units have twelve-hour working days. In the hot rolling units, workers take turns at the machine in order to cool off. So they spend some hours away from the machine, which are counted as working hours. At the polishing unit, Shobha receives INR3 000 per month for her twelve-hour shifts throughout the period; Ashima, at utensil packing, is paid INR4 000 per month. She has to use a pay-and-use public toilet as there is no facility provided for women at the workplace. Preeti, at the packaging unit, works from ten in the morning until nine at night. Her lunch break is not counted as part of her working hours. Her monthly salary is INR4 000; with payment for overtime work, she takes home INR7 000. She is aware of the minimum wage issue, and has participated in a strike for a wage hike at the factory. Triloki, who claims to have not received minimum wages his entire working life, pointed out that 'the condition of the labour can be assessed from the fact that a majority of them have continued working at a constant wage rate for over a decade'.

Living arrangements are organised with a certain logic. Yasin said:

> Mostly people from one village or type of work stay together. In many quarters around my shanty, people working in the factory in one shift stay together. Sometimes workers of night and day shifts stay together so that the work of cooking and fetching rations can be divided easily . . . I do not think finding a place to live in Wazirpur is difficult as only labourers like us live in this area, with or without the family.

In fact, for a family it may be difficult to pay the monthly rent of about INR1 500, and Zubeda indicated that she may have to return to her village with her children if things do not improve financially for them.

Ashima's husband drinks, but she explains:

> He never abuses us and he also works at home. I tell him to behave himself as it is very difficult to find living space in Delhi, and if we are thrown out it will be difficult to find a safe place

like this. We found a place in the inside street as we have two daughters, and also the houses around us accommodate families only; the houses where only men labourers live alone are a little farther away. Our street is also more hidden than other areas, so it is good. You may find it strange, but these things have to be thought about before taking a house. We never changed our house from here despite problems of water and electricity.

Ashima's family use a public toilet, and the females make sure that they go to use it before dawn as the walls of the toilets are broken. During the day they only access the toilet as a group because men are known to peep through the broken walls. Ashima's house has a bare look; the family stay in one room on the first floor and have to put up with roof leaks in the monsoons. The family members use a corner of their room to bathe.

Health problems for workers emanate from the nature of their work. Aniket had fallen ill due to the dust from steel cutting. Both he and Yasin said that they prefer to visit a private hospital in times of ill health. Aniket takes loans from friends when he needs to; this is how friends help each other. Ashima is not aware of social security as an entitlement. She questioned why women should get Employees' State Insurance (ESI) when their work is not hazardous. She too takes medicines from private medical practitioners. She thinks that unions can be of help in addressing harsh problems; but for routine issues, only the government can help. Preeti, who is more aware of entitlements than others, has demanded ESI from her employer. She gets a widow's pension of INR4 500 every quarter, and she uses her father's ration card to get provisions.

Future aspirations of the workers are clearly articulated. Mahesh hopes for less hazardous work with more stability. He finds that it is more difficult to settle down in Delhi now, as the government is harsher. Mohanlal had bought a *jhuggi* (mud and corrugated iron house) several months earlier, at a cost of INR100 000. Shobha does not see herself doing this work for long; she does not like it, and thinks that an office job would be more respectable. Male co-workers joke that the women are cleaning utensils at work too, just as they do at home. However, Shobha says that at work her task is part of the production process, but when she does the same activity at home, it is not even recognised as work. Ashima hopes that her daughters will get married sooner rather than later, as the kind of education that she and her husband are able to give them will not enable them to get good work. Once they are married, they can work in a factory if their respective husbands want them to, but she is not going to send her daughters to the factory. Preeti would like to join and work with a union, although not at present as she does not have time. Once her daughters grow up, she would be able to. Triloki, who has worked in the area longer than all of the other interviewees, is satisfied that he has done well for his family. He purchased a 25-square-yard plot in Shalimar Bagh in the city on which he has constructed a house, where he lives with his wife and four children. He also got a flat from the government as part of resettlement in another industrial area in lieu of a shanty he owned there.

Labour organising

The challenges to labour organising in the WIA could be categorised as union/collective-related and sociological in nature. The pattern of migrant workers settling in the area, and their interactions and relations, influence the potential for organising. In any case, the struggle is an arduous one:

> Alarming as the working conditions are, it is extremely difficult to organise the workers for the redress of the manifold problems and injustices . . . In the absence of any initiative from the labour department or any other government agency to help them, the odds are heavily against the workers in any struggle to assert their rights. Past experience tells them that they can expect hardly any help from the labour officials and the police will almost certainly side with the factory owners (Dogra 1989: 1802).

This assessment of the late 1980s holds true today, a fact that is reaffirmed by the struggle of GRMES and others in the WIA.

Wazirpur has seen trade union initiatives in the past. Brijwasi recalls that when a worker's hand was injured, the factory owners, instead of assisting with proper treatment, asked the worker to urinate on it in order to disinfect it. Sukhdev Laal, 38, the main machine operator in a hot rolling unit, said that he was injured while at the machine. When the owner helped with emergency medical treatment and gave him leave, he thought that he had a considerate employer, only to realise on his return to work that his wages for the days of absence and the cost of treatment had been deducted from his salary. He decided to join GRMES.

Such experiences led to a major strike in Wazirpur in 1983-4 by all sections of workers (including the steel line, rickshaw pullers and others), demanding the ESI benefit, sick leave, bonus payments, salary hikes and weekly holidays for all the workers. Subsequently, there were other similar initiatives, but they led to mixed results: demands for wages and better working conditions were agreed to by the factory owners, but further struggles by the workers were necessary to get the agreements implemented. Even then, the key issues of wages, work conditions and social security remained unsettled. Today GRMES, under the leadership of Anand, represents one of the collective efforts of workers in the area. Mobilisation of workers has evidently increased, with calls for strikes and rallies showing the numbers. However, resolution of the issues is still some way ahead, as is the process of building a strong collective.

GRMES is a group of workers that is not yet registered as a trade union although it is moving in that direction. The collective does not have a formal organisational structure. In 2013-14 GRMES had a president and vice president, nominated from among the workers of hot rolling units, with Anand as the collective's leader. The group holds meetings on the last Wednesday of every month to discuss issues of membership, minimum wages, ESI benefits and retrenchment of labour. The workers at the meeting also review the activities of the current month and plan for the next month's work. There are several students associated with the collective; they are able to help considerably with the paperwork. Recently GRMES has been focusing on a membership drive and has expanded its scope to include workers beyond the hot rolling units. Anand thinks that it is not a good time to register GRMES as a union, as there are too many factions among workers in the area. However, one of the gaps in the GRMES strategy is perhaps the fact that it is led by an individual. No capacity building of the union members has been done by engaging them on issues of labour rights, which appears to have been done by two other unions through street-corner meetings on Wednesdays and the distribution of information pamphlets.

GRMES also does not appear to have a consistently sustained activity, except for handling regular cases of retrenchment of labourers from different hot rolling units as and when they come up. Anand is seen by the workers as a local activist who is vocal and fearless in approaching the factory owners or their accountants with regard to various issues. In a few cases where labourers were dismissed because of underperformance or damage to the machinery, he has been able to negotiate with the factory owners to give workers another chance. However, in cases where the workers have been retrenched due to falling production and overstaffing (as a cost-cutting strategy), the chance of getting them back their jobs seems low because there is no sustained strategy of the collective.

GRMES has found it has not been able to collaborate with unions in the area. Wazirpur has two other active unions, which are seen by Anand as his rivals. He regards their strategies and ways of functioning as very confrontational and thinks they would not work in favour of labour. He offered an example: In May–June 2014, when the hot rolling workers went on strike to demand minimum wages and eight-hour shifts instead of the existing twelve-hour shifts, about 70 to 80 workers from different factories who were at the forefront of the movement were fired. Later, when the strike ended and the factory owners agreed to the demand of eight-hour shifts, these workers were not reinstated. Anand asked them to accompany him to meet with these factory owners for negotiation. In the meantime, in a parallel move, the fired workers had been contacted by one of the rival unions to file a case against their removal in the deputy labour commissioner's court. These workers (some of whom were active members of GRMES) later went on to register as a formal union. Anand says that in the GRMES-led strike, the rival union had given some support and assisted in organising the workers on a day-to-day basis, but in this process created a rift among the workers. Anand therefore refused to join that union when he was invited to do so, as he thought that it would not be not in the interest of the workers. He finds that the union's strategy of addressing issues through litigation is not appropriate as the workers do not have any way to stake a claim on their jobs. He also says that the decision for an eight-hour work shift was implemented in the factories for only fifteen days, as the factory owners sensed that there were factions among the workers; according to Anand, the rival union is to blame for this. The fired workers have still not been reinstated in their jobs, and their cases are yet to be decided in the labour court. They were forced to find petty jobs such as rickshaw pulling in the WIA. Meanwhile the rival union has continued its membership drive.

Notwithstanding this experience, Anand said that there is some scope to work with other unions on specific issues. It is an uneven experience – at times positive and at times otherwise. GRMES also gets assistance from federations of organisations working with the urban poor in Delhi.

For the past few years, the GRMES strategy for getting minimum wages for workers involved building pressure on the factory owners by going on strike. Anand thinks that this strategy will have to be changed as the morale of the workers is low because the implementation of an eight-hour work shift did not last long. The months of May and June were perfect for organising a strike as it is difficult for the workers to work in the rolling units in the extremely hot weather. But the steel product market was already down. Low market demand and low production in factories favour the factory owners as such conditions will justify a decision to retrench workers if a strike is called in summer.

Anand asserted that one of the biggest challenges they face is with regard to proving that specific workers have been working at a particular factory for a certain period of time. This is so because the factory owners do not issue a letter of appointment or an identity card to the workers; GRMES therefore finds it difficult to build a case with the labour department and argue for the workers. It is difficult even to prove that workers put in twelve hours of work a day. There are also differences in the key concerns of workers in different factories; hence building common opinion across the workers is a huge task. Due to the steady movement of workers between the city and the village, there are changes in the factories as workplaces and in their workforces, which makes it a challenge to keep records of workers' hours and other issues.

While there is member involvement in decision-making in GRMES, this appears to be constrained by its informal nature and by the fact that there is one individual who has initiated the collective, and a formal decision-making structure has not yet been put in place. Collective assessment of situations and strategy building could perhaps address concerns about the trough that the movement is going through. Given the size of the workforce in the area, there seems to be ample scope for multiple unions or coordinated functioning. As a context for labour organising, the tenuous work conditions, patterns of migration and nature of social networks make the challenge more nuanced for organising from within the area. To discuss the organising process without examining the sociological context would be an oversimplification. Some of these contextualising factors are highlighted in the following paragraphs. They are drawn from the interviews, and could be viewed as impressions of communities by 'others'.

The issues related to surviving in the city have shaped the priorities of workers. The profile of the WIA outlined earlier could be that of any semi-regulated industrial area and informal settlement in any large city in the country. There are several issues related to living conditions of this population that need to be addressed, and which probably consume considerable energy and resources of the workers. Jagan, a 60-year-old worker, pointed out that in his initial years here, workers needed to have basic documents and proofs of residence in the city in order to access other entitlements. Hence the workers sided with the political leaders who could facilitate this process for them, rather than with the union activists. He went on to say:

> Now that my sons are secure with voter identity card, ration card and a house, they can wage a struggle for their rights as workers ... I am able to differentiate between these things today ... when I was young I could not really see these two things – worker (*mazdoor*) and citizen (*nagrik*) separately.

The fragmentation of labour affects workers' connection with each other. The Babbage principle, related to division of labour in industrial settings, holds true in this industry. It states:

> In so far as the labour process may be dissociated, it may be separated into elements, some of which are simpler than others and each of which is simpler than the whole. Translated into market terms, this means that the labor power capable of performing the process may be purchased more cheaply as dissociated elements than as a capacity integrated in a single worker (Braverman 1974: 57).

The labour process in the utensil manufacturing industry, outlined earlier, fragments the workplace and the workers, making the task of forging a collective identity extremely challenging.

The sense of community along regional lines and work categories affects the potential for bonding among workers. The strong regional aspect to workers' sense of community and identity, and the caste to which they belong, are likely to have led to conditions of distress in their villages, and hence encouraged migration to the city. Migrants from particular regions may also be found predominantly in certain types of work. For example, the Mahobias come from the Mahoba district in the Bundelkhand region of Uttar Pradesh; they are engaged in construction work. Some workers think that the Mahobia people have not changed much with time; they still sport the same attire which signifies them to be Mahobia, and the entire family works as construction labourers. The Bundelkhand region is directly connected by train to Delhi, facilitating migration to this city. The women from this community are helpers in construction work with their husbands, and are also domestic workers; most of the men also prefer to work as security guards. The scheduled castes (the term used for historically disadvantaged castes that are listed in the first schedule of the Indian Constitution) in Bundelkhand villages were more oppressed and they were the ones more likely to migrate. In fact, those who have done well are still oppressed when they go back to their villages. However, it is now likely that even upper-caste people come to the city to work due to fragmentation of land among big families and the need to earn extra for sustenance. As another example, migrants from Jharkhand mostly work as rickshaw pullers and factory workers. They are relatively more educated than Mahobia or Bundelkhandi people and migrated in order to escape abject poverty in the villages. Satisfied with being able to feed themselves and their families in the city, they are not motivated to join protests and unions. Lastly, many of the supervisors are from Haryana. They consider the job of a supervisor more dignified than that of a worker who operates the machines. Interestingly, however, when they feel extra pressure from the owners, they become sympathetic towards the workers and also seek support from the labour unions.

While workers survive with support of these networks, community and identity also create fault lines across sections of workers that need to be bridged in order to build class consciousness. Circles of interaction and familiarity are important in this regard. Birbal Yadav says that many of the factory workers do not know other workers doing the same work in similar factories within the industrial area. Their social circle is limited to the people with whom they work or stay. Beyond that, the workers only know each other if they pray or worship together.

Seasonal migration has a bearing on the supply of labour at different times of the year. Most of the Mahobias own land in their villages, and they return there to live from October to March. Many workers stay in Delhi only in the summer; during that time not many festivals are celebrated that require people to come together. For important festivals such as Chhaat Puja or Diwali, workers prefer to go home. Around March, when workers return to the city, there is surplus labour, which may result in replacement of workers who are seen as troublemakers. In this way, the seasonal migration and its scale pose challenges to labour organising.

Bonds among workers are formed through various activities. Workers from Jharkhand stay together in close-knit groups as do other workers, but they stand out as they survive in minimal conditions and without their families so that they can save most of their earnings. Mahobias spend money on gambling and also take loans from each other to gamble. The Dalit workers from Jharkhand may not have an ESI card or even make the effort to obtain one, but when it comes to Hindu rituals they spend thousands of rupees. One can see workers bonding over card games on the street corners on Wednesday, which is a weekly day off; they interact with each other only for a short time and then return to their more regular circles. Mostly the groups of workers who come together to play cards are not friends but strategic partners who sit together for a game and sometimes even gamble for money, a pack of tobacco, a bottle of liquor or a non-vegetarian dinner. Some people such as labour contractors give loans to workers to gamble. After a game, fights sometimes break out on the streets, so card playing results in rivalries as well as bonding.

Because women are engaged in types of work that are not machine-related, they seem to be at the fringes of the manufacturing process and of collectivising. As yet, there is no concerted thought about involving them in the worker collective. One GRMES member said:

> We have women workers as well working in the factory but I have no idea about how women can have a union . . . Once we are able to fight . . . the benefits will trickle down to them as well. Why should we put them through the pain of fighting outside the

house? It is enough that they are able to come out and work and also look after their families.

Vinay, another worker, stated:

> The industrial work is such that in the past many years technology has made day-to-day things easier for people, but the technology in the utensil factory has not been worker friendly. It has put more pressure on the worker. Every change in technology has put pressure on workers to work with more speed and of course more strength, and women have not been able to cope with this.

The foregoing discussion underscores the fact that informal labour organising is a mammoth task. Union building in this sector is likely to go through many highs and lows before it stabilises. For an initiative such as GRMES, lack of financial support and resources makes this an uphill and frustrating task. A successful way forward depends on the collective's ability to build strong alliances with union federations and to enhance its resource base so that organising can be systematically approached.

Conclusion

Recent labour reforms in India are aimed at reducing the bureaucratic obstacles for owners and investors and streamlining the regulation and monitoring of industries, and have 'little to do with the real concerns of the working class or with protecting the interests of labour in the country' (*Frontline* 2014: n.p.). In this environment, the issues around precarious work and working conditions are likely to be pushed further to the periphery. That the WIA, one of hundreds of such manufacturing hubs in cities across India, continues to be characterised by extremely labour-unfriendly conditions highlights the need for central trade unions and federations in the informal sector to respond substantively and with urgency.

Notes

1. Government of India, Ministry of Micro, Small and Medium Enterprises. http://msme.gov.in/Web/Portal/New-Default.aspx (accessed 17 December 2014).

2. Planned industrial areas such as the WIA are developed and serviced with basic infrastructure through state support to help them grow into hubs of manufacturing and industry.

References

Braverman, H. 1974. *Labor and Monopoly Capital*. New York: Monthly Review Press.

Dogra, B. 1989. 'Laws Ignored.' *Economic and Political Weekly* 24(32): 1801–2. http://www.jstor.org/stable/4395189 (accessed 27 November 2014).

Frontline. 2014. 'Labour under Attack'. 14 November. http://www.frontline.in/cover-story/labour-under-attack/article6540729.ece (accessed 12 January 2015).

Kundu, A. 2003. 'Politics and Economics of Land Policies: Delhi's New Master Plan'. *Economic and Political Weekly* 38(34): 3530–2. http://www.jstor.org/stable/4413928 (accessed 25 November 2014).

Singh, R. 2001. 'Masculine Identity, Workers and HIV/AIDS'. *Economic and Political Weekly* 36(22): 1944–7. http://www.jstor.org/stable/4410686 (accessed 27 November 2014).

10

Organising Vulnerable Home-based Workers in India

Indira Gartenberg

India is the second most populous country in the world, with 1.2 billion inhabitants. Numbering 586 million, women constitute nearly half of its population (Census of India 2011).[1] Of the country's total workforce, a staggering 92 per cent represent men and women working within the informal economy (NCEUS 2007: 1). These workers lack any recognition or protection under national or international law, often work on the margins, do not have any social security benefits or safety net, and are typically not organised in trade unions or similar membership-based associations. Their 'informal' status facilitates – and is often instrumental in reinforcing – their vulnerability as workers and citizens. Social stratification in India based on gender, religion, region, caste and class causes further complexity. Presenting a global picture of women in the informal sector, Martha Chen (2001: 72) states: 'In India . . . the informal sector accounts for nine out of every ten women working outside agriculture.' Because women are an integral part of the informal economy in general, and constitute a large proportion of the urban poor in particular, a discussion on the ways in which informality and vulnerability affects them is significant and timely. Just as important are their coping mechanisms in the face of such vulnerability.

There are a number of scholarly discussions on women's conditions and exploitation in the informal economy. They point to the glaring disparities in men's and women's earnings, as well as female workers' poor health and nutrition, dismal working conditions, lack of social security, and their exploitation for maximising capital accumulation, all while they continue to perform unpaid domestic chores. These studies problematise these workers' systematic subjugation by shedding light on the interplay of factors that serve to hinder women's work (Nakkeeran 2003; Bhatt 2006; Gopal 2012; Krishnaraj 2012). Meena Gopal (2012: 302) narrates the case of home-based Beedi workers in the villages of Tamil Nadu, who, despite working in groups 'outside their homes under the shade of the neem trees', are not able to cement their relationships due to competition among them, depriving themselves 'of bargaining power and unity against the employer'. It is in this broad context that the present study is situated. While much has been written about the problems faced by women workers in the informal economy, there is relatively scanty scholarly work that describes the creative ways in which some of these women are collectively responding to the dual challenges of informality and vulnerability. Rina Agarwala (2013: 1) states: 'Informal workers in India *are* organizing, and more research on these movements is desperately needed' (emphasis in the original). In the present study, I attempt to address this lacuna.

This chapter highlights the case of a union of women workers in the informal economy – some of India's poorest – conjuring their collective spirit in their quest for identity and dignity. It attempts to uncover the wealth of information that exists in the gap between strategy and outcome of organising in the informal economy, focusing on the process. It seeks answers to questions such as: What does organising in the informal economy entail? Who are the agents that initiate this process? How is organising in the informal economy different from that in the formal sector? What can the broader labour movement take away as key lessons for new ways of organising?

Although I use the cohort of home-based workers to present the specific ways in which some of the poorest and most invisible workers in urban slums of India are collectively voicing their concerns, this chapter presents the consolidated effort of female workers engaged in different sections of the informal economy to assert their collective identity as women, which has the potential of benefiting all kinds of women workers and their families. While 'issues' help people to come together, and organising is usually around these 'problems' that are of immediate concern (such as harassment at the workplace or poor sanitation facilities in places of residence), I argue that the *process of coming together for each other* has a transformative potential of its own. It enables women to reimagine themselves as active agents of change, worthy of respect and dignity, rather than passively waiting at the receiving end of handouts based on the generosity of someone else (such as the state, an employer or civil society). This stands in stark contrast to the traditional conditioning of women as individuals whose 'labour of love' in the home is devalued or undervalued and almost always taken for granted. The process of women workers coming together begins a dialectic surrounding their dignity not just as workers, but also as women and as humans.

About Labour Education and Research Network and LEARN Mahila Kamgar Sanghatana

Most of the findings and reflections in this chapter are based on a trade union called LEARN Mahila Kamgar Sanghatana (LMKS), or LEARN Women Workers Union. As a trade union of urban female workers in the informal economy, LMKS has been engaged since 2006 in organising home-based workers, domestic workers, street vendors, garment factory workers and rag pickers in three cities of Maharashtra state in the western part of India: Mumbai, Nashik and Solapur.

LMKS is affiliated to, and born out of, a labour non-governmental organisation (NGO) called the Labour Education and Research Network (LEARN). Registered in 2000 (under the Societies Registration Act, 1860, and the Bombay Public Trusts Act, 1950), LEARN's core objectives are to generate research on labour and to use this research to form collectives of workers, especially those in the informal economy. As an NGO, LEARN receives financial support from national as well as international donors, aid agencies and some corporations (in both the public and private sector). It channels these resources to help LMKS run its operations effectively in all three districts.

In examining the work participation of women in the rural areas of developing countries, Bina Agarwal (2012) makes a strong case for micro-level studies to counter conceptual biases. Summarising her article, Padmini Swaminathan (2012: 5) writes:

> Agarwal points out that the inability to learn from insights provided by micro-level studies, combined with biases that underpin national level statistics which generally form the basis for development policies, not only means that coverage and comprehension of women's work is impaired but also that

the conceptualization of many schemes to help the poor is misdirected.

This is a micro-level study that analyses the work of the LMKS in the context of informal organising. It offers a direction to informal organising, but may also prove useful to certain sections of the government whose purpose is to promote labour welfare and decent work.

Contextualising home-based work

In 2002, at the 90th International Labour Conference, the International Labour Organization (ILO) passed a resolution expanding the scope of the definition of informality. This definition was accepted the following year by the International Conference of Labour Statisticians. Chen (2012: 8) sums up the components of the new definition thus:

> There are three related official statistical terms and definitions which are often used imprecisely and interchangeably: the *informal sector* refers to the production and employment that takes place in unincorporated small or unregistered enterprises . . . *informal employment* refers to employment without legal and social protection – both inside and outside the informal sector . . . and the *informal economy* refers to all units, activities, and workers so defined and the output from them. Together, they form the broad base of the workforce and economy, both nationally and globally (emphasis in the original).

In 2007, the National Commission for Enterprises in the Unorganised Sector (NCEUS) presented its authoritative and eloquently written *Report on the Conditions of Work and Promotion of Livelihoods in the Unorganised Sector*. It states:

> At the end of 2004–05, about 836 million or 77 per cent of the population were living below Rs.20 per day and constituted most of India's informal economy.[2] About 79 per cent of the informal or unorganized workers belonged to this group without any legal protection of their jobs or working conditions or social security, living in abject poverty and excluded from all the glory of a shining India (NCEUS 2007: 1).

It is in this context that we must examine home-based workers in India. Specific to this chapter are the urban home-based workers toiling in the slums of three cities of Maharashtra.

According to the ILO's (1996) 'C177 Home Work Convention', home-based work is work carried out by a person in his or her home or in other premises of his or her choice, other than the workplace of the employer, for remuneration, and which results in a product or service as specified by the employer. In my study, I use the term 'home-based work' to include both piece-rate workers and own-account workers. The former are end workers in a long value chain, whereas the latter have much shorter backward and forward linkages. As an example of piece-rate workers, home-based embellishment workers engage in 'job-work', wherein a middle-person delivers stitched, pre-embroidered garment pieces and provides materials for hand-sewn embellishment, specifies the pattern to be done on the garment, and picks up the completed order the same day or the next day.[3] Neither the worker nor the middle-person is aware of the end employer or end customer with whom the garment will eventually end up. This applies to the tens of thousands of items made in the slums for a larger supply chain. On the other hand, individuals who run a home-based mess service, which serves cooked meals to clients within the slum area, manage their own finances, buy their own ingredients and have a direct link to their end customers.

HomeNet South Asia (2015) estimates that women constitute approximately 80 per cent of around 50 million home-workers in South Asia.[4] The ILO (2013: xii) states that home-based workers constitute 18 per cent of the urban workforce in India. A study conducted by WIEGO (Women in Informal Employment: Globalizing and Organizing) indicates that in 2011–12, over 16 million women workers in India were engaged in home-based work and 7.34 million of them were in the urban areas (Raveendran, Sudarshan and Vanek 2013: 4).[5] Clearly, home-based workers constitute a huge and dispersed workforce. They live and work in challenging circumstances, earn paltry sums for their work and face several occupational hazards. The work itself tends to be monotonous, labour-intensive and isolating – especially so if done alone and not in a group.

One aspect of home-based work that distinguishes it from other informal economy trades, such as street vending or rag picking, is its relative invisibility. The work is undertaken at home or in common community spaces within the workers' low-cost urban settlements. As a result, home-based workers remain unseen and ignored by representative forums such as local trade unions or national trade union federations. With the exception of the Self-Employed Women's Association (SEWA) at the national level, and smaller initiatives by membership-based organisations at the local level, home-based workers are relatively invisible, under-researched and largely unrepresented. Trade union federations have largely ignored workers in the informal economy in their bargaining agendas. Organising initiatives in the informal economy function more or less independently of their formal counterparts and vice versa. In addition, unions of informal workers such as LMKS do not necessarily wish to replicate the functioning of heavily factionalised and fragmented formal sector trade unions and union federations with their exclusionary principles.

A characteristic and significant feature of home-based work is that there is no formal employer-employee relationship. An employee 'going to work' in her office or to a factory shop floor or a bank has several indicators of official identity. The principal employer is known to workers irrespective of their employment status (permanent, contract, temporary, casual, trainee). This is not the case for the home-based worker tied into a value chain. She is not aware of the end employer, which is ultimately to her disadvantage. Writing about the lace makers of Narsapur village, Maria Mies (2012: 59) states:

> The political-economic function of the separation of the sphere of production from the sphere of reproduction and the definition of women as housewives seems to be to create a readily available and disposable labour power whose day-to-day reproduction as well as its unemployment will not be the responsibility of either the capitalist, or the farmer or the . . . merchant.

In addition to remunerative home-based work, these women perform all domestic chores and look after their families' needs, their children's education and the cleanliness of their homes. However, this work is neither counted nor valued, and is almost always taken for granted. This devaluation also extends to the remunerative work that the women perform within their homes. Field findings indicate that most home-based workers and their families consider their work a pastime activity done to kill time, frequently referring to it as 'timepass'. Thus the workers hardly consider themselves as workers and earning members contributing to the household. The consciousness of being a worker is completely missing – it does not surface even in trying times when all other family members are rendered unemployed, and remunerative home-based work becomes the shock absorber and the 'employer of last resort'. In the face of the cruel politico-economic and financial system invariably favouring the rich, an interlocking of factors such as age, gender, religion, caste and class contributes to the overall vulnerability of home-based workers. Organising this huge workforce is therefore not merely significant, but also the need of the hour.

Home-based workers of Maharashtra: A short profile

The women workers whom I met and have interacted with over the years are engaged largely in low-paid manufacturing and services (Gartenberg 2011). The manufacturing tasks include embellishing, assembly and finishing work in various industries, such as electrical components, garments, footwear, trinkets, costume jewellery, food processing, utensils and electronics. Services such as *bhishi* (home-cooked meals service), women's beauty parlours and *mehendi* (henna) painting are also part of home-based work. For the most part, women engaged in low-income home-based work are from lower socio-economic groups, live in slums or low-cost housing settlements, and belong to the lower castes. In the case of cities such as Mumbai, many home-based workers are women who arrived in the city as newlyweds with their husbands who work there mostly as informal labourers in construction or as taxi drivers, among other things. Most often, their point of origin (the village) tends to be a constituent of one of the distressed states of India, where barriers created by caste-based employment do not permit any social or economic upward mobility. The younger workers are second-generation migrants, the children of these individuals. In all cases, irrespective of generation, the home-based workers earn very small sums for their work, especially those workers remunerated on a piece-rate basis.

Although the nature of employment in manufacturing work is different from that in service work, with each trade having problems specific to it, both types of labour face several similar issues. While workers engaged in manufacturing find the piece-rate payments very low, those in service work may face payment defaulters. Both kinds of workers experience inadequacies in their physical environment and the lack of access to their citizenship rights. For a trade union in the informal economy working for either group, it is therefore imperative to approach all organising issues at the level of specific trade, individual health and family well-being, community access to resources and lobbying for citizenship rights. Organising through LMKS clearly demonstrates this holistic approach.

The LMKS organising process

The LMKS organising process is semi-structured at best, in that the activists know roughly what to look out for and address while they 'go to the field'.[6] Usually the activists go in pairs to an area, and mostly this pairing is loosely based on their area of residence. They all wear their LMKS identity cards around their necks. In the Solapur branch of LMKS, the activists also wear identical sarees to indicate that they belong to the same union. They walk through various residential and commercial areas of a slum and look around to identify the different kinds of tasks performed by women, including remunerative work (*identification phase*). These areas may or may not be known to the activists.

As regards home-based workers, this method of organising works best because the activists are able to meet and talk to workers at their place of work (that is, their homes or common community spaces) while they are working. LMKS activists make themselves comfortable in any of these areas. I have been part of meetings in a variety of locations, such as a member's home, on a path created by a series of lids covering the gutters in a tiny bylane of a slum, on a raised platform at the entrance of a raincoat factory, and at the side of a road available equally for vehicular, animal and human thoroughfare. An informal setting sets the tone for an equally informal interaction, which works even better if the activists and the workers speak the same language. It is also a space for enrolling new members and renewing old memberships. In addition to asking the workers about their work and lives, activists can also observe the conditions of work, workers' posture and other occupational safety indicators while at work, workers' physical and cultural environment, and so on (*interaction phase*).

Through interaction, the women move to possible strategising, where activists solicit members' work-related details and problems, followed by possible resolution strategies from the members themselves. Although most women are quiet and shy in the beginning, they open up gradually and come up with ideas for their own issues (*strategising phase 1 – membership level*). This process is very powerful as it helps to plumb the intensity of the issues at hand, with the group 'sharing the burden' rather than an individual having to deal with it alone. In addition, discussing issues becomes a prompt for members to examine their own lives for similar experiences and to muster the confidence to voice them in such group brainstorming sessions. When necessary, the activists take notes in their notebooks. For their part, illiterate activists make 'mental notes', relying on their sharp memories. Upon their return from the field meetings, they enlist the help of their literate counterparts in the union to write their narratives (*taking field notes*). This is also an important indicator of cooperation among female activists in informal trade unions. While the illiterate activists proceed confidently in their interactions with members – discussing and resolving their problems, strategising with them, implementing their action plans and learning from them – they need not feel incapacitated by their lack of reading and writing skills, because their fellow trade unionists are available for completing the associated documentation.

The core group of activists meet once every week to discuss past field meetings and the members' grievances. The group goes through the brainstorming sessions, approaching the issues from different points of view based on a combination of activists' individual subjective positions and their exposure to information about laws, religious/caste taboos confronting the victims, and so on. Employing group consensus, the activists devise appropriate strategies and action plans to include collective negotiation with a host of stakeholders, such as family members, neighbours, key community members, employers, middle-persons, city councillors and other elected representatives, government officers and departments of the state machinery. For issues that stand out and affect all members and informal sector workers in general, demonstrations are planned (*strategising phase 2 – activist level*). These meetings of the core group also allow for discussions on prospective collaborations with like-minded organisations.[7]

The central focus of any field interaction, meeting, discussion, suggestion or action is the benefit to individual members. The clarity on this aspect in the minds of the activists promotes a healthy, critical cognitive process that leads them to stand by the worker's side in her times of acute need, so that she feels fully supported by a union made up of women just like her. This support could mean negotiating on her behalf or with her, and perhaps approaching the right organisations that could help with her specific issue (*implementation phase*). For instance, in cases of domestic violence, the activists take the concerned victim (not necessarily a member) to an NGO providing free legal aid and associated counselling. In cases of dire financial emergencies, activists might make small contributions from among themselves to help out. They may go to the hospital for a member's health issue and connect with the hospital social worker to redirect special help for the member. Once this happens, the member feels confident to repeat the process for someone else in the future, either by herself or by leading the person to LMKS. This snowballing process ensures the sustainability of LMKS efforts.

Over the years, word of LMKS work and activities has spread, mainly through the members themselves, who go to visit their relatives or friends in far-flung areas outside the main city and mention the work of LMKS. Activists get phone calls from women residing in such areas and the same process of organising is repeated. Phone calls also include rescue or distress calls, usually in cases such as domestic violence, family feuds, stalking or sexual harassment, and so on. Calls may also be made in cases where domestic workers are dragged to police stations for being falsely accused of theft by their employers. Cellphones feature prominently as informal organising tools for women to connect with each other, as a trust-building strategy ('You know you can call me any time'), as well as for networking with different individuals and organisations. They also help the activist to have an independent life of sociability outside the frame of her family and extended kinfolk. For a group that is not entirely computer literate or Internet-savvy despite the world's massive social networking buzz, cellphones serve as a means to communicate, interact and create a larger world of shared collective identity.

Organising home-based workers the LMKS way

The organising process of LMKS has been customised to address the unique situation of home-based workers. Even though the production processes of most company products are fragmented, with workers at various levels of skill sets spread out in different geographical areas, this very fragmentation also ends up clustering certain parts of the process. For instance, in the Amrut Nagar slum of Ghatkopar suburb in central Mumbai, one finds different sets of workers in the same lane working on different parts of the same necklace thread, until the finished product is completed at the end of the lane. Each completed set of items from one home is sent to the next worker's home for subsequent value addition. The process is repeated until the product is completed. In this sense, the lane itself becomes an invisible conveyor belt.

It must be borne in mind that this picture stands in contrast to formal sector organising, where workers in a corporation automatically assume the consciousness of being a part of a trade union in that workplace. It is not unusual to find the company's name incorporated in the name of the union. Informal organising, on the other hand, is not born on the factory shop floor and has no direct company allegiance or employer identity. Worse, informal workers, such as the home-based workers discussed here, do not even have the consciousness of being workers (see the idea of 'timepass' mentioned above). The concept of a workers' collective is therefore entirely new as well. The LMKS is very different from formal sector unions in that it uses community and neighbourly relations among people, their working conditions, the available urban infrastructure and civic amenities (or the lack of them), workers' domestic issues and their family's well-being as issues around which to devise a collective identity. An additional yet integral binding factor is the fact that remunerative work exists in the area for most women (as home-based workers, domestic workers, street vendors, and so on), which LMKS uses to reinforce their 'shared identity', making it possible to bring them under one umbrella of 'women workers in the informal economy'.

While most women and girls sit inside or outside their homes, often in groups, to work on these products, some workers also sit together in common community spaces while performing different tasks on the same items. This clustering of work and workers presents itself as an opportunity for trade unions in the informal economy to organise workers at their workplaces, within their homes or in public spaces in their residential slums. It must be remembered that slums are not homogeneous spaces, and the various markers of identity, such as region of origin, religion, caste and linguistic backgrounds, are often more divisive than inclusive in these spaces. Therefore, work itself presents the possibility of keeping these differences in the background (if not overriding them in the long run) and of uniting as a group of 'women workers'. In the same slum, one notices North Indian workers from the lower caste sitting beside Maharashtrian workers from the same caste group working on necklace threads. They perform different tasks and are paid differently as well (depending on the value addition they make to the item), but that does not deter them from developing bonds while at work. Further, they often sit in a common open space in the community near their homes, speak each other's languages and talk about a wide range of topics, from local politics, to the new happenings in their community, to their family problems. LMKS finds such a space to be apt for organising.

Community-based organising interventions have a high chance of being successful, which has been proved on several occasions by LMKS. For example, in 2013, one of the LMKS activists – herself a former home-based worker – conducted a series of meetings with home-based workers in an area called Muslim Nagar within Dharavi slum. She talked about these meetings as being a successful attempt at activating existing members in collective action. It is an important case which emphasises the importance of the organising process at the community level.

These members from Muslim Nagar are engaged in embellishing pre-embroidered pieces of ready-made garments with sequins. The garment pieces as well as the materials required for the embellishment are provided by the middle-person. The completed consignment is counted and picked up by the middle-person the next day. In the wedding season or during festivals, the pressure of orders is high and the time between drop off and collection of orders is much shorter, so that the completed consignments are picked up the same day.

The LMKS activist said that she wanted to find out more about the situation of these workers and their payment terms, because one of the members from the area had mentioned to her some problems associated with her work. The activist went to a regular meeting in the area and conducted a short survey. She said:

> I did the survey . . . it gave information about what is the work [that home-based workers do], how much money they make [in doing that work], how many pieces can be made in a day. I realised that the per-piece rate [from the middle-person] was too little, and the payment was heavily delayed.

She understood that the problem needed to be solved, and the first step was to make the members aware that this behaviour was unacceptable and should not be tolerated.

Another meeting in the same area was conducted soon after. The LMKS activist told the group:

> You all discuss among yourselves – this is the piece I have got, it takes this much time to make, and that the money should be paid within [maximum] three to five days. Irrespective of where we get the orders and which middleman gives it to us, we should first discuss this subject and then accept the order, so that our hard work is not wasted. If we [workers] find that the rates are very low, then everyone collectively does not take up the work. Only if *everyone* [in the group of that area] finds the rates feasible, then accept the order. Also [make sure] you do not wait for a week or a month to get your payment for the work; it should come within three to five days [of the completion of your work] so that we are not faced with a bigger problem. We will support you through the union.

After a brief discussion with the group, the activist added: 'And another important thing: if we face some trouble, then the middleman should help us out. If he does not have the capacity of giving us an advance [payment], then why should we give him completed work in advance?'

In reflecting on this particular meeting the LMKS activist said:

> We cannot trust the middleman. We [our members] were getting money very late, and several times the middleman would disappear after collecting the completed order [without paying the workers]. The hard work and hours put in by the worker were wasted. They would get tense about it [non-payment of the work] and this would create a stressful situation at home.

She told us that the same members now engage in at least some discussion before taking up work from any middle-person that comes to their area. However brief it may be, the discussion includes points such as the kind of work to be done on the garment, the minimum per-piece rate, the time allowed for returning the completed order and the middle-person's deadline for payment.

Key lessons

Home-based work is the new wave in the corporate world today. A series of recent articles featured in *The Economist* suggests the proliferation of skilled freelance workers of all kinds 'available at a moment's notice' (*The Economist* 2015a: 15) and a mushrooming of entrepreneurs who make the employer-employee match possible within seconds. The available workers 'get paid only when they work and are responsible for their own pensions and health care. Risks borne by companies are being pushed back on to individuals – and that has consequences for everybody' (*The Economist* 2015b: 7). While white-collar, well-educated graduates and the mainstream media may only now be waking up to this reality, this has been the situation of poor home-based workers for decades, especially so in developing countries like India. Overhead costs, such as a workplace, electricity and storage, were always borne by the home-based worker; her invisible and low status in the society caused her to be paid poorly; and her issues of personal well-being such as domestic violence and isolation kept her vulnerable and voiceless. Bringing her in touch with others like her is therefore the only way to break out of this helplessness-reinforcing deadlock. The organising attempts by LMKS indicate that some of these issues can be addressed directly, and that it possible to articulate one's story in a group without fear. Integrating a cross-section of workers from different parts of the informal economy further strengthens this process. The union identity cards reinforce the workers' shared identity as members of the same collective.

From the case presented above, LMKS presents some other key lessons for organising home-based workers in particular. First, economic relations embedded in social relations are the grounds for organising. The interlocking of religion, caste, gender and patriarchal roles makes it difficult to break out, while unionisation helps to imagine alternatives to this arrangement. The informal norm-setting by the group, as suggested by the LMKS activist to her members, is beneficial for all and certainly more powerful than the no-norm situation, which is beneficial to none. It also serves to eliminate competition among workers. Group decisions on topics such as terms of work, payment and deadlines, in addition to complaints about civic amenities and urban infrastructure, have merit in their own right, in that they create spaces for women to interact with each other and articulate their concerns not just as women and as workers, but also as citizens and human beings. Group discussion and decision making also have the latent function of unlearning ideas of low self-worth and fear induced in women through patriarchal conformity. Undergoing this process with others at the same time facilitates an individual's unlearning. Altogether, the organising process serves to build grassroots democracy, a 'working identity' of women, and solidarity within a fragmented workforce. This stands as an alternative to the existing patriarchal, exploitative and invisible structure in which the home-based workers find themselves.

Challenges

Although I speak optimistically in this chapter about the LMKS organising effort and its successful impact in the informal economy, I do not intend to suggest that it is a simple or linear process. In fact, the path of organising in the informal economy is dotted with a number of challenges and obstacles, not the least of which have to do with the deeply engrained ideas of inferiority among women themselves, and consequently their resistance to speaking up. If and when women pass this stage, the resistance from those whom they stand up to is equally grave. There are many categories that might have to be resisted – husband and others in the family, extended kin, the employer, local government agents, the police and several government offices. Worse, women themselves may stand in opposition to female activists ('the bad women'), who deviate from the customary subservience attributed to women and girls and ask others to follow suit. Convincing women to value themselves is perhaps one of the biggest challenges in organising informal workers.

Second, internal dynamics among women activists from diverse religious, linguistic and caste backgrounds cannot be ruled out as an impediment. A group of women who try to collectivise others like them clearly cannot instantly shed their lifelong conditioning of prejudices and stereotypical ideas regarding members of other communities, with whom they compete in the labour market. Organising presents an opportunity for women to go through a process of questioning ideas to which they had easily conformed not so long ago, and to face the painful discomfort that such questioning brings. This process of building trust among activists, their obvious differences notwithstanding, is a gradual one, and can often take several years of working together. For the most part, however, once trust firmly sets in, as it has in the oldest section of the LMKS in Mumbai, it stays put. The activists sit together to have lunch, look after each other's infants and maintain family contact, despite and through their sporadic, unpleasant fights.

Third, there is the issue of acceptability – by family, kin, neighbours, employer and society. Some of the activists in Mumbai experienced increased instances of domestic violence, mainly from husbands who did not know what to make of their wives' new-found independence and their support group, away from the family's complete control. In one case, when an activist resisted violent attacks by her husband, he cut her union identity card into pieces after beating her up. For activists, keeping their morale high in the face of such resistance is another challenge. Additionally, they are often encouraged by the union to participate in residential capacity-building workshops hosted out of town. In one instance, an activist was flatly refused entry back into her home and made to sleep outside on the streets as punishment for attending a SEWA workshop in Ahmedabad. But the fact that all LMKS activists have continued to be organised and have remained with the union, even while countering the wrath of several individuals and institutions in their sociocultural milieu, sufficiently proves that women workers do value being organised. This is reminiscent of a sentiment echoed in Ela Bhatt's (2006: 9) early impressions of organising women in the Textile Labour Association; she realised that 'a union is about coming together. Women did not need to come together *against anyone*, they just need to come together *for themselves*' (emphasis in the original).

The fourth obstacle has to do with resource mobilisation and consistent inflow of funds. Organisations require resources to keep going, especially when outreach efforts expand. LMKS charges its members a nominal annual fee; these monies are used mainly for making identity cards for members, travel expenses and small office expenses like stationery. For its overhead costs of an office space, honoraria for its full-time activists and other miscellaneous expenses, LMKS depends on national and international funding received by its mother organisation, LEARN. Relying on the union's membership dues for these expenses is not feasible, because that would mean reducing the number of full-time activists as well as substantially reducing the overhead costs. This would in turn be detrimental to expanding and sustaining the outreach of the union over time.

Fifth, organisations in the informal sector face a crisis of maintaining functional governance systems, keeping transparent financial records, and meeting cumbersome official requirements of running an organisation. These include, but are not limited to, filing annual income tax returns and foreign fund returns, providing periodic programmatic and financial reporting to its funders (in the case of the NGO), and submitting annual membership returns (in the case of the trade union). In most cases, these tasks are beyond the skill sets and capability of most grassroots activists, despite their enviable potential and outreach in organising, as well as their rich proficiency in resolving problems that most immediately affect the members.

Lastly, there is the uncomfortable subject of risks of all kinds. Here I focus on one of them. Resource mobilisation continues to be a challenge for LMKS, and reporting requirements of the funding agencies necessitate a dependence on LEARN as well as on educated individuals who can assist in NGO management and genuinely support the cause of informal workers' organising. This situation poses an important question: can unions of workers in the informal economy ever become truly independent or must they rely on lifelong help from well-intentioned individuals and agencies to support their activities? This reliance immediately exposes unions to the risk of granting entry to individuals and agencies with vested interests, ready to exploit them as potential target groups for securing personal funding from aid agencies, to employ their mass membership base for dangerously exploitative social entrepreneurial ventures, or to gain free-of-cost assistants for fly-by-night artists and researchers. Who is to decide which of these individuals and agencies are genuine supporters? Or, to put it differently, which of these are not potentially harmful for LMKS, its members and its cause? It continues to be a dilemma. Unfortunately, thus far LMKS has only found answers to this problem after going through experiences that taught the union that such collaborations were sometimes less than ideal. Not enough shock absorbers exist in the LMKS structure to guard it from these unforeseen, unexpected incursions. This is not to say that as an organisation LMKS is unique in facing such challenges. But given the union's informal nature, it requires much more time and effort to recuperate from even one such crisis than is required for its formal counterparts. Sufficient safeguards need to be devised within the government's labour office that can nurture and promote the formation and healthy functioning of unionising efforts in the informal economy, so that the dependence on individuals to handle the official reporting responsibilities is reduced substantially. These safeguards could include, for instance, engaging accountancy students doing their compulsory 'articleship' period not only to report the accounts, but also to build the capacities of trade unionists in the informal economy to gradually take up part, if not all, of this responsibility.

That said, the topic of challenges facing unions of workers in the informal economy is only roughly touched on in this chapter. It merits another research study altogether.

Reflections

Organising vulnerable workers in the informal economy is different from traditional forms of organising in the formal sector. First, the membership of LMKS constitutes poor women residing in slums and low-cost urban settlements. It is evident that for LMKS, organising is about inclusion. All kinds of women workers in the informal economy are welcome in the union, irrespective of their employment status, age, region, religion, caste and linguistic backgrounds. But the issues that are addressed need not be restricted to the members or to women. Rather, through the women, LMKS manages in its field of operation to encompass and influence the entire gamut of individuals living and working in those environments, such as families, neighbours, co-workers, middle-persons and, in some cases, also employers. The leadership of LMKS, too, comes from within this same base, making it easier for members to relate to their leaders, and strengthening the efficacy and sustainability of interventions and initiatives. Therefore, instead of being a top-down, elderly, male leadership, as is typically the case in formal sector unions, the leadership in LMKS is categorically grassroots, young and middle-aged females of mixed sociocultural identities representing different levels of education.

The steps followed by LMKS activists in organising are straightforward, and it is possible that any of the phases – identification, interaction, strategising and implementation – may not be uniform in each case or in each area; they may extend or shorten, and may overlap. Informality provides easy access to a diverse group of workers in a host of informal spaces available free of cost, which facilitates informal interactions. Due to a mass membership base, intervention strategies can also backfire, especially when an uncomfortable interaction ensues with powerful men and political heavyweights in the area. Although this prospect is frightening, talking about it to a support group as a victorious story afterward makes it bearable. Gradually, courage to take on more such confrontations is mustered, and the degree of resistance from the other side is often laughed at in afterthought.

The mobilisation of membership by LMKS is community based and focused on female workers, rather than factory-based mobilisation focused on male permanent workers. In contrast to the traditional formal sector, intervention of informal organising through LMKS crosses the doorstep of the worker's home, problematises the power structures within the family and community, enters into uncomfortable conversations in the private sphere of home and extended kin, and presents a mutually arrived-at conflict resolution. This approach is geared to the benefit of the member as a worker, a woman, a wife and a mother. It also presents itself as an alternative to formal sector trade union organising in which vulnerable workers are often 'talked down to' and left to their own devices while being excluded from the privileged group of organised permanent workers. Moreover, group mobilisation for collective negotiation helps to create informal solidarity among a fragmented workforce and to build grassroots democracy.

The LMKS organising process is unique in that it combines the ideology of the collective power of the trade union with a community-based mobilisation process akin to social work. Thus the conceptualisation of women as social beings in various roles is central to the entire organising process, including approach, interaction, strategising and implementation. Furthermore, the mobilising agents are themselves part of the same socio-economic milieu as those being organised. This too is an important aspect of the success of LMKS interventions. This is not to write off the merit of non-participant intervention, but instead to emphasise the feasibility of interventions initiated by women worker-activists who represent their constituents, due to the ease with which the latter can relate to the former.

As for the activists themselves, being representatives of the voiceless makes them empowered and famed individuals in their own families and communities. The activists' daily interactions with many different kinds of people, their weekly meetings as a core group, and their capacity-building inputs from various organisations sharpen their understanding of the scale and breadth of issues facing workers operating in the informal economy. Activists' close propinquity to each other in the weekly meetings (over shared meals and cups of tea) exposes them to viewpoints of other trade union activists like themselves, and forges strong bonds of collegial camaraderie and organic solidarity. Lack of literacy, as mentioned earlier, is hardly a hindrance. This also demonstrates that the language of empathy is fundamental for the success of building a strong grassroots movement.

Lastly, quantitative indicators that are 'acceptable' in world of academia, funding agencies and policy-making collectives hardly matter in a space where so much of the change is occurring at the individual's cognitive level. This change has a bearing on the transformations she is able to make in her immediate environment through her group. However, it is important also to bear in mind that this transformation is a result of a group process impacting on an individual's thinking and action. Each group success gives her more confidence; and her ability to take risks on an individual level is also enhanced if she feels reassured that she has a group's strong solidarity to fall back on.

In more ways than one, organising by LMKS is different from and a negation of the older, traditional factory-based unionisation characteristic of the formal sector. It is organising that intends to empower the women at all levels. Activating women's agency at the grassroots is possibly one of the few ways by which home-based workers and other workers in the informal economy can substantially improve their life conditions in a way that they find suitable. An equitable and inclusive structure like that of LMKS provides a platform where concerted collective efforts for such a transformation can take place.

Notes

1. This chapter is based on a paper presented by the author at the International Sociological Association (ISA) XVIII World Congress of Sociology held in Yokohama, Japan, 13–19 July 2014, as part of the RC44 Research Committee on Labour Movements. At the time of the presentation, this chapter was titled 'New Dynamics in Collective Bargaining in the Informal Sector: Impressions from India'.
2. Rs. 20 was approximately US$0.32 at the time of writing.
3. 'Middle-person' is a term used in this chapter to refer to both middlemen and middle-women.
4. HomeNet South Asia, established in 2000 following the Kathmandu Declaration, is a regional network of home-based worker organisations in South Asia. It was formed to give visibility to home-based workers and their issues, to advocate for national policies, to strengthen grassroots and membership-based organisations of home-based workers, and to create and strengthen South Asian networks of home-based workers.
5. Women in Informal Employment: Globalizing and Organizing (WIEGO) is a global network focused on securing livelihoods for the working poor, especially women in the informal economy. WIEGO believes that all workers should have equal economic opportunities and rights. It creates change by building capacity among informal worker organisations, expanding the knowledge base, and influencing local, national and international policies. See www.wiego.org (accessed 10 January 2015).
6. 'Going to the field' is a phrase used by the LMKS activists to refer to a broad range of their activities in the community. It includes exploring new areas for membership, informal interactions in existing membership areas (of which their residence could be a part), resolving conflicts at the community level and visits to government offices.
7. These could include a plethora of entities such as hospitals willing to conduct health camps, other NGOs wanting to conduct spoken-English lessons, charitable organisations looking for membership-based organisations to give away donations, or campaigns on various issues such as rights to affordable housing, sanitation facilities, improved access and quality of food grains in ration shops, and so on.

References

Agarwal, B. 2012. 'Work Participation of Rural Women in the Third World'. In *Women and Work*, edited by P. Swaminathan. New Delhi: Orient Blackswan.

Agarwala, R. 2013. 'Inventory of Informal Worker Organizations: India'. Los Angeles: IRLE, UCLA. http://www.irle.ucla.edu/research/documents/Agarwala-IndiaInventoryDec2013.pdf (accessed 10 January 2015).

Bhatt, E. 2006. *We Are Poor but So Many*. New Delhi: Oxford University Press.

Census of India. 2011. 'Gender Composition of the Population'. New Delhi: Government of India. http://www.censusindia.gov.in/2011-prov-results/data_files/india/Final_PPT_2011_chapter5.pdf (accessed 20 March 2015).

Chen, M. 2001. 'Women in the Informal Sector: A Global Picture, the Global Movement'. *SAIS Review* 21(1): 71–82.

———. 2012. 'The Informal Economy: Definitions, Theories and Policies'. WIEGO Working Paper No. 1. Cambridge, MA: WIEGO. http://wiego.org/sites/wiego.org/files/publications/files/Chen_WIEGO_WP1.pdf (accessed 10 January 2015).

The Economist. 2015a. 'There's an App for That'. 3–9 January: 15–18.

———. 2015b. 'Workers on Tap'. 3–9 January: 7.

Gartenberg, I. 2011. 'Mapping Exercise of Home Based Workers in Maharashtra'. Paper prepared for HomeNet India. www.learn-india.org (Research tab) (accessed 10 January 2015).

Gopal, M. 2012. 'Disempowered despite Wage Work: Women Workers in Beedi Industry'. In *Women and Work*, edited by P. Swaminathan. New Delhi: Orient Blackswan.

HomeNet South Asia. 2015. 'HomeNet South Asia and Overview'. http://www.homenetsouthasia.net/HomeNet_South_Asia_and_Overview.html (accessed 10 January 2015).

ILO (International Labour Organization). 1996. 'C177 Home Work Convention'. Geneva: ILO. http://www.ilo.org/dyn/normlex/en/f?p=1000: 12100:0::NO:: P12100_ILO_CODE:C177 (accessed 10 January 2015).

———. 2013. *Women and Men in the Informal Economy: A Statistical Picture.* 2nd ed. Geneva: ILO. http://www.ilo.org/wcmsp5/groups/public/~dgreports/~stat/documents/publication/wcms_234413.pdf (accessed 10 January 2015).

Krishnaraj, M. 2012. 'Women Craft Workers as Security for Family Subsistence'. In *Women and Work*, edited by P. Swaminathan. New Delhi: Orient Blackswan.

Mies, M. 2012. 'Dynamics of Sexual Division of Labour'. In *Women and Work*, edited by P. Swaminathan. New Delhi: Orient Blackswan.

Nakkeeran, N. 2003. 'Women's Work, Status and Fertility: Land, Caste and Gender in a South Indian Village'. *Economic and Political Weekly* 38(37): 3931–9.

NCEUS (National Commission for Enterprises in the Unorganised Sector). 2007. *Report on Conditions of Work and Promotion of Livelihoods in the Unorganised Sector.* New Delhi: Government of India.

Raveendran, G., R.M. Sudarshan and J. Vanek. 2013. 'Home-based Workers in India: Statistics and Trends'. WIEGO Statistical Brief No. 10. http://wiego.org/sites/wiego.org/files/publications/files/Raveendran-HBW-India-WIEGO-SB10.pdf (accessed 10 January 2015).

Swaminathan, P. 2012. 'Introduction'. In *Women and Work*, edited by P. Swaminathan. New Delhi: Orient Blackswan.

11

Collective Agency and Organising among Domestic Workers in Ghana

Angela D. Akorsu and Amanda Odoi

Although domestic work is hardly a recent phenomenon, it has generated renewed interest among academics, trade unions and civil society organisations for various reasons. The most compelling has been the associated vulnerability, which is typical of informal economy work forms. While acknowledging the fact that all informal work generally shares common features, such as being outside the ambit of national social protection provisions, some peculiarities, which have implications for organising, exist with domestic work and are worth highlighting (Lindell 2010).

Domestic work in particular emerges as a work type with unique social relations. It draws a significant number of its workforce from among women, children and immigrants (Ramirez-Machado 2003; D'Souza 2010; ITUC 2010), and tends to be invisible because it occurs in private homes. It is characterised by unique vulnerabilities and needs, and yet is difficult to define, organise and protect. Domestic workers are a category of heterogeneous workers. They are 'an important army of workers [who] perform domestic tasks in private households in exchange for remuneration and/or lodging and board' (Ramirez-Machado 2003: 1). These workers constitute the world's housekeepers, cooks, caregivers, drivers, gardeners, laundry (wo)men and security guards. As is obvious from this list of activities, the services of domestic workers are in high demand and domestic work has become an increasingly indispensable work type. However, domestic work continues to lack recognition and is susceptible to and characterised by exploitation and abuse (Ramirez-

Machado 2003; Moreno-Fontes-Chammartin 2004; ILO 2009; Tsikata 2009; Bonner 2010; D'Souza 2010; ITUC 2010). Unlike other forms of non-standard work, which have been and are being created by the current wave of neoliberal economic policies, and are slipping out of the purview of state regulation and protection, domestic work has never been within the ambit of state regulation and protection, nor has it been regarded as work.

According to the International Labour Organization (ILO 2009), 4 to 10 per cent of total employment in developing countries is in domestic work. This suggests that there are about 100 million people working in domestic services, and Asha D'Souza (2010) posits that the sector still has a high capacity for labour absorption. Domestic work constitutes a significant component of informal work, and the informal economy accounts for over 80 per cent of non-agricultural employment, over 60 per cent of urban employment and over 90 per cent of new jobs created in Africa over the past decade or more (ILO 2002).

Several authors report that women are in the majority in domestic work in most countries. For instance, Gloria Moreno-Fontes-Chammartin (2004) indicates that 81 per cent of all Sri Lankan women migrant workers and 38 per cent of Filipinos are employed in domestic work. Martha Chen et al. (2005) report that in South Africa domestic work represents about a quarter of women's informal employment. D'Souza (2010) states that in Ecuador 98.7 per cent of domestic workers are women. Underpinning this trend in the sharp increases in the demand for and supply of domestic workers worldwide is the increase in female labour force participation, the intensification of work, the ageing of societies, the problems in balancing family life and work, the decline in household care services, structural adjustment programmes, devastation of the agricultural sector and economic crises (Tsikata 2009; Bonner 2010; D'Souza 2010; ITUC 2010).

The gendered nature of domestic work can be located within the broad socio-economic context. Domestic work is strongly gendered on two scores. On the one hand, it relieves women of their domestic responsibilities to enable them to participate effectively in other forms of economic activities – an important indicator of gender equality – and, on the other hand, it is dominated by women (Tsikata 2009; Bonner 2010; D'Souza 2010; ITUC 2010). The predominance of women in domestic work is a result of gender segregation in the labour market and reinforces the gender division of labour, which treats women's work in the home as less important and non-economic. Hence, the paternalism associated with the concept of housewives and with benevolent breadwinners is transferred to domestic workers.

Undoubtedly, the exploitative conditions under which domestic workers work are also a reflection of gender discrimination. For instance, Alcestis Abrera-Mangahas (1996: 9) writes: 'Traditional attitudes wherein women are regarded as subordinate or as having stereotyped roles perpetuate widespread practices of coercion, violence, and abuse; such prejudices and practices may justify gender-based violence as a form of protection and control of women.'

In Ghana, the current character and form of domestic work is largely dictated by the socio-economic contexts in which it occurs. It has been reported that the lack of decent employment options has generated a massive supply of domestic workers (Tsikata 2009). Economic liberalisation and its ensuing informalisation have led to increases in informal work, of which domestic work is a part. Although over 86 per cent of Ghana's working population is located in the informal economy (Ghana Statistical Service 2008), the proportion of domestic workers continues to be unaccounted for in national statistics due to its 'invisible' nature and disguised status. It is characterised by the usage of unpaid family relations and under-aged children, who often lack appreciation of themselves as workers. The absence of accurate statistics on domestic workers is further informed by the fact that domestic work, in its myriad manifestations, defies a single definition. For instance, according to Dzodzi Tsikata (2009), the definition of domestic work in Ghana's Labour Act (Act 651 of 2003) is restrictive and exclusive of various categories of domestic workers such as those who foster children and those involved in the running of informal economy businesses. Without attempting to address all the complexities associated with the definition of domestic work in Ghana, the above perspectives underscore the need for research on domestic workers' organising since organising is, in fact, the first step to securing protection for them.

This chapter seeks to complement the others in this volume by presenting insights into how domestic workers in Ghana constitute themselves as active agents rather than passive victims of exclusion.

The chapter also attempts to explore the interaction between individual agency, collective action and external organising either by traditional trade unions or by non-governmental organisations (NGOs). Some specific issues addressed include the labour force types and needs, the forms and strategies of organising among domestic workers, the sources of power that they engage, and how trade unions and NGOs are engaging with organised domestic workers.

The study reported on in this chapter adopted a purely qualitative design for empirical data collection. Specifically, semi-structured group discussions and structured interviews with individual domestic workers and employers were conducted in Accra. These were complemented with key informant interviews with organisers, recruitment agents and some trade union officers. A total of 33 informants participated, including 7 key informants, 22 domestic workers and 4 employers. The first phase of data collection was undertaken from 16-18 June 2014, and a follow-up was carried out on 9-10 October 2014.

The discussion that follows is organised into five sections. The first section focuses briefly on conceptions of power and agency. In sections two, three and four, the empirical findings are discussed, highlighting labour force types and needs, the forms and strategies of organising among domestic workers, and the sources of power that they employ in doing so. The final section contains concluding remarks and implications.

Power and agency among domestic workers

George Ritzer (2004) describes humans both as volitional actors and agents, individual or collective, that can associate or disassociate with other agents to form networked associations, which in turn define, name and provide them with substance, action, intention and subjectivity. This description seems to suggest that it is through associations that human actors derive their nature or essence. In addition, Bruno Latour (1996) posits that the strength in associations comes not merely from unity, but also from careful lacing, weaving, netting and plaiting of heterogeneous actors.

Norman Long and Ann Long (1992) argue that underpinning the interest in social actors is the belief that it is theoretically problematic to limit any analysis of organisational strength to external forces. In the case of domestic workers, this point is explicitly illustrated by the well-documented difficulties in trade union organising and in sustaining domestic workers' organisations (IRENE and IUF 2008; ILO 2009). In addition, Chris Bonner (2010) reports that networking, alliance building and organising initiated by and among domestic workers is on the rise as a direct response to their specific circumstances. Any intervention by trade unions is thus best focused on facilitating this trend and empowering domestic workers. In the view of Long and Long (1992), this requires recognising the crucial role of human/social actor consciousness. They further indicate that instead of viewing social actors as passive recipients of intervention, or as disembodied social categories (based on gender or some other classificatory concept such as class), they should rather be conceived as active participants with the ability to make informed choices. Thus, regardless of how disadvantaged the social agents may be, the exact direction of change and the significance of that change cannot be imposed externally. Any social organisation is often the result of negotiations and social struggles among different kinds of actors, and agency is an integral part of that.

The concept of agency refers to people's capabilities and their related actions and/or behaviour, rather than to the actors or agents themselves. The inherent implication is that in as much as social structures may be inhibiting for individuals, they tend to transform their circumstances in ways that attribute the capacity to devise coping mechanisms to the individual actor, even under the worst of conditions. This coping may be positive with respect to interventions or negative with respect to endurance. In this context, domestic workers who initiate alliance building and networking qualify as social actors, with agency or the capacity to alter their circumstances. Albert Bandura (2001: 1) distinguishes between three modes of agency: 'direct personal agency, proxy agency that relies on others to act on one's behest to secure desired outcomes, and collective agency exercised through socially coordinative and interdependent effort'. Bandura (13) further explains that because people often have no direct control over their social conditions, they tend to seek 'valued outcomes through the exercise of proxy agency'. In this sense, trade union intervention may be seen as a form of proxy agency for domestic workers. Chris Bonner and Dave Spooner (2011) argue that when non-standard workers, such as domestic workers, collaborate with trade unions in their organisational efforts, their mutual needs and benefits are satisfied. As the non-standard workers acquire organisational experience and clout, trade unions 'retain and re-build their influence and legitimacy as a voice for the broad working class' (Bonner and Spooner 2011: 102). This seems to suggest that both collective agency on the part of domestic workers and trade union organising are crucial.

Sarah Mosedale's (2004) analysis of power suggests that the relationship between domestic workers and their employers potentially generates power as a zero-sum game, where any increase in the power of the domestic worker threatens the quantity of power of the employer. This means that in order to perpetuate employer *power over* domestic workers, employers will resist domestic workers' efforts by preventing them from organising and manipulating their consciousness to make them incapable of doing so. Successful organising by domestic workers therefore requires other types of power. According to Mosedale, the first type of power as a positive-sum game is *power within*, which is the internalisation of assets such as self-esteem, self-confidence and belief that one's actions can have effects. The second type of power is *power to*, which increases the boundaries of what is possible for one without compromising someone else's power. The third type is *power with*, which is the recognition that more can be achieved by a group working together than by individuals on their own. Organising domestic workers is essentially about leveraging their power to negotiate the terms and conditions under which they work. The empowering potential of such organising lies in collective representation as well as in democratic participation. According to Reyna Hayashi (2010), collectively bargaining for better conditions goes far beyond a rights regime that simply opens up avenues for nominal protection. It presents vulnerable workers with the opportunity to assert and exercise their rights to achieve what they want in terms of working conditions.

Labour force types and needs

While most of the domestic workers in this study are female, there are some male domestic workers. There is, however, an obvious gender division of labour in the kinds of activities they perform, even within the domestic arena. For instance, gardeners and drivers are predominantly males, while care work, laundry, cleaning and cooking are performed mainly by females. Furthermore, the domestic workers in the study varied from those with no formal education to the highly educated. Thus, study respondents included a male gardener with secondary education, and a female with a degree in human resources management who has been a domestic worker for twenty years and is currently serving as a cook and cleaner for two different families.

Domestic workers identified in this study can be categorised according to mode of recruitment, employment, living arrangements and level of formalisation. Note, however, that the mode of recruitment has implications for the level of formalisation in the sense that when domestic workers are recruited through relations and friends, their engagements often take place without a written contract. However, those recruited through placement agents tend to have their engagement formalised by means of contracts. While the interactions with the placement agents enhance the workers' propensity for collective action and create some awareness of unions, the contracts further determine the working conditions. Since the contracts often stipulate the job description and the commensurate remuneration, in this study instances of abuse were fewer among domestic workers with contracts. The role of the agents as gatekeepers cannot be completely ruled out, as workers can easily contact the agents with complaints and requests for relocation if necessary. Thus, the informally employed tend to be the most disadvantaged, with longer working hours, flexible pay and elastic job descriptions.

With regard to living arrangements, the most prevalent as well as the most preferred category, both for workers and their employers, is the live-in type, where the domestic worker lives in the home of the employer. These workers receive board and lodging as part of their remuneration. Whether live-in or live-out, these workers are often engaged as gardeners, cooks, drivers, laundry men/women, cleaners, as well as carers of the elderly and of children. There are also those who perform all the above activities as complete housekeepers, and these are mostly live-ins. All domestic workers experience similar work conditions, but the interviews revealed that the conditions of live-in and live-out workers have different merits and demerits (see Table 11.1). Live-in domestic workers, for instance, found the restrictions on their social life as the most unbearable demand from employers. As one gardener put it, 'When you are a live-in, employers do not allow you to bring your girlfriend into their houses and that can be hard, you know?'

Table 11.1 Differences in working conditions for live-in and live-out domestic workers

Type of domestic worker	Merits	Demerits
Live-in	Proximity to work No rent and utility bills Food provided Receives in-kind benefits	Restricted social life No privacy More prone to sexual abuse No closing time; longer work hours Lower income No opportunity to undertake work to supplement income
Live-out	Freedom and opportunity to engage in other income-generating activities More likely to have a closing time and to have rest days Less prone to sexual harassment	Transportation to work can be a problem Need to cater for own accommodation, utilities and some meals in a day

Source: Field data, 2014.

Besides these differences among live-in and live-out domestic workers, the spatial location of tasks performed within the domestic space predisposes domestic workers to specific forms of vulnerability. Drivers and gardeners, for example, are more distant from their employers than are housekeepers and caregivers, and by implication are less likely to be abused. A worker engaged as a steward for six years pointed out that although they work for the same employer, cooks and drivers are treated better than stewards with respect to incentives, regardless of the fact that stewards tended to suffer more physical and verbal abuse.

Perhaps the most revealing of working conditions is the gendered dimension to the nature and source of abuse suffered in domestic work. There were more reports of domestic workers suffering emotional, verbal and physical abuse from female employers, while incidents of sexual harassment and violence tended to be by male employers against female workers. Indications are that the background of employers with regard to education and nationality plays a critical role in perpetuating abuse. There were more reports of abuse from Lebanese employers than from

Ghanaian and Western employers, for example. The more educated the employers, the better they treat their domestic workers.

Generally, the provision of working tools and equipment, including protective gear, is neglected by the employers, as are health care, pensions, leave and rest periods. Insecure employment and low wages, often below the state-approved minimum wage,[1] were additional complaints from the respondents. A bone of contention was the mode of payment – cash versus in-kind. While some domestic workers alleged that their employers hide behind the various forms of in-kind payments to justify the meagre wages paid them, others are very happy with the worth of the various in-kind payments. A 46-year-old worker, for instance, prefers the in-kind payments to an increased monthly wage. According to this worker, who is paid GH₵200, or US$62.11, per month, she appreciates the frequent gifts, loans and other welfare support that she receives from her employer, and would under no circumstance trade such favours for a higher wage.

Unlawful termination was another source of concern for domestic workers. They generally lamented that their employment could be terminated at the slightest provocation. Even complaining about poor conditions of work could mean losing one's job, a situation that increases the vulnerability of non-standard workers.

Organising forms and strategies

The willingness to organise was prevalent among all the categories of domestic workers encountered. This willingness is motivated by deplorable working conditions and informed by the belief that if workers organised, their working conditions would improve. However, some workers refuse to organise to avoid offending their employers, since that could mean losing their jobs. Four organising forms among domestic workers in Ghana were identified: member-based organisations; individual organising; trade union organising and NGO organising. Trade union approaches to organising non-standard workers have included direct recruitment, granting affiliation status to already existing informal economy associations, and simply providing support to independent associations (Webster and Von Holdt 2005; Britwum 2010). Domestic workers in Ghana are increasingly organising and are being organised to fill their representational gap.

Member-based organisations
Member-based organisations can take the form of welfare associations, with dues-paying members who democratically elect their leaders to represent them. The Cooks and Stewards Association in Kumasi is an example. Such a group aims for solidarity and serves as a safety net in times of need. The Cooks and Stewards Association relied on tribal connections and utilised the snowball method to recruit members. This association served members' welfare needs to a very large extent, providing a support group where members could share experiences and help one another in times of need. They had no intention of becoming empowered to collectively fight for rights at work. The success of this association can be traced to the unifying effect of members originating predominantly from Northern Ghana, the mix of male and female members, and the elite employers they predominantly worked for.

The Cooks and Stewards Association demonstrates domestic workers' ability to organise into associations and reflects the human/social actor consciousness described by Long and Long (1992), as well as workers' awareness of their *power with*. Regardless of how disadvantaged domestic workers may be, their agency, individual or collective, is more crucial in altering their circumstances than any external efforts may be. This explains Bonner's (2010) assertion that networking, alliance building, and organising initiated by and among domestic workers for their specific circumstances is increasing worldwide. The pertinent question, however, is whether these associations can develop into a strong political voice for the membership. In the view of Alison Brown and Michal Lyons (2010), these micro associations rarely influence decision-making to their advantage against established interests, unless they are formalised in ways that grant them access to institutional spaces.

Individual organising
The key informants from both the Trades Union Congress (TUC) and the Industrial and Commercial Workers Union (ICU) indicated that they find direct organising of domestic workers a daunting, even an impossible, endeavour. This is so regardless of the realisation that 'there are compelling practical and political reasons for trade unions to take the lead in such organizing if they are to retain or rebuild their influence with employers and governments, and their legitimacy as the voice and

true representatives of the broad working class' (Bonner and Spooner 2011: 88).

The study revealed that the rather incidental approach of using individual volunteer organisers proved successful. In one instance, a volunteer organiser for the TUC managed to mobilise 400 domestic workers (see Box 11.1). Once the domestic workers came together, they functioned first and foremost as a member-based group, with dues-paying status. Unlike most member-based organisations, however, these workers have worked hard at seeking union coverage, with the hope that they can then secure better working conditions. Currently, this group of domestic workers has received official recognition as a union with a certificate dated 2015.

> **Box 11.1 Organising experience of an individual volunteer**
>
> In 2010, the TUC received sponsorship from Women in Informal Employment: Globalizing and Organizing (WIEGO) to organise domestic workers in Ghana. Clueless about how to proceed with this task, the head of TUC's organisation department was introduced to a woman who agreed to help organise domestic workers for the TUC. This woman, who was then a student of the Certificate in Labour Studies programme, was promised employment at the TUC afterwards. Without being given any resources, she embarked on gathering domestic workers and brought 50 domestic workers to a TUC/WIEGO meeting. Since then she has continued her organising work, and has managed to bring together some 400 domestic workers (approximately 300 females and 100 males). These workers are organised in sixteen suburbs in Accra. Each of the suburbs has a representative, who is mainly responsible for organising other domestic workers in the suburb.
>
> The lead organiser employed the following organisational strategies: personal relations and networking; announcements in church; door-to-door solicitation; snowballing; social media; and letters of authority from political figures (such as Members of Parliament [MPs] and assemblymen). She also intimated that she is planning a television series with the twofold objective of highlighting

> the fact that domestic workers are workers, as well as presenting the need for and the benefits of allowing them to organise.
> Organisational challenges include the lack of funds for organising. The lead organiser indicated that her organisational strategies incur large transportation and communication costs, which she claimed she has had to finance herself. She has appointed an interim executive committee consisting of a president, vice president, secretary and treasurer, based on seniority, education and commitment.
> *Source: Field data, 2014.*

In another instance, a volunteer organiser was used to mobilise 900 individual domestic workers directly into the ICU. (His efforts are described more fully in a later section of this chapter.) The ICU key informant described this volunteer as follows:

> [He was] passionate about the agenda to provide a collective voice to domestic workers, and this was because he is the son of a retired domestic worker, a cook. This volunteer organiser used snowballing to access most of the domestic workers, and this was facilitated by the ethnic connections that existed among the workers.

The motivations and effectiveness of the individual actors used by the unions to recruit domestic workers present an interesting theme for analysis. Efforts by these two individual organisers were based on different motivations. The ICU organiser volunteered to mobilise individual domestic workers directly into the union, and his motivation, according to the key informant, was that as a son of a retired domestic worker, he was passionate about providing a collective voice for domestic workers. He was in employment and mobilised the domestic workers part-time, without any financial expectations. The TUC organiser, on the other hand, was not employed, and she expected to be hired by the TUC as a reward for her organising work. Her greatest motivation was the employment opportunity, and indications are that the fact that this has not materialised is threatening the future prospects of the recently unionised group and is likely to negatively influence her zeal for future organising. Regardless of the differences in their motivations, both organisers can be described as effective: they organised 900 and 400 domestic workers respectively. Despite the success of this approach in terms of the number of domestic workers mobilised, it does not fit the conception of individual agency or collective action on the part of the domestic workers themselves. The organising effort is external, and this does not empower workers enough for them to claim rights at work.

NGOs

An NGO effort at organising domestic workers is seen in the work of the Ghana branch of Leadership and Advocacy for Women in Africa (LAWA), an NGO of female lawyers who focus on legislative advocacy for children and women in particular. LAWA's mission is to assist with legal reforms to end practices that discriminate against women and children in Ghana. Their main tools are research and advocacy. According to the LAWA key informant, the NGO veered into domestic workers' organising in 2003 by organising a few workers in Accra, Kumasi and Kpando, but its efforts were constrained by a lack of funds. LAWA did manage to organise sensitisation workshops about placement contracts. Although this effort could not be sustained, the sensitisation has the potential to help prepare those domestic workers to build agency for possible future collective action.

Some studies are very clear in stating that in addition to domestic workers' own agency and trade union organising, NGOs are also effective in organising domestic workers (Bonner 2010; Hayashi 2010). However, this statement is not confirmed by this study, which found that LAWA is the only NGO that has done work with domestic workers in Ghana, and it has not been successful in organising them as active agents with power to secure better working conditions. In the view of Hayashi (2010), even if NGOs are successful in organising domestic workers, they can at best achieve nominal rights protection for them; providing such workers with the opportunity to assert and exercise their own rights to achieve what they want in terms of working conditions is improbable. Bonner (2010: 6) implicitly confirmed the limitation of NGOs to provide domestic workers with organisational empowerment and clout: 'Their primary strategies are social/welfare, provision of services and policy advocacy for and/or with domestic workers.' As revealed in this study, LAWA's work with domestic workers in Ghana has focused on policy advocacy, specifically working towards securing legal protection. This is an example of what Hayashi (2010) calls nominal rights protection, which is at best only a means to an end.

Trade union organising

Two national unions, the TUC and the ICU, emerge as having worked at organising domestic workers in Ghana. In both cases, the initiative was driven by external funding – from WIEGO, for the TUC; and from the Women Workers Union in Denmark (KAD), for the ICU. The study depicts two organisational approaches: direct individual recruitment of domestic workers, and affiliating a domestic workers association to a trade union, both of which are among the documented approaches that trade unions have used to access non-standard workers (Webster and Von Holdt 2005; Britwum 2010). While the TUC resorted to direct individual recruitment, relying heavily on a volunteer organiser (described above in Box 11.1), the ICU affiliated the Cooks and Stewards Association while resorting to direct individual recruitment in Accra (see Box 11.2).

Box 11.2 The ICU's experience of affiliating and organising domestic workers

The organisational strategy used by the ICU is twofold. The ICU started organising domestic workers in 1999. In Kumasi, the ICU adopted the Cooks and Stewards Association, expanded it to include all other forms of domestic workers, and inaugurated it as the Domestic Workers Union, affiliated to the ICU.

In Accra, a volunteer was used to mobilise individual domestic workers directly into the ICU. The ICU received funding from the KAD in Denmark to support activities for the domestic workers and also for organising domestic workers in Accra. Domestic workers were then organised in three suburbs of Accra – Airport, Cantonments and Tesano. It is important to note that these suburbs are elite communities, where diplomats, expatriates and the wealthy reside. In view of this, the workers tended to be relatively enlightened and educated. About 900 domestic workers were organised by the ICU; they met weekly, on Sundays at 2.00 p.m.

The ICU organised a number of sensitisation and training workshops for the domestic workers. These workshops focused on their rights and responsibilities, as well as on grievance procedures. Beyond equipping them to handle grievances properly, the ICU often intervened in the settling of disputes between domestic workers and their employers. These interventions often ended in either restoring them to their employment or claiming compensation for them. In one such case, the ICU was able to claim a GH₵25 000 settlement for a worker through arbitration.

In addition to these services, the ICU developed employment contract guides to facilitate the formalisation of domestic workers' engagement. Three different types of contract guidelines were developed to cater for employers of different economic status and for differences in the willingness to adhere to the provisions demanded. Some of the provisions in the contract guide relate to details of pay rates, hours of work, job specification, disciplinary and termination procedures, conditions of leave, as well as injury and compensation provisions. Each member of the Domestic Workers Union paid GH₵1 per month, which limited what the union was able to do.

The ICU's efforts in organising domestic workers were fraught with a number of challenges, including:
- inadequate funding to support programmes since the domestic workers' monthly contributions were minimal and KAD funding eventually ceased;
- resistance from formal sector employees associated with the ICU against the use of their dues to support domestic workers, who paid relatively little in terms of dues;
- dominance of a particular ethnic group in the executive positions, which made conniving possible and changed the internal power dynamics among the executives; and

> • inability of the domestic workers to be present at meetings. Their absence was often due to fear of their employers. The workers could attend meetings only by deception and so meetings tended to be brief and not well patronised.

With regard to union awareness and the need to join a union, the study revealed that domestic workers with some level of education and exposure, and/or those formally employed, tend to have both a high need for collective action and a need to join a union, needs not shared by other domestic workers. Further questioning showed that the domestic workers had high expectations of unions in terms of the potential benefits: they believed that unionising would offer some sense of belonging and pride in their work. For instance, one worker stated: 'In case of wrongful termination of contract, [the union] can stand by us and advocate for us.'

As Bandura (2001) indicates, proxy agency that relies on others, such as a trade union or an NGO, to secure valued and desired outcomes is crucial in view of the limitations of individual and collective agency. In this sense, the affiliation of the Cooks and Stewards Association to the ICU may be viewed partly as a form of proxy agency for domestic workers, where they derive benefits that go far beyond a rights regime that simply opens up avenues for nominal protection (Hayashi 2010). This is not to suggest that trade unions have nothing to gain in such partnerships. Bonner and Spooner (2011) posit that when non-standard workers like domestic workers collaborate with trade unions in their organisational efforts, their mutual needs and benefits are satisfied. As domestic workers gain organisational experience, exposure and clout, trade unions can regain their influence and legitimacy as a voice for the broad working class, which is fast eroding due to membership loss, among other factors. Regardless of this recognition, and despite the TUC's direct engagement with non-standard workers, which began with the affiliation of the Ghana Private Road Transport Union in 1967 (Britwum 2010), this study has found a rather reactive attitude on the part of Ghanaian trade unions in reaching out to domestic workers. For instance, the ICU informant confessed that the partnership between the ICU and the Cooks and Stewards Association was 'initiated by the association; otherwise, we did not know there was any such association'. The partnership was also said to have been possible only because of funding from KAD in Denmark. On the part of the TUC, its efforts to reach out to organise domestic workers only started when it had WIEGO funding to do so. Even so, the TUC only reached out to a group of domestic workers, and this was organised by an individual.

Claiming rights over the domestic workers organised by individual volunteers emerged as the greatest threat to the sustainability of the mobilised domestic workers in both instances. In the case of the TUC, it is clear that it was the union that requested the woman to organise domestic workers in exchange for an employment opportunity and not for remuneration. Although the TUC acknowledged her role by nominating her for participation in an international programme for domestic workers, employment with the TUC has not materialised. Now that it has become apparent that she will not be employed by the TUC, the organiser is reluctant to hand over the organised domestic workers to the union and has indicated her intention to establish an NGO instead. According to her, she feels used by the TUC, especially when she financed the organising herself. The TUC official confirmed this, but he is of the strong opinion that the idea of forming an NGO may have been suggested to her by a rival union. However, he does not rule out influences of the exposure she received at the international programme for domestic workers. The members interviewed expressed their frustration at the state of affairs and are beginning to wonder if it was worth organising at all. Although a few of the domestic workers are happy to interact directly with the TUC for benefits such as travelling abroad for TUC-sponsored programmes, the majority seem to remain loyal to their organiser. It is unclear what the future of this group of domestic workers will be. However, the organised domestic workers are currently registered as a union and have affiliated with three different international bodies: the International Union of Food, Agricultural, Hotel, Restaurant, Catering, Tobacco and Allied Workers' Associations; the African Domestic Workers Network and the International Domestic Workers Federation.

A similar issue of allegiance was also seen in the ICU case. According to the ICU key informant, the greatest challenge that finally collapsed the association was ethnic influences. For instance, instead of consulting the ICU to intervene on behalf of the domestic workers, these executives would step in to demand compensation for the workers, and they would take as much as 10 per cent for themselves. Members therefore began to lose confidence in the association. By the time the ICU became aware of this, membership decline was beyond repair. By 2005, after about six years of organising domestic workers, the ICU lost all the members. This supports the assertion that there are many difficulties in organising and sustaining organisations of domestic workers (ILO 2007, 2009; IRENE and IUF 2008).

Sources of power utilised in organising domestic workers

Given the subordinated position of domestic workers in relation to their employers, it was not surprising to find that employers' use of power over domestic workers sometimes interfered with their individual agency. Employer hostility to organising was reported by almost all respondents and confirmed by the four employers interviewed. None of the employers saw the need for domestic workers to organise. According to one employer, collective organising would expose the workers to negative influences: 'It is not necessary for the domestic workers to organise; they will learn bad things such as conniving with others to rob their employers.' This inhibition notwithstanding, domestic workers in Ghana have counteracted employers' power over them with their own power sources as described below:

- *Power within* – Illustrated in the self-consciousness that individual domestic workers displayed in wanting to alter their circumstances. This is the source of individual agency observed in the two volunteer organisers (a former domestic worker and a son of a domestic worker).
- *Power to* – The successful use of the snowball method suggests that individual domestic workers see the need, and the responsibility they have, to act to increase the boundaries of what is possible.
- *Power with* – The recognition that more can be achieved by a group working together than by individuals on their own, as seen in the case of the Cooks and Stewards Association.

The utilisation of these power sources is significant in the sense that they emanate from the domestic workers themselves. As suggested by Mosedale (2004), it is these power sources that actually empower individuals and not paternalistic power sources.

External sources of powers utilised in recruiting domestic workers have included religious leaders and politicians. The TUC organiser indicated that because people have confidence in their religious leaders, she gets them to make announcements in church about the need to have domestic workers organised, and these announcements have often dealt with employers' hostility. She also resorted to the use of political power when an MP gave her an introductory letter for clout in her door-to-door solicitation. The placement agencies also emerged as empowering agents for domestic workers and potential actors in the organising of domestic workers.

Trade union influence and clout was the main source of power that the workers used in their attempt to seek rights at work. As a group, the Cooks and Stewards Association saw the ICU as a source of power. The awareness of this power source was a result of an individual's agency or use of *power to*. A worker who served as a cook for a bank manager was eventually employed at that bank. From his experience with the ICU's activities at the bank, he alerted his former colleagues about the possibility and benefits of joining a union; hence their engagement with the union. While acknowledging the important role of trade unions in empowering domestic workers' groups, Bonner (2010) cautions that any intervention by trade unions is best done in their role as facilitators and not as patronising agents. Table 11.2 lists some power sources available to the domestic workers and their specific purposes.

Apart from these power sources, various embassies and high commissions also emerged as potential sources of power for claiming rights at work for domestic workers, although these have not yet been utilised. The ICU official indicated that in interactions with employers of domestic workers, some expatriate employers said they would prefer the ICU to place the sample recruitment contracts at the various embassies and high commissions so that expatriates could be made aware of their responsibilities as employers even before they attempt to recruit domestic workers.

Table 11.2 Power sources and their purpose

Power source (or actor)	Purpose
Religious leaders	Making church announcements about the need to allow domestic workers to organise
Politicians and MPs	Providing letters of introduction to facilitate house-to-house solicitation
Media	Sensitising general public on the need to organise domestic workers and snowballing on social media
Placement agencies	Including organising provisions in their terms of engagement
Trade unions	Providing political clout and influence

Source: Field data, 2014.

Conclusions and implications for future organising

The study reveals that self-organising is possible among domestic workers since they feel a strong need to alter their circumstances, and that such self-organising is spontaneous in nature but unable to develop into a strong political voice for the membership. Meanwhile, the adoption of self-organised groups by unions has been shown to be disruptive due to rights-claiming struggles. Trade union organising of domestic workers, on the other hand, is seen to be reactive and dependent on donor funding.

Regarding organisational efforts of trade unions to reach domestic workers, the study depicts two approaches: direct individual recruitment of domestic workers, and affiliating a domestic workers' association to a trade union. Both approaches have been fraught with challenges. With regard to direct recruitment, trade unions have relied on organisers outside the union, and this has resulted in rights-claiming struggles between the organisers and the union. Affiliating existing domestic workers' groups to unions has also not actually led to any acceptable level of representation for domestic workers.

The implication is that trade unions need to be more proactive in their quest to organise domestic workers, and this requires changes in their attitudes, approaches and structures. Only then can unions effectively ally with domestic workers' groups. In the meantime, instead of adopting spontaneously organised domestic workers' groups, trade unions could provide groups with support in the form of nurturing, while guarding against claiming rights over them. It seems from this study that it is only by addressing the challenges inherent in self-organising and by harnessing their strengths that domestic workers can gain a political voice, and it is only by gaining a political voice that their vulnerable circumstances can be transformed.

Note
1. The national minimum wage at the time of data collection in 2014 was GH₵6 or US$1.86 (US$1 = GH₵3.22).

References
Abrera-Mangahas, A. 1996. 'Violence against Women Migrant Workers: A Philippine Reality Check'. Paper prepared for the Expert Group Meeting on Violence against Women Migrant Workers, 27–31 May, Manila.

Bandura, A. 2001. 'Social Cognitive Theory: An Agentic Perspective'. *Annual Review of Psychology* 52(1): 1–26.

Bonner, C. 2010. 'Domestic Workers around the World: Organising for Empowerment'. Paper presented at Social Law Project Conference, 7–8 May, Cape Town.

Bonner, C. and D. Spooner. 2011. 'Organising in the Informal Economy: A Challenge for Trade Unions'. *Independent Publishing Guild* 2: 87–105.

Britwum, A.O. 2010. 'Union Democracy and the Challenge of Globalisation to Organised Labour in Ghana'. PhD thesis, University of Maastricht, Maastricht.

Brown, A. and M. Lyons. 2010. 'Seen but Not Heard: Urban Voice and Citizenship for Street Traders'. In *Africa's Informal Workers: Collective Agency, Alliances and Transnational Organizing in Urban Africa*, edited by I. Lindell. London: Zed.

Chen, M.A., J. Vanek, F. Lund, J. Heintz, R. Jhabvala and C. Bonner. 2005. *Progress of the World's Women: Women, Work, and Poverty*. New York: UNIFEM.

D'Souza, A. 2010. 'Moving towards Decent Work for Domestic Workers: An Overview of the ILO's Work'. Working Paper 2/2010. Geneva: ILO.

Ghana Statistical Service. 2008. 'Ghana Living Standards Survey: Report of the Fifth Round (GLSS V)'. Accra: Ghana Statistical Service.

Hayashi, R.R. 2010. 'Empowering Domestic Workers through Law and Organising Initiatives'. *Seattle Journal for Social Justice* 9(1): 486–535.

ILO (International Labour Organization). 2002. 'Resolution and Conclusions Concerning Decent Work and the Informal Economy, 90th Session'. Geneva: ILO.

———. 2007. 'Decent Work for Domestic Workers'. *Labour Education* 3–4 (148–9). Geneva: ILO.

———. 2009. 'Decent Work for Domestic Workers'. Report IV(1) International Labour Conference, 99th Session. Geneva: ILO.

IRENE (International Restructuring Education Network Europe) and IUF (International Union of Food, Agricultural, Hotel, Restaurant, Catering, Tobacco and Allied Workers' Associations). 2008. 'Respect and Rights: Protection for Domestic/Household Workers'. Report of the international conference held in Amsterdam, 8–10 November 2006. www.domesticworkerrights.org (Research tab; accessed 22 July 2013).

ITUC (International Trade Union Confederation). 2010. 'Decent Work, Decent Life for Domestic Workers'. ITUC Action Guide. Brussels: ITUC.

Latour, B. 1996. 'On Actor-Network Theory: A Few Clarifications Plus More Than a Few Complications'. *Soziale Welt* 47: 369–81.

Lindell, I. 2010. 'Introduction: The Changing Politics of Informality: Collective Organizing, Alliances and Scales of Engagement'. In *Africa's Informal Workers: Collective Agency, Alliances and Transnational Organizing in Urban Africa*, edited by I. Lindell. London: Zed.

Long, N. and A. Long (eds). 1992. *Battlefields of Knowledge: The Interlocking of Theory and Practice in Social Research and Development*. London: Routledge.

Moreno-Fontes-Chammartin, G. 2004. 'Women Migrant Workers' Protection in Arab League States'. In *Gender and Migration in the Arab States: The Case of Domestic Workers*, edited by S. Esim and M. Smith. Beirut: ILO-ROAS.

Mosedale, S. 2004. 'Assessing Women's Empowerment'. Paper presented to the WIDE Annual Conference, 20–22 May, Bonn.

Ramirez-Machado, J.M. 2003. 'Domestic Work, Conditions of Work and Employment: A Legal Perspective'. Conditions of Work and Employment Series No. 7. Geneva: ILO.

Ritzer, A. 2004. 'Actor Network Theory'. *Encyclopedia qxd*.

Tsikata, D. 2009. 'Domestic Work and Domestic Workers in Ghana: An Overview of the Legal Regime and Practice'. Conditions of Work and Employment Series No. 23. Geneva: ILO.

Webster, E. and K. von Holdt (eds). 2005. *Beyond the Apartheid Workplace: Studies in Transition*. Pietermaritzburg: University of KwaZulu-Natal Press.

Contributors

Angela Dziedzom Akorsu is a Senior Research Fellow at the Institute for Development Studies (IDS), University of Cape Coast, Ghana. She holds a PhD from the University of Manchester. Her research interests focus on employment, labour and gender issues. She has authored several publications covering labour standards, gendered employment, informal economy workers, labour relations, human resource planning, employee training and trade unionism.

Sharit Bhowmik was Professor and Chairperson of the Centre for Labour Studies at the Tata Institute of Social Sciences (TISS), Mumbai. He engaged in labour studies throughout his working life, focusing on plantation labour and informal work. He was a member of the Subgroup on Plantation Labour of the National Advisory Committee (India) and a member of the Expert Committee on Street Vendors in Mumbai.

Owusu Boampong is a Research Fellow at the Institute for Development Studies (IDS), University of Cape Coast, Ghana. He holds a PhD in international development from the University of Birmingham, England. His interests are in the areas of small enterprise development and the dynamics of the informal economy. He has carried out research into the network enablers and constraints of the Ghanaian craft export industry, organising in the informal economy, and decent work and private sector participation in waste management. He is part of an IDS research team exploring the value chains, policy regimes and organising efforts in the informal waste management sector in Accra.

Akua Opokua Britwum is an Associate Professor at the Centre for Gender Research, Advocacy and Documentation (CEGRAD) at the

University of Cape Coast, Ghana. Her publications cover gender-based violence, gender and economic participation, trade union democracy, and labour force organisation in the informal economy.

Malati Gadgil is an activist with Kagad Kach Patra Kashtakari Panchayat, a waste workers' union in India, and is working on building strong enterprises for the union members. She is involved in advocating for better policy implementation to safeguard and upgrade the livelihoods of waste pickers. She holds a master's degree in gender and medical sociology.

Indira Gartenberg is a PhD scholar at the Tata Institute of Social Sciences (TISS), Mumbai, and a former fellow of the International Center for Development and Decent Work (ICDD) at the University of Kassel, Germany. She has been working as the organising secretary of LEARN Mahila Kamgar Sanghatana (LEARN Women Workers Union), which collectivises poor working women in urban slums in India. Her research interests include urban informal labour, women's work, trade unions, children's activism and performing art.

Carmen Ludwig is a postdoctoral researcher at the Institute of Political Science, University of Giessen, Germany. From 2012 to 2014 she was a visiting scholar at the Decent Work and Development Initiative cluster at the Society, Work and Development Institute (SWOP), University of the Witwatersrand. Her current research interests focus on organising strategies along global value chains.

uMbuso we Nkosi holds a BA degree in international relations and sociology, a BA Honours in economic and industrial sociology, and an MCom in development theory and policy. He is currently reading for his PhD in development studies at the University of the Witwatersrand. He was selected for the Archibald Mafeje Scholarship for Advanced Study by the Tiso Foundation in 2015. He is currently a co-editor of the *Global Labour Column*.

Amanda Odoi holds an MPhil in sociology from the University of Cape Coast, Ghana. Her research interests are in gender, sexuality and women's studies. She currently works as a Principal Research Assistant with the

Centre for Gender Research, Advocacy and Documentation (CEGRAD) of the University of Cape Coast. She has conducted research into perceptions around forced sex in marriage, young women's perspectives on healthy sexuality in Ghana and Burkina Faso, culture as a pathway to gender violence in Ghana, and creating a decent work agenda for domestic workers in Ghana. She has also assisted in teaching a number of gender-related courses at the University of Cape Coast.

Melanie Samson is a Senior Lecturer in Human Geography at the University of the Witwatersrand. She holds a PhD in political science from York University, Canada. She previously worked for the South African Municipal Workers Union and the National Union of Metalworkers of South Africa. Melanie was also the Africa Waste Sector Specialist for Women in Informal Employment: Globalizing and Organizing (WIEGO). She continues to work closely with WIEGO and waste picker movements around the world.

Benjamin Yaw Tachie is a Research Fellow at the Institute for Development Studies (IDS), University of Cape Coast, Ghana. He holds an MPhil in development studies from the University of Cape Coast and is pursuing a PhD in entrepreneurship in the informal economy at the same university. His research interests include vulnerable groups in the informal economy, human resource development, and leadership. He is a member of an IDS research team exploring the value chains, policy regimes, working conditions and attempts at organising in Accra's informal economy.

Mouleshri Vyas is Professor in the Centre for Community Organisation and Development Practice at Tata Institute of Social Sciences (TISS), Mumbai. Her areas of teaching, research and field action are communities and development, community organisation, informal labour, and programme planning and evaluation in development practice.

Edward Webster is Professor Emeritus in the Society, Work and Development Institute (SWOP) at the University of the Witwatersrand. Among his more than 100 scholarly publications is *Grounding Globalization: Labour in the Age of Insecurity* (Blackwell, 2008), written with Rob Lambert and Andries Bezuidenhout; the book won the American Sociological Association's Labor and Labor Movements Section Distinguished Scholarly Monograph Prize.

Jesse Wilderman got his start in organising while working in a metal factory, where he joined his co-workers in standing up to form a union. He has worked for nearly twenty years as an organiser with trade unions and other social movement organisations. He holds master's degrees from the Harvard Kennedy School of Government and from the Global Labour University programme at the University of the Witwatersrand, where he completed research on organising among farm workers. Following this research, Jesse served as a fellow at the Chris Hani Institute in South Africa, as well as providing organising training to trade unions and social justice groups in several African countries. He is currently the Executive Vice President of a 30 000-member health-care workers' union in the United States.

Index

Accra Metropolitan Assembly (AMA) 22, 126, 127, 128, 130, 134, 139
Adhav, Baba 146, 147
Adivasi Vikas Parishad (AVP, Tribal Development Council, India) 67-8, 69, 70, 71
Adivasis (Assam) 68
African Domestic Workers Network 244
African National Congress (ANC) 78, 174, 181
Agbogbloshie Scrap Dealers Association (Ghana) 137, 138, 139-40
Agricultural Products Marketing Co-operative (India) 21
All India Gorkha League 59, 66
All India Trade Union Congress (AITUC) 7-8, 61
Anand (GRMES leader, India) 191, 192, 198-9, 200
Anti-Privatisation Forum (South Africa) 173
Asadu Royal Waste (Ghana) 22, 133
Assam Company 56

Bai, Mangal 152
Bengal-Assam Rail Road Workers' Union 58
Benin, women traders 10
Benso Oil Palm Plantation (BOPP, Ghana) 48

Bharatiya Mazdur Sangh (Indian Workers' Union) 61
Black Municipal Workers' Union (BMWU, South Africa) 170
Brazil, farmers and farm workers 110-11
British East India Company 56
Bruce, Robert 56

Cairo, informal economic activity 9-10
Cape Town Municipal Workers' Association 170
cellphones and social media 19, 22, 87, 215
child labour 57, 151, 154, 240
  India 72 n.1, 189
Chipko movement (India) 146
Civil and Local Government Staff Association (Ghana) 23, 135
civil society 21, 24, 34
Commission of Enquiry on the Conditions of Tea Plantation Labour in India and Ceylon (Rege Commission, 1944) 57
Communist Party of India (CPI) 58, 66
Communist Party of India (Marxist, CPI(M)) 66
Congress of South African Trade Unions (COSATU) 86, 171, 173
Cooks and Stewards Association (Ghana) 237, 241, 243, 244, 245, 246

254

cooperatives 143-4, 151-61, 162-3
Coordination Committee of Tea
    Plantation Workers (CCTPW,
    India) 70, 71

Dalit people (India) 147, 163 n.1, 203
Darjeeling Gorkha Hill Council
    (DGHC) 67, 68
deregulation 1
domestic workers 6, 22, 23, 228-30,
    231-3, 237, 240-1, 243, 247-8
  Ghana 230-1, 233-40, 241-7
  India 208
  South Africa 229
Domestic Workers Union (Ghana)
    241, 242
Dooars Planters Association (DPA,
    India) 58, 59, 72 n.2

Employees' State Insurance (ESI, India)
    196, 198
empowerment 148, 151, 162
Environmental Service Providers
    Association (ESPA, Ghana) 126,
    129, 133, 134, 139
Ethiopia, solid waste management 135
EurepGAP (Euro-Retailer Produce
    Working Group) 101, 112, 115 n.3
Expanded Public Works Programme
    (EPWP, South Africa) 177

Farm Worker Coalition (South Africa)
    86
farm workers
  Ghana 17, 18, 20, 35-6, 38-51
  India 17-18, 19-20, 55-8, 59-60,
    61-5, 66, 67, 68-71, 72 n.1
  South Africa 5, 16, 18-19, 20, 74-5,
    76-7, 78-85, 87-90, 91, 92-3, 94,
    98-9, 104, 105-6, 107-10, 112,
    113-14, 115, 167
farmers
  Ghana 38, 40

  India 20-1
  South Africa 20, 74, 77, 78, 79-80,
    81, 82, 83, 89, 90, 92-3, 99,
    101-2, 103, 104, 105, 107-8, 109,
    110, 111, 112-14, 115
Food and Allied Workers Union
    (FAWU, South Africa) 107, 108
Fruit South Africa 103

Garam Rolla Mazdoor Ekta Samiti
    (GRMES, worker collective, India)
    188, 197, 198-9, 200, 203-4
General Agricultural Workers Union
    (GAWU, Ghana) 5, 36, 43, 44,
    45-50, 51
Ghana
  comparisons with India and South
    Africa 9
  domestic workers 230-1, 233-40,
    241-7
  faith organisations 47, 51, 246
  farmers 38, 40
  housing of workers 45, 47
  informal economy groups 34, 123,
    128-9, 131-4, 137-40, 140 n.1,
    230
  labour law and regulations 40, 42,
    230
  land pressure 2
  Lebanese employers 235
  market traders 8
  migrant workers 125, 136-7
  mineworkers 9
  minimum wage 130, 236, 248 n.1
  oil palm industry see Ghana Oil
    Palm Development Corporation
    (GOPDC)
  oil palm workers 17, 18, 20, 35-6,
    38-51
  port workers 10
  solid waste management 126-7,
    128-34, 137-40
  strikes and protest 45, 136

trade unions 3, 5, 7, 18, 20, 23-4, 36, 43, 44, 45-9, 51, 135-6, 140, 231, 236, 237-40, 241-5, 246
traditional leaders 47, 50
transport of workers 41-2, 44
waste management workers 6, 22, 23, 24, 121, 123-4, 125, 126, 128-34, 135-40
women workers 38, 39, 41, 42, 130, 229-30, 233-4, 240
Ghana Oil Palm Development Corporation (GOPDC) 35, 36, 37-42, 44-6, 47, 49, 51
Ghana Private Road Transport Union 243
Ghana Trades Union Congress (TUC) 126, 135, 237, 238-40, 241, 243, 244, 246
Ghising, Subhash 67, 68, 69, 72 n.5
GlobalGAP 112
Global South 3-4, 8-9
Global Union Federations 6, 33
globalisation 1-2, 24, 33, 97-8
Gorkha Janmukti Morcha (GJM, Gorkha Liberation Front) 69, 70, 71
Gorkha National Liberation Front (GNLF) 67, 68, 69
Gorkhaland movement (West Bengal) 65-7, 68, 70, 72 n.5
Greater Accra Metropolitan Area (GAMA) 128
Greater Johannesburg Metropolitan Council (GJMC) 22, 23, 24, 172, 173, 178, 183 n.4
Green Advocacy (Ghana) 139-40
Growth, Employment and Redistribution (GEAR, South Africa) 171, 172
Gurung, Bimal 69

Hamal Panchayat (trade union, India) 146

Hind Mazdur Sabha (HMS, Indian Workers Council) 61
home-based work 6, 207, 210-11, 219, 226 n.4; *see also* India, home-based workers
HomeNet South Asia 210, 226 n.4
housing of workers
 Ghana 45, 47
 India 60, 63, 191, 192, 195-6
 South Africa 19, 76, 77, 78, 82, 102, 105

iGoli 2002 (Johannesburg) 172, 174, 175, 180-1, 184 n.10
India
 child labour 72 n.1, 189
 communal clashes 2
 comparisons with Ghana and South Africa 9
 construction workers 202
 domestic violence 221
 domestic workers 208
 elections 5, 10
 farmers 20-1
 garment factory workers 208
 Hindu fundamentalism 2
 home-based workers 207, 208, 210, 211-13, 216-21, 224, 225
 housing of workers 60, 63, 191, 192, 195-6
 informal sector 7, 8, 10, 65, 187-8, 206-7, 209, 211
 labour law and regulations 59-60, 71, 187, 197, 204
 malnutrition deaths 64
 migrant workers 2, 65, 197, 202, 203
 minimum wage 195, 200
 plantation schools 63-4
 rail workers 58
 rickshaw pullers 202
 scheduled castes 72 n.4, 202
 shipbreaking workers 10

steel utensil manufacturing 22, 188, 189, 191, 192-202, 203-4
street vendors 8, 208
strikes and protest 19-20, 22, 69, 71, 195, 198, 199, 200
tea industry 54, 55-7, 58, 59, 60, 64-5, 71
tea plantation workers 17-18, 19-20, 55-8, 59-60, 61-5, 66, 67, 68-71, 72 n.1
trade unions 3, 6-8, 17-18, 19, 20, 23, 24, 57-8, 59, 61-3, 66, 68, 70, 71, 143-4, 146, 147-62, 188, 197, 198-9, 200, 201, 204, 208, 211, 213-25
tribals 18, 27 n.4, 62, 65, 66, 67-8, 69, 72 n.4
waste management workers 24, 125, 134, 143-4, 145-62, 194, 208
women workers 23, 145-6, 148, 159, 194, 195-7, 203-4, 206-9, 210, 211-15, 216-21, 223-5
India Tea Association 72 n.2
Indian Labour Conference (ILC) 59, 72 n.3
Indian National Trade Union Congress 61
Indian Tea Planters Association (ITPA) 58, 59, 72 n.2
Industrial and Commercial Workers Union (ICU, Ghana) 237, 239, 241-4, 245, 246
informal sector workers 6, 9, 11-14, 24-5, 34-5, 124-5, 143, 146, 160, 162-3, 209
informalisation of work 1, 2-3, 4, 7, 10-14, 17, 22, 33, 166
International Domestic Workers Federation 244
International Labour Organisation (ILO) 11, 47, 48, 103, 105, 209, 210, 229
International Monetary Fund 121

International Trade Union Confederation (ITUC) 5, 6
International Union of Food, Agricultural, Hotel, Restaurant, Catering, Tobacco and Allied Workers' Associations 244

Jalpaiguri District Congress Committee (India) 59
Jharkhand people (India) 202, 203
Johannesburg City Council (JCC) 168, 169, 172, 179, 181, 183 n.1

Kagad Kach Patra Kashtakari Nagri Sahakari Pat Sanstha (KKPKNSPS, credit cooperative, India) 151-3, 158, 159, 161
Kagad Kach Patra Kashtakari Panchayat (KKPKP, trade union India) 125, 143-5, 147-51, 152, 153, 154-5, 156, 157, 158-9, 160, 161, 162, 163
Kaneshi Amaalataba Association (waste worker association, Ghana) 137, 138, 139
Kashtachi Kamai (cooperative scrap shop, India) 153-4, 158, 159, 160-1
Kaya Bola see Ghana, informal economy groups

labour
  codes of conduct and standards 34, 98
  scholarship 9
Labour Education and Research Network (LEARN, India) 208, 222
labour law and regulations
  Ghana 40, 42, 230
  India 59-60, 71, 187, 197, 204
  South Africa 78, 102, 103, 104, 105, 171

Land Bank (South Africa) 103
Leadership and Advocacy for Women in Africa (LAWA, Ghana) 240
LEARN Mahila Kamgar Sanghatana (LMKS, LEARN Women Workers Union, India) 208, 211, 213-16, 217-20, 221-5, 226 n.6, 226 n.7
Local Government Workers Union (Ghana) 23, 126, 135-6, 137, 140
Luxemburg, Rosa 172

Mahobia people (India) 202, 203
Marikana massacre (August 2012, South Africa) 5
Mawubuye Land Rights Movement (South Africa) 86
migrant workers
  Ghana 125, 136-7
  India 2, 65, 197, 202, 203
  South Africa 2, 8, 79, 80, 81, 87, 107, 110, 112, 114, 115, 169
mineworkers 5, 9
minimum wage
  Ghana 130, 236, 248 n.1
  India 195, 200
  South Africa 74, 76, 77, 78, 89, 106
mobile phones *see* cellphones and social media
Mohite, Baby 150
Mumbai Port Trust, Dock and General Employees' Union 10

Nanavre, Mohan 147
National Adult Education Programme (India) 145
National Association of Street Vendors of India (NASVI) 8
National Commission for Enterprises in the Unorganised Sector (NCEUS, India) 209
National Commission on Labour (India) 57

National Economic Development and Labour Council (NEDLAC, South Africa) 15, 171, 183 n.3
National Fresh Produce Markets (NFPMs, South Africa) 20, 99-100, 111, 112-13, 115 n.1
National Rural Employment Guarantee Scheme (NREGA, India) 193
National Union of Metalworkers of South Africa 181
National Youth Authority (Ghana) 139
Nepali language 66-7
New Trade Union Initiative (NTUI, India) 188
Nigeria, trade unions 7
non-governmental organisations (NGOs) 23

outsourcing and subcontracting 1, 7, 33, 40, 176-8, 180

paternalism 19, 75, 79-80, 81, 82, 83, 105, 220, 230
Pikitup (Johannesburg) 22, 166, 175-7, 178-9, 180, 181, 184 n.16, 184 n.17, 184 n.18
Plantation Labour Act (PLA, 1951, India) 60, 63, 64, 72 n.1
populism 1-2
power resources approach 15-17, 23, 24-5, 166-8, 181, 182-3
precariat 3, 4, 21, 22
privatisation 22, 35, 122, 128, 170, 171, 172, 173, 174, 181
Progressive Tea Workers Union (India) 68
public-private partnerships (PPPs) 121-2, 123, 126-7, 128, 140
Pune Municipal Corporation (PMC) 21-2, 154, 155, 156-7, 159, 161, 162, 163

Index 259

Rashtriya Swayamsevak Sangh (Hindu fundamentalist body, India) 61
Reconstruction and Development Programme (RDP, South Africa) 171
Rege Commission, 1947 57
Revolutionary Socialist Party (RSP, India) 58, 61
Rural Waste (Ghana) 132

Scheduled Tribes *see* India, tribals
Self-Employed Women's Association (SEWA, India) 3, 6, 8, 61, 211, 221
Shivnur, Tipavva 154
Siat Group (Belgian company) 37
SNDT Women's University (Pune) 23, 147, 155
social movement organisations 34, 91, 92, 93-4, 165, 167, 168
Social Security and National Insurance Trust (SSNIT, Ghana) 37-8, 44
solid waste management 121-3
  Ghana 126-7, 128-34, 137-40
  South Africa 174-81
  see also waste management workers
Solid Waste Collection and Handling (SWaCH, cooperative, India) 22, 125, 143-4, 154, 155, 156-7, 158-60, 161-2, 163
solidarity 5, 25-6, 37, 181, 182
South Africa
  agriculture 77-8, 79-80, 83, 93, 97, 99-101, 103-4, 105, 113-15
  clothing workers 8
  comparisons with Ghana and India 9
  corruption 166, 179, 180, 181
  domestic workers 229
  farm workers 5, 16, 18-19, 20, 74-5, 76-7, 78-85, 87-90, 91, 92-3, 94, 98-9, 104, 105-6, 107-10, 112, 113-14, 115, 167

farmers 20, 74, 77, 78, 79-80, 81, 82, 83, 89, 90, 92-3, 99, 101-2, 103, 104, 105, 107-8, 109, 110, 111, 112-14, 115
grocery chains 20, 78, 98, 100-3, 105, 109, 111, 112-13, 115
housing of workers 19, 76, 77, 78, 82, 102, 105
labour law and regulations 78, 102, 103, 104, 105, 171
legal advice offices 5
mechanisation 113-14
migrant workers 2, 8, 79, 80, 81, 87, 107, 110, 112, 114, 115, 169
mineworkers 5, 9
minimum farm wage 74, 76, 77, 78, 89, 106
municipal workers 166-7, 168-9, 170, 174
post office workers 181
solid waste management 174-81
strikes and protest 23, 74-5, 77, 82-94, 108, 109-10, 166, 169, 170, 174, 179-80, 181, 183 n.1
trade unions 23, 24, 75, 76-7, 82, 86-7, 90, 92, 99, 105, 106-9, 114, 115, 166, 168, 169-71, 172-4, 178-9, 181-2
waste management workers 24, 174-7, 178-80, 181, 182, 184 n.16, 184 n.17
women workers 83
South African Municipal Workers Union 23, 165-6, 167, 170, 171, 172-4, 178-9, 180, 181, 182-3, 184 n.16, 184 n.17
standard employment relationship (SER) 1, 33, 34, 35
Stofland (Western Cape) 82
street trashing 179-80
street vendors 6, 8, 208
strikes and protest
  Ghana 45, 136

India 19-20, 22, 69, 71, 195, 198, 199, 200
South Africa 23, 74-5, 77, 82-94, 108, 109-10, 166, 169, 170, 174, 179-80, 181, 183 n.1
Sumanbai (Pune waste worker) 154

Taxi Bola see Ghana, informal economy groups
Tea Board of India 55, 72 n.1
television, role in protest 84-5, 90
Textile Labour Association (India) 221
trade agreements 34
trade unions 21, 25-6, 33-4, 35, 91, 163, 165, 232-3, 247-8
  Ghana 3, 5, 7, 18, 20, 23-4, 36, 43, 44, 45-9, 51, 135-6, 140, 231, 236, 237-40, 241-5, 246
  India 3, 6-8, 17-18, 19, 20, 23, 24, 57-8, 59, 61-3, 66, 68, 70, 71, 143-4, 146, 147-62, 188, 197, 198-9, 200, 201, 204, 208, 211, 213-25
  power resources 15-17, 23, 24-5, 166-8, 181, 182-3
  South Africa 23, 24, 75, 76-7, 82, 86-7, 90, 92, 99, 105, 106-9, 114, 115, 166, 168, 169-71, 172-4, 178-9, 181-2
Transkei 169
Transport and General Workers Union (TGWU, South Africa) 183 n.2
Trinamul Congress (India) 69, 71
Twifo Oil Palm Plantations (TOPP, Ghana) 48, 49

United Front (South Africa) 181-2
United Trade Union Congress (India) 61

Verryn, Paul 8

waste management workers 21, 122, 163

Ghana 6, 22, 23, 24, 121, 123-4, 125, 126, 128-34, 135-40
India 24, 125, 134, 143-4, 145-62, 194, 208
South Africa 24, 174-7, 178-80, 181, 182, 184 n.16, 184 n.17
see also solid waste management
Wazipur Industrial Area (WIA, India) 22, 188, 189-92, 201-3, 204, 205 n.2
West Bengal
  government 66, 67, 69, 71
  tea industry 54-5; see also India, tea industry; India, tea plantation workers
Western Cape uprising 5, 75, 77, 82-93, 114, 167
Women on Farms (South Africa) 83
Women in Informal Employment: Globalizing and Organizing (WIEGO) 6, 210, 226 n.5, 238, 241, 244
women workers 6, 10
  Ghana 38, 39, 41, 42, 130, 229-30, 233-4, 240
  India 19-20, 23, 145-6, 148, 159, 194, 195-7, 203-4, 206-9, 210, 211-15, 216-21, 223-5
  South Africa 83
Women Workers Union (KAD, Denmark) 241, 242, 244
World Bank 121, 172, 183 n.5

xenophobia 1, 2

Yakub (WIA resident, India) 191

Zilla Cha Bagan Mazdur Union (District Tea Plantation Workers Union, India) 58
Zoomlion Ghana Limited 22, 132-3, 137